The Time of Darkness

The Time of Darkness

local legends and volcanic reality in Papua New Guinea

R. J. Blong

University of Washington Press
Seattle and London

1982

Printed in Australia

Published in the United States in 1982 by the University of Washington Press, in cooperation with the Australian National University Press, Canberra.

Library of Congress Cataloging in Publication Data

Blong, R. J. (Russell J.)
  Time of Darkness.
  Includes bibliographical references and index.
  1. Volcanic ash, tuff, etc.—Papua New Guinea.
2. Volcanic ash, tuff, etc.—Papua New Guinea—
Folklore. 3. Legends—Papua New Guinea. I. Title.
QE461.B554   551.2'1'09953   81-11484
ISBN 0-295-95880-4   AACR2

Acknowledgments

In the course of the research on which this volume is based I have become indebted to a very large number of people.

My most important debts are to Professor Jack Golson of The Australian National University who first provided the opportunity for me to work in Papua New Guinea and with whom I have spent many days of convivial fieldwork and invaluable discussion and to Dr Colin Pain of The University of New South Wales who has accompanied me (some would say, led me!) on numerous happy tephra-hunting expeditions.

During various sojourns in Papua New Guinea I have met, been assisted by, and relied on, numerous people both Papua New Guinean and European. My thanks to them all; in particular I have enjoyed and benefited from the company on various field forays of Dr Ernst Löffler (CSIRO), Dr Neil Enright (McGill University), Dr Jeremy Smith (University of New England), the late Rob Cooke and Chris McKee (PNG Volcanological Survey), Jim Porter and my wife Tina.

My fieldwork has been financed by Macquarie University, the Wahgi Project (ANU), the Myer Foundation and, in largest part, by the Australian Research Grants Committee.

In matters geochemical I have received an enormous amount of assistance from John Bedford and Dr Dick Flood of Macquarie University and from Dr Wally Johnson of the Bureau of Mineral Resources.

Dr Lionel Wilson of the University of Lancaster Lunar and Planetary Unit has made valuable comments on some of the material in Chapter 6. Professor George Walker of the University of Hawaii has commented on the entire manuscript and encouraged me in a number of other ways.

On the question of dating I have benefited from discussions with Dr Richard Gillespie and Dr Mike Barbetti of the University of Sydney Radiocarbon Laboratory, Henry Polach and John Head of the Australian National University Radiocarbon Laboratory, Professor Frank Oldfield of the University of Liverpool, and Dr Eldon Ball of The Australian National University. I must, however, absolve them from any responsibility for statements I have made on dating the time of darkness; I fear that it would be impossible to write so as to please them all.

Amongst the social scientists, my primary debt is to Professor Peter Lawrence of the University of Sydney who encouraged me to write this book and helped with several matters of interpretation. I have also benefited greatly from discussions with Professor Jim Watson of the University of Washington, Professors Bob Glasse and Mervyn Meggitt of the City University of New York, Dr Rod Lacey of the University of Papua New Guinea, and Dr Nick Modjeska of Macquarie University. Numerous other anthropologists, but particularly Drs Stephen Frankel, Buck Schieffelin, Aletta Biersack, Roy Wagner, Paul Wohlt and Nancy Bowers, have assisted me with matters of fact and interpretation.

My debt to various personnel of the Summer Institute of Linguistics will be evident in later chapters but I must acknowledge the assistance provided by Barry Irwin, Marshall Lawrence, Dorothy Drew, Audrey Payne, Karen Adams, Linda Lauck, Gordon Bunn and Bruce Hooley. Without the assistance of S.I.L. personnel I would have had only a slender collection of legends with which to work.

Much of the first draft of the manuscript was written in the Quaternary Research Center of the University of Washington. I thank the Director, Dr Estella Leopold and JAKJAP for many kindnesses.

At Macquarie University Dean Oliver, Ken Rousell and Rod Bashford drafted all the diagrams and Ruth Sefton typed much of the manuscript. Jane Clarke provided valuable comments on a draft version. I thank the rest of my colleagues, both academic and technical, for all their comments, both advisive and derisive!

Sydney, 1981   R.J.B.

Contents

Tables

Figures

1 Introduction

Volcanic eruptions have long fascinated people. Almost everybody knows something about the 1883 eruption of Krakatau (Indonesia), commonly regarded as the biggest during recent earth history. Such knowledge stems from the detailed field investigations of the Dutch geologist Verbeek (1886), the compendium of the Krakatoa Committee of the Royal Society of London (1888), the popular account of Furneaux (1965), the deaths of some 36,000 people, mainly at the hands of the ensuing seismic sea waves, the rapid spread of news of the calamity on the telegraph, and the subsequent brilliant optical effects observed all over the world. The newspapers and scientific journals of the time were full of items concerning the eruption as returning sea captains, ministers of religion, and natural historians reported their observations. Even Alfred, Lord Tennyson was inspired to begin his poem *St Telemachus*:

> Had the fierce ashes of some fiery peak
> Been hurl'd so high they ranged about the globe?
> For day by day thro' many a blood-red eve, . . .

Although the 1883 eruption of Krakatau has captured the public attention as *the* great eruption there are, in fact, numerous contenders for the title. The eruption of Tambora (Indonesia) in 1815 produced more volcanic ash (*tephra*)*, than did the Krakatau eruption and resulted in the deaths of over 90,000 people, primarily as a result of starvation (Neumann Van Padang, 1971, p.60). The AD 79 eruption of Vesuvius entombed the Campanian towns of Pompeii and Herculaneum, and produced the largest literature on the effects of an eruption (see Leppmann, 1966) as well as one of the world's great tourist attractions.

More recently, detailed archaeological investigations on the Greek island of Santorini (Thera) have revealed the Minoan (c 1500 BC) town near Akrotiri buried by an eruption essentially similar in style to those

---

*Volcanological terms are defined in the Glossary.

of Krakatau and Vesuvius but undoubtedly greater in magnitude. Various authorities have speculated about the role of this eruption in the rapid decline of Minoan Crete during the fifteenth century BC and the part of Thera in the Atlantis legend of Plato (see Luce, 1969; Galanopoulos and Bacon, 1969). Less firmly based speculations have also related the ten plagues of Egypt and the Moses-led exodus to atmospheric and seismic phenomena associated with the Thera eruption (van Bemmelen, 1971; Vitaliano, 1973).

Other great eruptions have their claims to fame. The 8 May 1902 eruption of Mt Pelée on the Caribbean island of Martinique completely destroyed the town of St Pierre and all but one or two of its 30,000 inhabitants in a period of only a few minutes (Heilprin, 1903). On the other hand, the 1912 eruption of Katmai and Novarupta in Alaska killed no one even though the volume of tephra ejected was much greater than that from Mt Pelée. This difference in the extinction of human life is, of course, an accident of location, the Alaskan volcanoes being sufficiently remote from human settlements that even the role of the volcano Novarupta in the 1912 eruption was not fully appreciated until more than fifty years later (Curtis, 1968).

In 1980 the eruption of Mt St Helens (USA) captured the attention of the world's media and initiated the most intensive and diverse scientific investigation of a volcano and its effects to date.

The effects of such major eruptions are varied and widespread. Earthquakes, seismic sea waves, acid rains, optical effects, atmospheric sound waves and the tephra fall itself can extend hundreds and even thousands of kilometres from the volcano. For example, houses shook perceptibly in East Java 780 km from Tambora during the 1815 eruption (Raffles, 1830), tidal gauges registered oscillations of 1 to 3 m more than 700 km from Krakatau along the Sumatran coast during 26 August 1883 (Wharton, 1888, p.106), acid rains destroyed the weekly wash of some Vancouver housewives 2400 km from Katmai-Novarupta in 1912 (Herbet and Bardossi, 1968, p.68), optical effects were experienced over North America and Europe following the eruption of Mt Agung on Bali in 1963 (Lamb, 1970, p.525), atmospheric sound waves from the Soufrière, St Vincent, eruption of 1812 were heard nearly 1300 km away on the Orinoco River (Heilprin, 1903, p.240), and tephra fall from Tambora in 1815 was observed on the island of Bangka more than 1500 km to the west (Petroeschevsky, 1949).

Such cataclysmic events as major volcanic eruptions are, not surprisingly, long remembered. Spinden (1919), for example, notes that Nicaraguan Indians still fix their ages and other events in relation to 'La Oscuridad Grande' — the Great Darkness, a reference to the darkness accompanying the ashfall from the great eruption of Coseguina in 1835.

Although it can be readily demonstrated that tephra falls can have effects long remembered even at great distances from the eruptive centre, the connection between source and effect depends on efficient communications. Where such communication does not exist the source of the tephra fall or atmospheric disturbance may not ever be discovered and, amongst the relatively unsophisticated, the connection between the tephra fall and a volcanic eruption may not be realised even though the event is much discussed and stories are passed from generation to generation. However, detailed examination of volcanic sediments can also indicate the extent of tephra from individual volcanic eruptions. Such studies have been particularly successful where the volcanic ash stratigraphy record involving detailed examination of deposits at numerous sites can be combined with lengthy historical records such as those available in Iceland (e.g. Thorarinsson, 1958, 1970).

This volume is concerned almost entirely with the documentation of a cataclysmic volcanic eruption which occurred in Papua New Guinea some 300 years ago. In Papua New Guinea the historical record is far from complete for the period before about 1870 even for coastal areas, while the interior highlands were not penetrated by Europeans until the 1930s. Documentation of the eruption, its magnitude and its effects thus must rely both on the stratigraphic record and on local legends.

The present investigation began in 1970 at an archaeological site in the Western Highlands Province of Papua New Guinea where numerous thin layers of inorganic sediments were identified in Kuk swamp. Studies of the mineralogy and stratigraphy of these thin layers (Chapter 2) revealed that many of them were volcanic ash but it was not known if these tephras were produced by nearby volcanoes or whether they represented the furthest fallout from some distant source. As opportunities arose to collect tephra samples from a wider area of the Papua New Guinea highlands, it became necessary to test the possibility that the tephras represented at one site were the same as those at another a hundred or more kilometres distant. The relatively simple geochemical techniques used and the results achieved with respect to two tephras are presented in Chapter 3.

The geochemical data, together with measurements of tephra thicknesses and particle sizes, helped to define the area covered by the two ashfalls. It became clear that the uppermost tephra, here named Tibito Tephra, was the product of a volcanic eruption of considerable magnitude. Investigations then centred on possible source volcanoes, both in the highlands and along the north coast of mainland Papua New Guinea. Detailed stratigraphic studies of some volcanoes, geochemical variations from volcano to volcano, and knowledge of local eruptive histories were used to eliminate most potential sources from further consideration. These various lines of evidence (Chapter 4) indicated that Long Island in the Bismarck Sea was the most likely source of both thin tephras. Tephrostratigraphic and geochemical investigations confirmed (Chapter 5) that Long Island was the source of Tibito Tephra.

Pinpointing the source of Tibito Tephra allowed the construction of an isopach map showing the distribution of the tephra and calculations of tephra volume. These calculations indicate that the eruption of Long Island was equal in magnitude to the 1883 eruption of Krakatau. Chapter 6 outlines a number of theoretical considerations and compares the eruption of Long Island with other famous eruptions.

At the time that the field investigations of tephra layers were proceeding at Kuk I became aware of a 'time of darkness' legend told by the Melpa-speaking people of the area to Vicedom in the 1930s. A free translation of Vicedom and Tischner's (1948) account, as told by Ko, follows:

> Once upon a time, in olden days, men saw to the south the whole land was covered with dark clouds. A storm was on its way and there was a rustling and whistling in the air. They asked what this meant, and heard that it was raining ashes in those parts, so that the people could not go out to dig up their food crops. So they themselves went out and gathered in stores. The ash-storm reached them and they had to stay inside their houses for four or five nights. By this time they were either terribly hungry or else they actually did starve to death. They were badly shocked by the event and were sure they would all be annihilated and that their spirits had deserted them, although they continued to pray. Gradually over a two day period it grew light again, till they were able to emerge and saw their crops and fields were ruined. They were in great need as their stores were finished and they had to plant new crops while they were still hungry. After a month nearly all of them died. A few remained and through time increased again. The plants we grow were handed down to us from those survivors. People today do not know that the ash-storms once took place. Men have increased again and it is said that a new race of men lives (translated from Vicedom and Tischner, vol. 3, p.50).

A somewhat similar story was recorded by Dr James B. Watson amongst the Agarabi of the Kainantu area, some 200 km east of Mount Hagen. Watson, who first heard the story in 1954, reported it in 1963:

> On a certain morning long ago . . . the people of our village awakened to find that the day did not lighten. Thinking at first that it was still night, they stayed by their fires; but after a while they decided that it would not get light. They did not know what to make of the darkness and they were afraid. Most of them stayed in their houses. However, when they went outside, they found everything covered with sand — like the sand in a stream. There was sand on the ground and sand on the thatch of the houses.

When they went out to the gardens to replenish their food, they found they had to push the sand away with their hands in order to get to the plants.

The second morning it was just the same. It was still dark and they had to light torches to go out to the gardens to get their food.

The third day was like the first two and now the people decided they must do something to make it light again. They killed a white-skinned pig. The morning of the fourth day it got light once more (Watson, 1963, p.152).

In reply to Watson's paper, R.M. Glasse outlined an event, believed to have occurred several times, which the Huli people at Tari called *bingi*. Glasse (1963, p.271) does not report the Huli legend verbatim but outlines the story thus:

Thunder, lightning and tremors herald the advent of *Bingi*. On the first day the sky darkens when it should be morning. For the next three days, a white pumiceous silt falls from the sky. It covers the sweet potato mounds (which are two or three feet high), chokes the streams and destroys unprotected crops. Afterwards many trees lose their foliage and birds and animals die. For a time food is short but people quickly replant their crops and these flourish in the enriched soil.

The legend (*mana*) of *Bingi* contains practical and ritual precautions for survival. Members of kin groups build communal houses at the first sign of *Bingi*. They lay in food and vessels of water to last four days and gather their pigs and dogs. They cover some of their gardens with grass. As sexual intercourse is dangerous at this time, all wives return to their natal groups. During the actual fallout no one leaves the communal house except for men who are last surviving sons. If these precautions are not followed, *Bingi* turns into a holocaust, destroying all life.

Figure 1 indicates that these three stories were collected in widely spaced regions of Papua New Guinea. Although Watson had suggested Krakatau and Glasse had proposed Doma Peaks near Tari, as the respective sources of the Agarabi and Huli ashfalls, it is possible that these three versions and the others recounted in Chapter 7 stem either from the one cataclysmic eruption with widespread tephra fall or that the legends originated at a point and then diffused across the highlands.

The question of diffusion is always difficult, but the three versions presented here are so different that 'parallel invention' seems, to me, more likely. The Huli legend has a strongly futuristic component while the Agarabi version concentrates on what happened during the time of darkness. On the other hand the Melpa version emphasises the

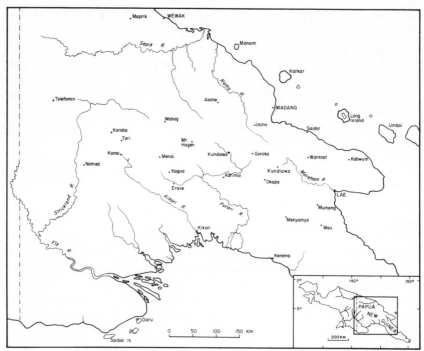

Fig. 1   *General location map*

aftermath. Diffusion seems unlikely, unless these are all remnants of the one much longer account. While each legend has a different emphasis, the common theme of a time of darkness, a fall of material from the sky, and consequences stemming from this event can be found in all three and in the other versions presented in Chapter 7.

Perusal of the literature and circulation of a questionnaire to anthropologists, missionaries, linguists and others produced information about 56 versions of the legend which seem to describe a fall of volcanic ash and its aftermath. Consideration of the diversity of sources of this material and obvious variations in its quality lead to a brief examination of some of the limitations of oral history (Chapter 7).

In Chapter 8 the areas over which Tibito Tephra is known to have fallen is compared with the presently known distribution of the time of darkness legends. Most importantly, by reference to key sites, the area within which Tibito Tephra is quite clearly the stratigraphically uppermost layer of volcanic ash is shown to coincide with most of the areas from which time of darkness legends have been collected. Geochemical analysis of materials purported to have fallen from the sky during the time of darkness strengthen the conclusion that most of the legends resulted from the fall of Tibito Tephra. In many ways Chapter 8 is the crucible of the thesis because it is there that the geological sciences and oral history are fused.

The subsequent examination of the folklore material centres on only two aspects of the legends; the physical characteristics of the material that fell from the sky and the effects of the ash fall. The available material from each legend is summarised in a series of maps and tables and briefly described in Chapters 9 and 10. Discussion then centres on variations in the legends and possible sources or causes of this variation. Elements of stylisation and embellishment and logical inconsistencies are also noted but most of Chapter 11 is devoted to a discussion of the significance attached to the time of darkness as revealed in the folklore material.

However, the time of darkness legends have a significance far beyond that accorded to a relatively unimportant local story. Because most of the versions of the legend stem from the fall of Tibito Tephra, a volcanic ash identifiable on the ground and with ascertainable effects, legend can be compared with reality. The veracity of the time of darkness legends is testable in three ways. Firstly, the physical characteristics of the material that fell from the sky as described in the legends can be compared with the present (and past) character of Tibito Tephra (Chapter 12).

Secondly, the effects related in the legends can be compared with the effects of tephra falls of similar thickness described in the literature. Chapter 13 sets out material drawn from a worldwide survey of the effects of specific thicknesses of tephra on houses, gardens, and people *inter alia* and compares the conclusions with the results described in the legends.

Finally, legend can be compared with reality by examining the question 'when did the time of darkness occur? The legends contain data which can be used to estimate genealogical dates. At the same time, the eruption of Long Island and the fall of Tibito Tephra can be estimated using radiocarbon dates and other techniques from the so-called 'hard' sciences. Historical evidence, largely of a negative nature, also bears on the dating question. The results of this analysis (Chapter 14) are not entirely conclusive but they do, once again, allow a comparison of legend and reality.

The significance of the time of darkness legends extends far beyond their importance as a collection of stories. They attain significance not only because they are revealed here as a coherent group of legends about the one event but also because they are shown to have originated with one of the great volcanic eruptions of the last millenium, yet an eruption that was not witnessed by European man. More importantly, it is because the veracity of the stories can be tested against physical reality that the stories attain real significance. Complete (and satisfying) as the conclusions reached here are, the investigations have raised numerous questions of a volcanologic, anthropologic and folkloric nature. Chapter 15 summarises the conclusions reached in this volume and outlines some of the issues raised.

2. Tephra identification and characterisation

Introduction

Volcanic ash or tephra attains considerable stratigraphic importance because it is erupted in an instant of geologic time (i.e. it is not time transgressive) and because it can mantle enormous areas allowing the establishment of a chronology amongst widely separated sites. The tephra cloud drifts on the wind, the deposit usually being elliptical in shape with thickness (Fig. 2) and particle size both decreasing with increasing distances from the source volcano.

After deposition the tephra is subject to wind drifting, erosion by water, compaction, and reworking by flora, fauna and the activities of man. An initially continuous tephra mantle may eventually be preserved only as a series of discrete lenses. The state of preservation depends on the environment of deposition, the thickness of the original mantle and the time elapsed since emplacement of the tephra. Correlation of the remnants of the tephra mantle can be, in adverse circumstances, a difficult task.

The use of tephra layers for stratigraphic purposes involves answering a number of questions relating firstly to the identification of sedimentary layers as tephras and secondly to the correlation of discrete layers from site to site.

The first set of questions which aid the recognition of sediments as tephras might include questions such as: (1) does the sediment have the characteristics of an aeolian deposit?; (2) is the deposit well-sorted?; (3) does the sediment occur on topographic highs as well as topographic lows?; (4) does the layer form a sharp boundary with underlying sediments?; (5) does particle size decrease upwards, i.e. does graded bedding occur?; (6) does the sediment have the mineralogical and geochemical characteristics of a volcanic rock? However, weathering of tephra, reworking and mixing with adjacent sediments all complicate the issues and recognition of sedimentary layers as tephras may not prove as simple as it first appears.

The second set of questions, involving correlations from site to site,

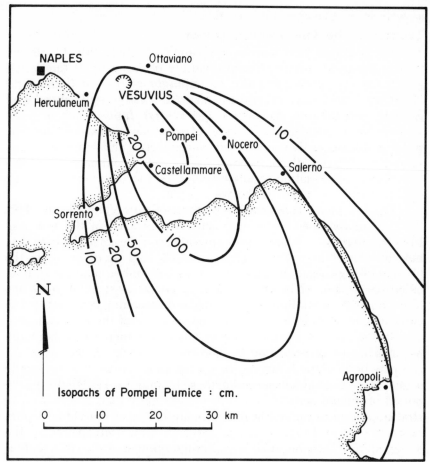

Fig. 2   *Isopachs of Pompeii Pumice*

revolve around the problem of characteristics of tephra remnants. Field characteristics which have proved useful include: colour, particle size range, bedding, fabric (arrangement of aggregates), readily identifiable minerals, thickness and general stratigraphic position. Such criteria are likely to be useful only within a limited area as all of these characteristics are likely to change with distance downwind and with distance from the long axis of the depositional ellipse (Fig. 2). More precise characterisation and correlation is likely to depend on *chemical fingerprinting* of tephra layers by one or more of a wide variety of techniques.

Satisfactory answers to the second set of questions allows the establishment of a *tephrostratigraphy* in which other sedimentary layers have locations stratigraphically above or below known recognisable tephras which can be correlated from site to site even where sites are many kilometres apart. If dateable materials lie adjacent to the tephras, a *tephrochronology* can be established whereby absolute as well as relative ages are known.

Tephras at the Kuk prehistoric site

Across the Papua New Guinea Highlands, airfall of thin (< 10 cm) tephra apparently occurred onto a variety of surfaces: (1) forests, (2) grasslands of *Leersia hexandra* or *Imperata cylindrica* (kunai), (3) *Phragmites karka* swamps, (4) garden surfaces and recently abandoned gardens, and (5) into prehistoric agricultural drains. Each of these surfaces has a considerable micro-relief; some have pockets of standing water or diffuse partly channelised overland flow and some have been subject to differential compaction by overlying sediments. All sites experience precipitation > 2500 mm/yr, falling in intense afternoon storms, particularly during the wet season.

There is thus considerable reworking of thin tephras even where they are undisturbed by human activity. However, at the Kuk pre-historic site (Fig. 3), where tephra investigations began and where they have been most intensive, prehistoric activity apparently involving the tending of pigs began at least 9500 years BP* and agriculture with an extensive system of barets (ditches) began at least 6000 years ago (Golson, 1977, 1978). Both pig keeping and gardening have resulted in considerable disturbance of the uppermost 1 m of the Kuk swamp.

Shallow (< 1.5 m) drains at the Kuk site, which totals about 200 hectares in area, provide more than 40 km of exposure. Some 10 tephras can now be identified, ranging in age from more than 30,000 years to c.240 years BP. Although several of these tephras have fallen during the period of human activity, few sites expose more than two tephras in stratigraphic position and at few sites are lenses of individual tephra more than 2 m long. Thus, at the Kuk site, disturbance of the stratigraphy is extreme; at all but a limited number of sites thin tephras have been incorporated into the topsoil and the stratigraphic entity of the tephras destroyed.

Elucidation of the prehistoric agriculture activity at the Kuk site is largely dependent on the tephrostratigraphy; without the tephras, identification and dating of prehistoric structures is almost impossible in the undifferentiated swamp sediments. Although accurate field identification of all the tephras at Kuk was essential, the present concern is only with the youngest, here formally named *Tibito Tephra*, and with the second youngest, here named *Olgaboli Tephra*. These two tephras are similar in field characteristics and liable to be confused with one another whereas the other tephras found within the period of human occupation are reasonably distinctive.†

Although codes of stratigraphic nomenclature normally demand

---

*BP. = Before Present = Before 1950.

†Although a later chapter is devoted to determining the age of Tibito Tephra it is worth noting now that ^{14}C dates suggest an age of about 240 years BP. Olgaboli Tephra has a ^{14}C age of 1100-1200 years BP.

reference to a type site for each formally proposed stratigraphic unit, rigorous adherence to such a principle poses several problems in relation to discontinuous small lenses of thin volcanic ashes. Vucetich and Pullar (1969) have proposed that type areas rather than type sites be defined for tephras. The two tephras in question are best exposed and most continuous on grassed surfaces at elevations > 3500 m, but such sites are rather inaccessible. On the other hand, Kuk Tea Research Station where the tephras were first discovered and where they have been most thoroughly investigated is undergoing continued agricultural development. Furthermore, even tiny remnants of one or other tephra are absent across large sections of the Kuk basin. It is intended, therefore, to propose the readily accessible crater of Mt Ambra (Fig. 3) as the type site. Descriptions in this report, however, refer particularly to the nearby Kuk Tea Research Station (Kuk prehistoric site).

Tibito Tephra (known to the field investigators as Z) was first recognised in an exposure on the east bank of Tibito Creek, on Block A4, Kuk Tea Research Station (1546 m asl):

0-29	cm	fibrous *Phragmites* peat
29-31	cm	olive-grey silty fine sand (Tibito Tephra)
31-42	cm	fibrous *Phragmites* peat
42-92	cm	compact, largely oxidised, finely divided black peat.

Olgaboli Tephra (formerly known as Q), the second youngest tephra, was first identified on Block A9 at Kuk. Here Olgaboli Tephra occurs as a 4-6cm dark grey silty sand on the floor of prehistoric barets.

Mt Ambra Crater exposes the following sequence:

0-10	cm	grey-brown crumb structured topsoil
10-14	cm	red and green pellets of reworked Tibito Tephra in grey fine crumb structured matrix.
14-18	cm	Tibito Tephra — green fine sand.
18-47	cm	grey organic clay with oxidised root channels.
47-54	cm	organic clay and reworked Olgaboli Tephra.
54-58	cm	Olgaboli Tephra — grey fine sand.
58-61+	cm	grey organic clay.

Depths and thicknesses vary even across the small area of the infilled Ambra crater — gardening activity has occurred even there!

Binocular microscope and radiographic examination of the Mt Ambra sediments emphasises the sharp basal contact of Tibito Tephra, the more diffuse upper boundary and mixing with overlying sediment, the density of the tephra relative to surrounding sediments, and the penetration of the tephra by biotic channels. Bedding of the tephra is rarely evident and the boundary between *in situ* airfall tephra and the overlying reworked tephra is not always discernible. Detailed examination of Olgaboli Tephra reveals essentially the same features.

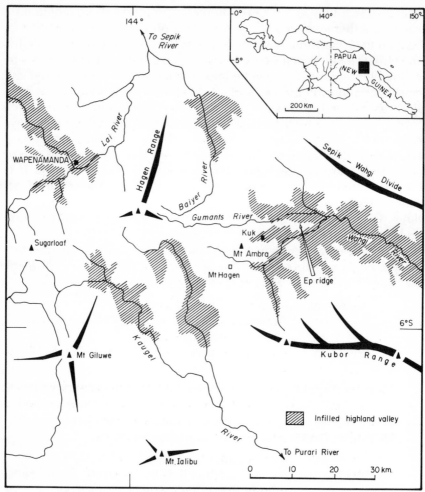

Fig. 3   *The central highlands of Papua New Guinea*

Tibito Tephra

The colour of Tibito Tephra is olive-grey but variable. The field colour in Munsell notation is 10Y3/1, dark yellowish-grey. The clay fraction from the tephra dried on a glass plate is 5Y7/1, light yellowish-grey. Where the layer is less than 2-3 cm thick and much penetrated by channels it frequently takes on some colour from the surrounding sediment, thus darkening the tephra. At some sites where it is lightly cemented, wide red iron oxide veins penetrate through the layer. Nevertheless, the olive-grey or greenish hue of Tibito Tephra is its most readily identifiable field characteristic.

Tibito Tephra freqently occurs at depths of from 20-40 cm. However, the best preservation occurs in large prehistoric barets at depths of more than 80 cm. In such sites current bedding is frequently evident.

The true airfall thickness of Tibito Tephra at Kuk is not known but is believed to be 3-4 cm. Individual exposures reveal all variations between discontinuous lines of tephra balls (1-2 cm in diameter) and reworked baret fills up to 12-14 cm thickness.

Because reworking is universal, particle size characteristics also cannot be determined with accuracy. Some collected samples have had varying proportions of fines removed, others are probably the winnowed and redeposited portions. Three particle size curves for the fraction coarser than 3.75 ϕ (0.074 mm) show that the mean particle size is a fine sand (Fig. 4). Variations in maximum particle size ($D_{10\phi}$) also indicate that considerable reworking has occurred.

When dry and not cemented by iron oxides Tibito Tephra forms soft, slightly coherent masses which crush very easily with light pressure to a dark green sandy powder, the colour of which cannot be accurately described using the usual Munsell Soil Colour Chart. The fines from this powder, moistened and smeared on the finger and then left to dry, leave a dark green film. This powdery consistency and smear colour test help distinguish Tibito from Olgaboli Tephra. The smear test colour seems to be characteristic of, and specific to, Tibito Tephra for most doubtful samples.

A low to intermediate allophane content is indicated for Tibito Tephra using a Fieldes and Perrot (1966) field allophane test kit.

The mineral fraction of the Tibito Tephra samples is dominated by subequal grains of pale to medium green pyroxene and plagioclase. In some samples the feldspar is unweathered. Most of the grains, however, are unaltered pumiceous glass. The glass shards are angular, colourless, and highly vesicular. The vesicles have occasional haematite coatings but are unfilled. Some of the glass is opaque and oxidised but most is clear and fresh. No quartz was visible in any samples.

Olgaboli Tephra

Olgaboli Tephra, a thin grey-black medium silty sand, has a general Munsell colour of 2.5Y N3/0 (grey-black), but where graded bedding is found the finer upper parts have a much more grey-brown colour. The clay fraction dried on a glass slide has a Munsell colour of 10YR 7/1, light yellow-brown grey. Like Tibito Tephra, this tephra takes on some of the colour of the surrounding sediment.

At some sites on Block A9 Olgaboli Tephra preserved as a baret fill appears to have three graded beds, all fining upwards and becoming browner upwards. However, at the Mt Ambra Crater site, the tephra shows no graded bedding; the lowermost 4 cm appears undisturbed. The uppermost 6 cm, washed in from the gently sloping crater walls, shows no upward fining or other discernible bedding.

Particle size analyses for Olgaboli Tephra (Fig. 5) show the tephra to be a fine sand. Marked variations in maximum particle size ($D_{10\phi}$) emphasise that reworking of the tephra has occurred.

Olgaboli Tephra is rather more cemented than Tibito Tephra.

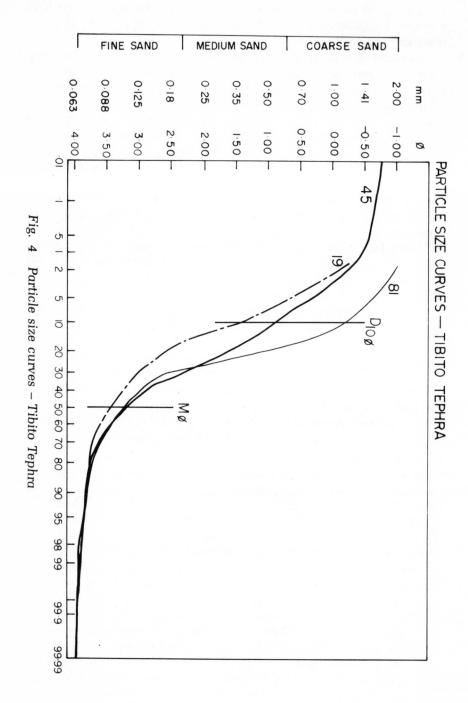

Fig. 4   Particle size curves – Tibito Tephra

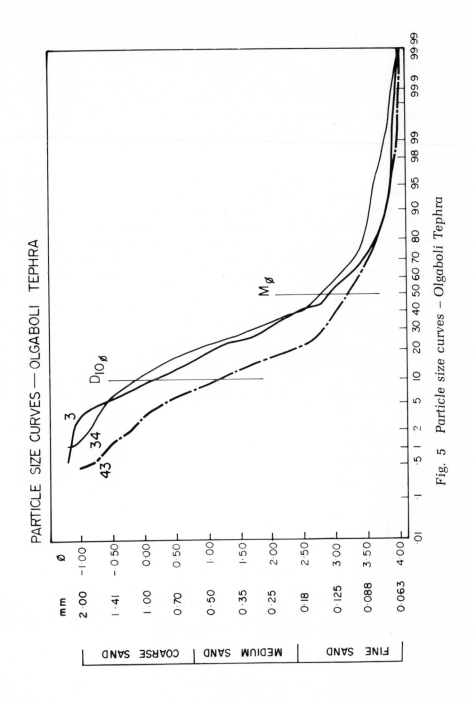

Fig. 5   *Particle size curves – Olgaboli Tephra*

Aggregates, particularly of the coarse basal layer, are difficult to crush and are enriched by iron oxide especially along root channels. Aggregates are usually blocky. Where the tephra is not sorted the ash powders in the same way as for Tibito Tephra but more pressure is required. The smear test produces a dark grey to black film on the finger.

Under a low power microscope the ash is a greyer colour than Tibito Tephra and usually has more iron oxide visible as films on grains and surfaces. Aggregates are more common and firmer. The volcanic glass appears to be colourless. Thin sections of Olgaboli Tephra indicate that most mineral grains are plagioclase. Minor amounts of pale green augite occur but no quartz was found. Angular, vesicular oxidised glass dominates the samples. One fragment of fine grained glass with microlites of plagioclase was observed.

In summary, Tibito and Olgaboli tephras are similar in particle size and in most field characteristics. However, they can frequently be distinguished by colour, by stratigraphic position where both are present and, with practice, by minor differences in consistency and 'feel'. Discontinuous lines of tephra balls are much more common in Tibito Tephra though this difference could result from a site or age factor rather than from inherent differences. Some samples are difficult to identify positively on field criteria alone.

3 Chemical fingerprinting and distribution of Tibito and Olgaboli Tephras

Chemical variations resulting from particle sorting and admixture

The spread of volcanic debris from an eruptive centre is broadly dependent upon particle radius, particle density, launch velocity, angle of elevation and release height (Wilson, 1972). Downwind velocities and rates of lateral wind shear determine the ratio of long and short axes of the depositional ellipse (Fig. 2), while particle shape, in addition to the factors already mentioned, influences settling time.

Obviously bubble-rich glass or pumice fragments of low density are liable to drift further downwind than crystals or lithic fragments. Consequently tephra composition can vary with distance from source (Fig. 6). With the concentration of particular trace elements in specific mineral assemblages of the tephra, downwind changes in trace element concentrations may also occur, though this appears to have never been demonstrated. While such variations are unlikely to be significant within the relatively small area of the upper Wahgi Valley (Fig. 3), chemical correlations across wider areas reported later need to take such possibilities into account.

From the knowledge that specific mineral assemblages have particular particle sizes, densities and shapes and hence differing fallout times (down times from release height), it follows that coarse and fine size fractions at the one site may have differing mineral assemblages and thus varying trace element concentrations. Therefore the removal of fines by surface water (or wind?) winnowing or the concentration of coarse size grades is likely to increase element variation between samples of the one tephra.

Reworking of the tephra by geomorphic, biologic or human agency is also likely to increase element concentration variability by inclusion of foreign mineral (and biologic) material. In extreme cases of mineral admixture the element concentrations will tend towards those

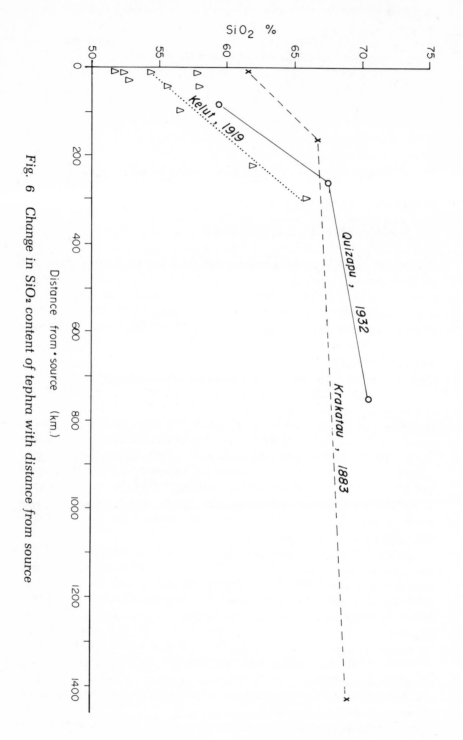

Fig. 6   Change in SiO₂ content of tephra with distance from source

characteristic of the substrate or overburden material. Admixture of organic material raises loss on ignition but the selective uptake of elements by specific plants (cf. Brooks, 1972) may influence total element concentrations through ignition residue.

A further problem arises through weathering of the tephra. With increasing age there is a selective loss of mobile elements such as Sr and Rb and a progressive concentration of 'stable' elements such as Ti, Y and Zr. Furthermore, the rate and the character of mineral weathering at the base of an abandoned drainage ditch may be rather different from that continuing on an abandoned garden surface.

Given these varying influences, it is unreasonable to expect highly accurate analyses of tephra deposits. Influences resulting from weathering may be unimportant in tephra as young as Tibito and Olgaboli, but this cannot be stated with any certainty.

Chemical fingerprinting of the type undertaken in this study will only be satisfactory for correlation purposes where gross differences in element concentrations are present and where large numbers of sample analyses providing some sort of statistical basis for comparison are available.

A further discussion of the influence of tephra reworking and altitudinal and environmental controls on the analytical results, with particular reference to Olgaboli Tephra, is presented in Appendix 2.

Analytical methods

Chemical analyses of highlands tephra were undertaken with the aim of 'chemically fingerprinting' tephra so that individual samples of uncertain field characteristics could be identified accurately. Various techniques of chemical identification have been utilised elsewhere, including element concentrations in magnetites using powder cameras (Kohn, 1970), microprobe analyses of glass or magnetite separates (Westgate, et al., 1970) and neutron activation analysis of glass shards (Borchardt and Harward, 1971). The basic analytic technique used here is set out by Norrish and Chappell (1967) in their paper 'X-ray fluorescence spectrography'. Analyses were performed using a Siemens SRS Sequential X-ray Spectrometer.

Initially fingerprinting of the tephra was attempted using the magnetic fraction only, but difficulties were experienced using Kohn's (1970) technique for extracting pure samples of this fraction in sufficient quantities to make fused lithium borate-lanthanum glass discs. Furthermore, the time taken for sample preparation was unacceptably long.

Second, whole sample analyses were undertaken for major elements. Again, sample preparation was time consuming for a large number of samples but more importantly for the present discussion, the major element concentrations for the two tephras are so similar that the analyses do not discriminate between them.

Third, whole sample analyses for trace elements were undertaken.

Samples were oven-dried, obvious plant roots and other contaminants removed, the samples crushed in a Tema mill, and formed into a pressed pellet with a boric acid backing (Norrish and Chappell, 1967. p.204). Preparation time per sample was only a few minutes.

The pressed pellets were, at first, analysed for the following trace elements: Ti, V, Cr, Co, Ni, Cu, Zn, Ga, Rb, Sr, Y, Zr, U and Th. The first seven of these elements must be analysed under vacuum. Problems were found with many samples breaking up so that attention was directed toward the last seven elements determined without vacuum. Where mass absorption coefficients were determined by the Compton scatter method, storage in the PDP-8 octal computer controlling the Siemens XRF analyser was inadequate so Ga analyses were sacrificed. Of the remaining elements, U and Th are present in only very small quantities (< 5 ppm) in Tibito and Olgaboli Tephras and accurate determinations were not possible.

The four elements Rb, Sr, Y and Zr have thus been used in the present investigation. Of these elements, Sr and Zr have previously been used by Jack and Carmichael (1969) for the chemical fingerprinting of acid volcanic rocks in California, while Cann (1970) has recommended the use of Y and Zr (with Ti) for discriminating between basalts from various volcanic environments.

Not all of the 230 or so samples considered here were analysed by precisely the same method. Mass absorption coefficients were measured directly or estimated by measuring the intensity of Compton-scattered radiation. Corrections for 'loss' of volatiles were appled to some samples, while some samples were ignited at 800°C for one hour prior to analysis. Other samples were analysed after extraction of the magnetic fraction or after removal of a particular size fraction. The variations in analytical techniques were imposed because of the small size of some samples, the time required for sample preparation, and, it must be admitted, inexperience with the method.* The form in which each sample was analysed is recorded in Appendix 1.

These variations in the precise method of analysis and calculation do not improve the reliability of the results, but they do not, it will be shown, prejudice the conclusions reached here for the samples considered, the elements analysed, and the accuracies required.

Analytical results: within sample variation
Figures 7 and 8 indicate the range in sample values resulting from

*The preferred method of sample treatment is: (1) remove obvious contaminants such as plant roots and ignite at 800°C for one hour, (2) keep residue in sealed airtight container to prevent hygroscopic clays from absorbing water, (3) measure mA or calculate using major element analyses. Whole samples should be used with no fraction removed; however, it would be worthwhile analysing the sand fraction alone providing aggregated allophane can be successfully deflocculated and removed.

repeated analysis of the one sample. Each plotted point represents the mean value for pressed pellets prepared from the one sample crushing. Two plotted points with differing analytical numbers with a connecting line indicate that two sets of pellets were prepared from the one field sample. Analytical numbers and field descriptions of samples are listed in Appendix 1.

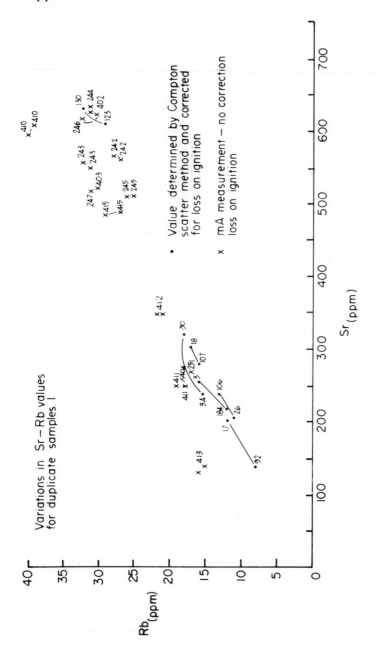

Fig. 7   Variations in Sr-Rb values for duplicate samples

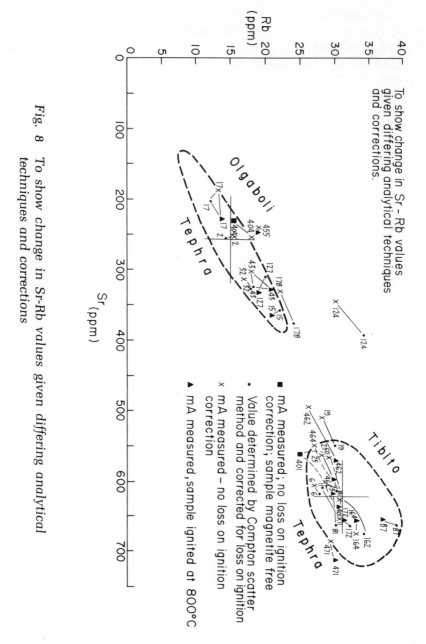

Fig. 8   To show change in Sr-Rb values given differing analytical techniques and corrections

Several points are worthy of note:

1. (Figure 7)   Substantial variations in values for identical samples occur, particularly for those samples analysed by the Compton scatter method and with corrections applied for loss on ignition. The variations between samples appear to result from poor values for loss on ignition and from the use of only one loss on ignition

value per field sample.

2.   (Figure 7)   Samples analysed using a measured mass absorption value and no loss on ignition correction show a significantly lower and more acceptable level of variation.

3.   (Figure 8)   Where samples have been re-analysed using a different technique or some variation in sample quality (e.g. magnetic fraction removed) there is also a change in Sr and Rb values. The removal of the magnetic fraction from a sample has less effect on Sr, Y and Zr contents (see Appendix 1) than on Rb values.

4.   (Figure 8)   Samples that have undergone ignition at 800°C usually provide the highest values. Analyses with loss on ignition corrections generally provide higher values, as expected, than the same samples with no loss on ignition correction. Not surprisingly, if the values with measured mass absorption are corrected for loss on ignition, they plot much more closely to the already corrected values.

The possible effects of these analytical variations need to be kept in mind when interpreting the grouping of samples on subsequent scatter diagrams.

Tibito Tephra

Fifteen analyses of Wahgi Valley samples of Tibito Tephra are plotted on Fig. 9. A few of the samples in this plot come not from Kuk but from the Gumants Basin a few kilometres to the north (Fig. 3). The values for Y and Zr as well as those for Sr and Rb can be found in Appendix 1.

The mean values and standard deviation of the fifteen samples are given in Table 1 and reproduced on Fig. 9. The values are also surrounded by a dotted line which encloses all those samples from the Upper Wahgi firmly believed, on the basis of field evidence, to be Tibito Tephra. Thus the scatter diagram indicates a chemical confirmation of the field evidence despite the varied methods of analysis.

The point with the highest Sr and Rb values is in fact the sample from the original type site on Block A4 at Kuk (Chapter 2). The two points at the other end of the ellipse both have no loss on ignition correction. It is quite clear, for sample 19 at least, that this would plot much closer to the sample 19 with loss correction (Sr=550, Rb=30) if the correction had been applied (see Fig. 8).

Olgaboli Tephra

A Sr-Rb plot for thirty-seven samples identified in the field as Olgaboli Tephra also shows a neat grouping of values that are easily enclosed by an elongate ellipse (Fig. 9). Sample statistics for Olgaboli Tephra are presented in Table 2.

It is clear from the sample statistics that Olgaboli Tephra is more variable than Tibito Tephra, particularly in terms of Sr, but whether this is due to a longer period of weathering, more sample reworking, more included volatiles (mainly organic material) or greater variability in determination of loss on ignition values is not known.

Table 1

Trace element sample statistics — Tibito Tephra

		Sr	Rb	Y	Zr
Mean	$\bar{x}$	600	30	28	72
Standard deviation	o	49	3.9	2.8	10.7

Table 2

Trace element sample statistics — Olgaboli Tephra

		Sr	Rb	Y	Zr
Mean	$\bar{x}$	261	15	27	84
Standard deviation	o	63	3.7	3.8	22.6

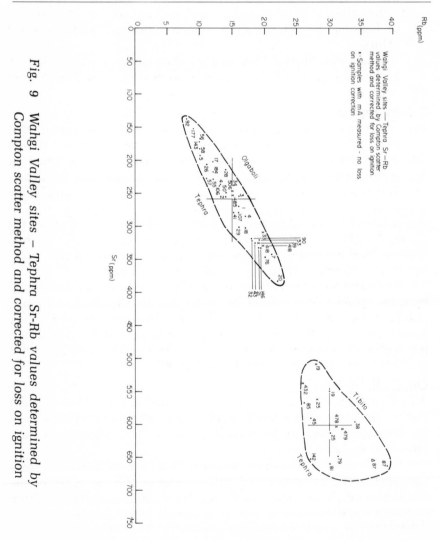

Fig. 9   Wahgi Valley sites – Tephra Sr-Rb values determined by Compton scatter method and corrected for loss on ignition

The high values, samples 7 and 20, for example, are coarse basal layers of Olgaboli Tephra with low loss of ignition corrections (5.4 and 3.1 per cent respectively). Furthermore, sample 20 comes from Nonnymuk Lake near Mt Ambra and is likely to represent a relatively unweathered tephra because of its deposition in a semi-permanent water body.

On the other hand the samples at the opposite end of the ellipse, Nos. 92, 177, 56, 143 and 58 are all samples collected from sites such as baret fills where admixing with surrounding material was probable and collection of a sample of pure tephra difficult. All five samples have relatively high loss on ignition values (17.4, 37.6, 16.5, 15.6 and 8.0 per cent respectively).

A full discussion of the possible interpretations of the range of values for Olgaboli Tephra is given in Appendix 2.

The distribution of Tibito and Olgaboli Tephras

As already mentioned Tibito and Olgaboli tephras are preserved only occasionally at Kuk Tea Research Station and only rarely will they both be found at one site. Absence from a site, however, does not necessarily mean that the tephra was not deposited.

In the attempt to extend the known distribution of the two tephras by working outwards from Kuk, attention has been concentrated on high mountains, swamps, and sites on the perimeter of the known distribution. The problems of field identification and correlation described earlier make positive identification of the tephra at isolated sites even more difficult. Field identification criteria are inadequate when the nearest site with positive identification is tens of kilometres distant and increasing reliance must be placed on chemical criteria.

Chemical evidence

Samples believed, on the basis of field exploration, to be either Tibito or Olgaboli (or other tephras from key sites) have been treated and analysed in the same way as those from the Upper Wahgi Valley.

Figure 10 illustrates the scatter of Rb and Sr values for samples from outside the Upper Wahgi Valley. The two dotted ellipses contain the scatter of Upper Wahgi Valley samples of Tibito and Olgaboli Tephra as shown on Fig. 9. Means and standard deviations of the Upper Wahgi Valley samples are also shown.

Tibito Tephra

Figure 11 shows the location of some twenty-five sites with a total number of forty-six samples of putative Tibito Tephra stretching from Koroba and Tari in the west to Mugil (near Karkar Island), Madang and Saidor in the east. The maximum east-west spread of sites is thus c.500 km and the maximum north-south spread from Mugil to Mt Michael is about 130 km.

There seem to be no problems with any samples that plot within the ellipse defined by Tibito Tephra samples from the Upper Wahgi

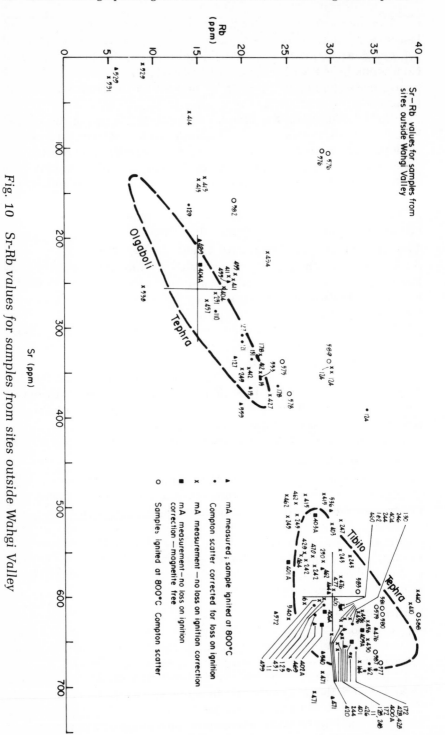

Fig. 10   Sr-Rb values for samples from sites outside Wahgi Valley

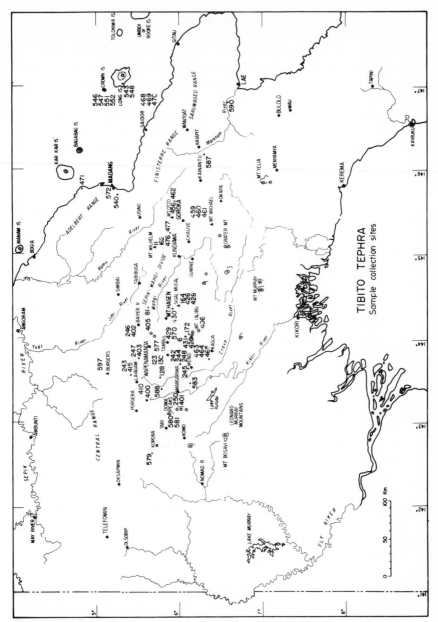

Fig. 11   Tibito Tephra – sample collection sites

Valley. It can be ascertained from Appendix 1 that each of these samples has expectable Zr and Y values and there is no reason to doubt onfield or chemical criteria that these samples are other than Tibito Tephra. There is nothing sacrosanct about the Tibito Tephra ellipse based on the Upper Wahgi Valley samples. A far greater number of samples is now considered — by definition some samples (about a third) should fall outside one standard deviation from the mean. However, samples lying outside the ellipse are now discussed individually:

540   Gogol floodplain (collected by Dr C.F. Pain): although this sample has a low Rb value a more accurate analysis on an 800°C ignition residue plots within the ellipse.

471   Mugil-Karkar: three analyses all plot outside the ellipse with high Sr values. These samples were collected from a beach ridge-foredune system. The possibility of Sr contamination in this environment is high. Though the collection site lies close to Karkar and Bagabag volcanoes and the sample is rather darker coloured than usual for Tibito, its general appearance, stratigraphic position and trace element chemistry suggest that it probably is a sample of Tibito Tephra.

572   Kranket Island, Madang: A careful analysis indicates a rather low Rb value. On field and general stratigraphic evidence there can be little doubt that this sample is Tibito Tephra. It is also worth noting that all of the coastal samples (469, 470, 471, 540 and 572) plot rather low on Fig. 10. This may result from differential weathering in the lowland environment (all other sites are above 1500 m elevation) or from variations in particle size and mineralogy on the margins of the known distribution.

401   Margarima: As shown on Fig. 8, magnetite-free samples tend to have low Rb values. Sample 250 is a duplicate.

245   Quen, 1.5 km N of Mendi: Duplicate analyses plot close together. There is no reason to doubt that it is Tibito Tephra.

462   Mt Otto: Duplicate analyses plot close together. Another Mt Otto sample (456-3 analyses) plots well within the defined field. A careful analysis of 462 with prior ignition at 800°C and measured mA also plots within the field.

415   Ipea-Sirunki Ash 4 (Ash A in Oldfield et al., 1977; collected by Prof. F. Oldfield): Duplicate analyses plot close together. This sample was probably contaminated by organic residues.

536   Yumbis-Wage Z-1: Although a good analysis of this sample plots very close to the Tibito Tephra ellipse the sample in the field directly overlies Tibito Tephra (sample 400). It is clearly younger than Tibito Tephra, occurs at the collection site as a yellow-brown clay c.2.5 cm thick and could not be confused on field characteristics. Although Sr and Rb values of 505 and 30 ppm suggest this sample is similar to Tibito Tephra, Zr and Y values of 274 and 40 ppm indicate that it is quite distinctive. Nothing further is known about this tephra.

403   and 247 Sangulapa, Wabag (collected by Nita Pupu): Duplicate analyses plot close together. A third analysis on a magnetite free sample (403A) plots within the ellipse but close to 403 and 247.

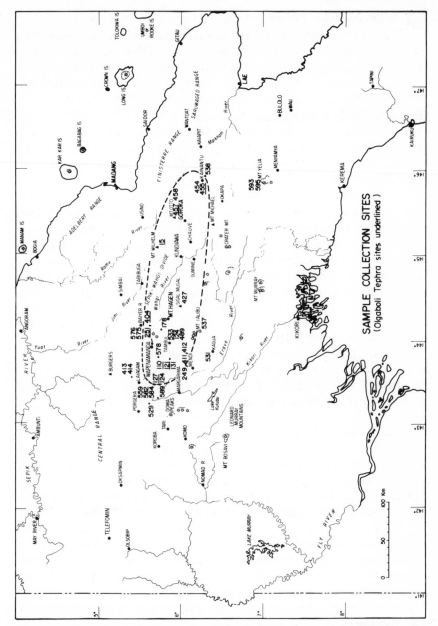

Fig. 12   Sample collection sites (Olgaboli Tephra sites underlined)

410 Laiagam (collected by Tim Payakalya): Duplicate samples with high Rb contents. Other values indicate that this is Tibito Tephra (Appendix 1). In fact the sample plots very close to sample 87 from the site where Tibito Tephra was originally identified.

580 Tari Gap: This sample plots inside the ellipse but has a Zr value of 105 ppm. On stratigraphic grounds and correlation with 581 it is

believed to be Tibito Tephra.

There is no chemical, field or stratigraphic evidence to suspect that any of the samples plotted close to or in the Tibito Tephra ellipse as shown in Fig. 10 are not in fact Tibito Tephra with the exception of sample 536 which seems to be a younger tephra. Figure 11, then, illustrates the currently known distribution of Tibito Tephra.

Olgaboli Tephra and other tephras

The Sr-Rb ratios for a variety of non-Tibito Tephra samples are shown in Fig. 10 with site locations shown on Fig. 12. Some of these samples are known not to be Olgaboli Tephra on the basis of stratigraphy and field characteristics.

No samples plot within the ellipse below the mean value for Rb. This perhaps accords with the deductions made in Appendix 2 where some evidence suggested that the high values of Sr and Rb and lower values of Zr represented the uncontaminated Olgaboli Tephra. In general, samples collected outside the Wahgi Valley are less contaminated and/or less weathered than those collected at Kuk because: (1) they are generally from higher elevations; (2) they were collected later when problems associated with sampling had already become apparent, and (3) better sample preparation and analytical techniques were normally used.

Thus, taking those samples with Sr values above 300 and Rb values above 18, and examining the additional chemical data and the field evidence, it is quite clear that all the samples in this section of Fig. 10 are samples of Olgaboli Tephra with the exceptions of samples 124 and 559:

124 Ipagua-Tambul 132/1 Ash 1 (collected by Dr C.F. Pain): On three analyses this sample has high values of Zr and Rb. This sample was believed to be Tibito Tephra at the time of collection; chemical fingerprinting indicates that it is not.

559 Sirunki (collected by Dr P. Hughes): This sample has high values of Zr and Y, although it was believed to be either Tibito or Olgaboli Tephra at the time of collection. Subsequent examination of this field area suggests that sample 559 represents a much older tephra.

The second group of samples plotted on Fig. 10 having above average Rb values but Sr values about the mean for Olgaboli Tephra contain a number of samples some of which are clearly not Olgaboli Tephra on field characteristics and stratigraphic evidence. Each is discussed briefly:

251 and 404 Tchak Valley, Wapenamanda (informant: Wia Tabai): Analyses of three differing fractions by different techniques indicate that the samples are clearly Olgaboli Tephra.

110 Mendi Road — W side of Mt Giluwe: Olgaboli Tephra.

457 Mt Otto summit: This sample has a rather greenish-yellowish tinge in the field and rather high Zr (94 ppm) but it is probably Olgaboli Tephra.

455 Kainantu Airstrip — SW corner of football field: Compact greenish-black tephra c.4 cm thick, grading finer upwards. A good analysis using a previously ignited sample indicates that this is Olgaboli Tephra.

454 The same site as 455 but collected from a 1 cm thick reworked layer: On field evidence samples 454 and 455 were believed to be the same layer. This sample with high Zr and Y values may be contaminated by organic matter or it may, in fact, represent a different ash from sample 455.

489 Tambul — Ash Kau 2 (Pain, 1973, collected by Dr C.F. Pain): Other details are required but it seems unlikely that this tephra is Olgaboli Tephra. An analysis on a sample ashed at 800°C showed a Zr value of 260 ppm and a Y content of 35 ppm.

411 Egari 2 60-61 cm (Ash C of Oldfield et al., 1977; collected by Prof. F. Oldfield): This sample cannot on field evidence be Olgaboli Tephra as it stratigraphically underlies Egari 2 40-41 cm Ash B which has been analysed (sample 412) as definitely Olgaboli Tephra. The high Zr and Y values (107 and 19 ppm respectively) might also indicate that the sample is not Olgaboli Tephra but organic contamination could produce a similar result. Only very small amounts of sample were available for analysis.

Only eleven other samples are depicted on Fig. 10: of these, samples 529, 531, 538, 582 and 584 are old, very weathered clay-rich yellow-brown tephra. There was no possibility of confusion with Olgaboli and Tibito Tephra on field identification criteria. Nevertheless, it is gratifying to note that there was also no possibility of confusion chemically given the trace element values presented in Appendix 1.

Sample 129, from Sugarloaf, stratigraphically underlies sample 127 which is clearly Olgaboli Tephra on stratigraphic, field and chemical criteria. However, 129 is not particularly distinctive on chemical grounds as it has Zr and Y values of 111 and 32 ppm respectively. These values are not dissimilar to many of those samples of Olgaboli Tephra with low Sr and Rb values and high Zr values. However, sample 129 has a loss on ignition of 45 per cent; thus the analytical results are in some doubt.

414 Oldfield (1976) believed that this sample (Ash B in Oldfield et al., 1977) is Olgaboli Tephra and correlated with Ash B at Egari (sample 412). The chemical values established here suggest it is not a sample of Olgaboli Tephra and that it is not correlated with Ash B at Egari (which clearly is Olgaboli Tephra). Both Sr and Zr values are too low (60 and 38 ppm respectively).*

413 This sample stratigraphically underlies 414 but it is not particularly different chemically from many Olgaboli Tephra

---

*Both 414 and 413 were analysed as single samples, not enough sample being available for duplicate analyses.

samples except in its Sr-Rb ratio: on current evidence it is not possible to clarify the relationship of this sample to others.*

578 T83A Q, Tomba: Although the Rb value is high (26 ppm) this sample is clearly Olgaboli Tephra.

575 and 576 Baiyer River: These two samples, collected from a depth of 20-30 cm on a colluvial hillslope, were believed to be either Tibito or Olgaboli Tephra, but Sr values are low (80-100 ppm) and Zr values are c.300 ppm. Good samples were difficult to collect without contamination. These samples appear to represent a previously unknown tephra. Some field evidence suggests that this tephra is older than Tibito but its relationship to Olgaboli Tephra is unknown.

589 Kondo, drainage ditch — S of Kandep. At the time of collection this sample was believed to be Tibito Tephra and identical to sample 599 (which is Tibito Tephra). However, the ash layer is buried to depths of up to 150 cm on < 6° colluvial surfaces and no other tephras are present. The sample on geochemical grounds is certainly not Tibito Tephra, probably not Olgaboli Tephra, and Zr values suggest it is also a different tephra from that represented by sample 124.

The probable known distribution of Olgaboli Tephra is marked on Fig. 12 by a dotted line. More refined analyses and a denser spread of samples will allow greater accuracy and firmer conclusions to be drawn but it should be pointed out that the dotted distribution does not indicate the total distribution of this tephra. Small reworked remnants of tephra are difficult to find in the field and Olgaboli Tephra may eventually be proved to occur at sites already examined but outside the shown distribution. On the other hand some of the samples currently included may be shown to belong to another tephra distinct from Olgaboli Tephra. This is believed to be an unlikely possibility (Appendix 2) but the stratigraphy of many of the sites distant from the Upper Wahgi Valley is quite uncontrolled and it has not always been possible to examine sites in any detail, particularly where short duration helicopter landings have been made on isolated high mountain sites.

The collection of a number of thin tephra beds from a wide variety of sites with minimal stratigraphic control reveals the presence of a number of poorly known tephra of unknown age but generally older than Olgaboli Tephra. Insufficient samples are available yet to make meaningful correlations or even to define the geochemistry of the tephra. These older tephras are of no further concern in the present analysis.

4 Potential sources of Tibito and Olgaboli Tephras

Figures 11 and 12 indicate that although the complete distributions of the two tephras are not known the results of chemical fingerprinting suggest that both Tibito Tephra and Olgaboli Tephra are very widespread.

As the two tephras were first identified in the Upper Wahgi Valley, the initial search for sources was concentrated within a 100 km radius of the Kuk prehistoric site. Other potential sources requiring investigation included the highlands volcanoes outside this radius, Krakatau (suggested by earlier investigators) and the volcanoes of the Bismarck Sea to the north of the Papua New Guinea mainland.

Potential sources close to Kuk prehistoric site

The major volcanoes of the highlands are much eroded (Ollier and Mackenzie, 1974), the youngest K-Ar dates on Mt Hagen and Mt Giluwe lavas providing ages of 200,000-220,000 years (Page and Johnson, 1974; Löffler, 1976). Pain and Blong (1976) indicate that the last major tephra eruption from Mt Hagen occurred more than 50,000 years BP and that this tephra fall was the last major fall from any centre in the area with the exception of Birip (Pain and Blong, 1979). The last eruption from Birip was certainly late Pleistocene, possibly about 18,000 years BP (Dr C.F. Pain, pers. comm.).

Minor volcanic centres near to the upper Wahgi Valley include Mt Ambra 4 km west of Kuk, Mt Malia, a parasitic cone on Mt Hagen, Terek in the Nebilyer, the Kraildung centre on the northern side of the Gumants (not previously recorded), and the string of small tuff rings, cones and maars along the SE side of Mt Giluwe (Fig. 13).

All of these vents can be fairly easily eliminated from consideration as potential sources of Olgaboli and Tibito Tephra. Both tephra are found in the crater of Mt Ambra, which has also been dated by a basal peat within the crater to have been inactive for at least 32,000 years (ANU-1466). Terek, Kraildung, Malia (probably) and in fact Mt Ambra are all overlain by Tomba Tephra, the tephra identified and named by Pain and Blong (1976) as at least 50,000 years old. Similarly, at least some of the small vents (possibly as young as 1000 years according to Blake and Löffler, 1971) along the south-eastern side of Mt Giluwe are overlain by Bune Tephra, a tephra coeval with Tomba Tephra (Pain and Blong, 1976). Furthermore, on morphological grounds, none of these southern Giluwe vents could have produced any significant tephra. Finally, ample evidence will be produced later to show that neither Olgaboli nor Tibito Tephra thicken toward any of these vents (cf. Fig. 2).

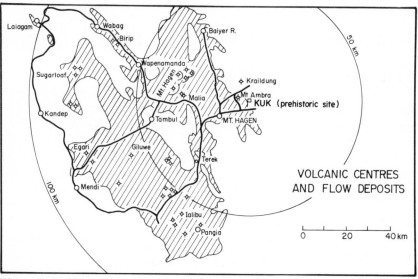

Fig. 13   *Minor volcanic centres within 100 km of Kuk prehistoric site*

Other highlands sources

The distribution of major volcanoes in the highlands is shown on Fig. 14. All of these volcanoes can be regarded as extinct (Cooke and Johnson, 1978) except for Doma Peaks and Mount Yelia, which still show some signs of thermal activity, and are also the locations of some seismic activity (Mackenzie, 1976, p.223). In fact, across the highlands from west of Tari to east of Kainantu, Tomba Tephra is the youngest tephra from a highlands source or the youngest tephra present is coeval with Tomba Tephra (Pain and Blong, 1976, 1979; Pain and Wood, 1976). This generalisation does not apply, however, to Mt Yelia and there is some doubt about Doma Peaks because of its solfataric activity.

Mt Yelia

Mt Yelia lies 125 km south of Goroka in the Eastern Highlands Province. The general geology of the volcano has been described by Mackenzie (1973). Some cool fumarolic areas occur near the summit, 2737m asl (Branch, 1967). No detailed tephrostratigraphy of the Mt Yelia area has been undertaken but preliminary investigations (Blong, unpubl.) suggest that the last significant tephra eruption of Mt Yelia was a classic Plinian-Pelèan sequence which deposited about 1.5 m of

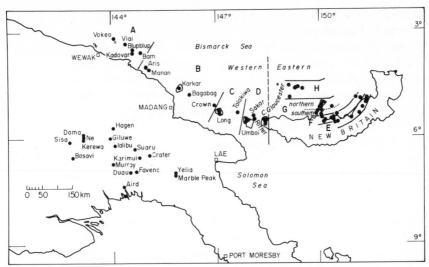

Fig. 14   *Major volcanic centres – Bismarck Arc and Papua New Guinea highlands*

pumice lapilli in the Marawaka area, a few km from the volcano, probably about 18,000 years BP (SUA-836). This airfall deposit is overlain by variable thicknesses of pyroclastic flow material. Younger tephra eruptions may have occurred on Mt Yelia but reconnaissance observations suggest not.

Doma Peaks

Doma Peaks, a stratovolcano about 2900 m high, is located (Fig. 14) in the Southern Highlands. The morphology and petrography of the volcano have been described by Mackenzie (1973). As a result of local legends about an eruption and the reports of airline pilots that sulphur smells emanated from the summit area, a brief volcanological investigation was undertaken by Taylor (1971). Taylor noted the presence of several solfataras near the summit and concluded that the date of the last eruptive activity was inconclusive but in the period 90 to 400 years previously. This age estimate is, in reality, based on Glasse's (1963) version of the Huli legend of *bingi*.

Blong's (1979) brief investigation of the Doma Peaks area confirms Taylor's (1971) view that a volcanic mudflow or lahar emptied the crater lake through a breach in the western wall, laying down an extensive deposit in the Wabia area. One radiocarbon date (SUA-697) on wood included in the deposit in the drained crater lake indicates that this event occurred about 800 years ago, and certainly more than 600 years ago. Furthermore, Dr C.F. Pain (pers. comm., 1978) has argued convincingly that the lahar or mudflow event did not produce any significant tephra, the last major tephra eruption in this area being that of Tomba Tephra, more than 50,000 years ago. Certainly, the lahar event was the last significant activity at Doma, although solfataric and earthquake activity continue to the present.

Chemical analyses

Although minor centres within a 100 km range of Kuk Tea Research Station are definitely not sources of either Tibito or Olgaboli Tephra and although only Doma and possibly Mt Yelia are likely to have been active in Holocene time, it is worthwhile examining the major and minor element geochemistry of the highlands volcanoes in relation to that of Tibito and Olgaboli Tephras.

Tables 3 and 4 present major element analyses of Tibito Tephra and Olgaboli Tephra respectively. The two tephras are very similar. Plotted on MacKenzie and Chappell's (1972, p.5) nomenclature diagram (Fig. 15) both tephras are low Si-andesites or high K-low Si andesites.

Figure 16 indicates that both tephras have very different TiO_2-SiO_2 ratios from Yelia rocks. However, on a K_2O-SiO_2 plot some Doma rocks plot close to the tephra samples.

Table 3
Major element analyses* — Tibito Tephra
Upper Wahgi Valley

Sample No.	25	75	79	81	87	87	424
SiO_2	54.75	53.71	55.18	53.37	55.46	53.15	56.77
TiO_2	.87	.77	.76	.79	.79	.80	.66
Al_2O_3	23.24	17.52	16.58	18.47	20.50	19.21	17.25
Fe_2O_3	9.12	12.69	12.89	12.19	9.88	11.62	11.50
MnO	.15	.26	.04	.02	.16	.01	.18
MgO	2.84	3.33	3.35	3.25	3.23	3.43	3.21
CaO	6.13	7.57	7.06	7.15	6.76	7.35	7.79
Na_2O	1.80	2.47	2.37	2.55	2.12	2.69	2.22
K_2O	.90	1.65	1.56	1.56	.98	1.59	1.05
P_2O_5	.65	.33	.33	.43	.33	.49	.21
Total	100.46	100.30	100.10	99.78	100.21	100.33	100.84

*Total Fe as Fe_2O_3. Samples ignited at 800°C before analysis.

On a Na_2O-K_2O plot the two tephras fall well below Hagen, Giluwe and Ialibu analyses. They also have much lower Na_2O contents than the Doma and Yelia samples, though sodium is one of the first elements likely to be leached in the weathering of the tephras.

Trace element analyses for Doma and Yelia rocks have not been published but it appears from MacKenzie's (1976) data that Rb contents of rocks from Hagen, Giluwe, Murray, Duau, Favenc and Bosavi are high compared with Olgaboli and Tibito tephras. Sr covers the range of Tibito Tephra but no analysed samples are as low as Olgaboli, Y values are similar and Zr values are generally higher than those for Tibito Tephra.

Additional trace elements were measured on one sample of Olgaboli (Sample 7) and two samples of Tibito (Samples 11 and 19) by Dr B. Chappell (Australian National University) and Dr R.W. Johnson (Bureau of Mineral Resources). These analyses are presented in Table 5.

Comparison of MacKenzie's Table 1 (1976) with these data indicate that the two tephra are considerably higher in V and Cu than any analysed Highland rocks but no other trace element values allow differentiation.

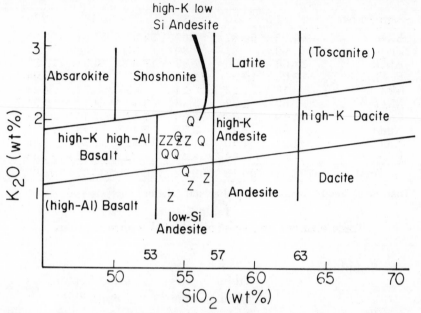

Fig. 15   Nomenclature diagram after MacKenzie and Chappell (1972) showing Tibito and Olgaboli Tephra

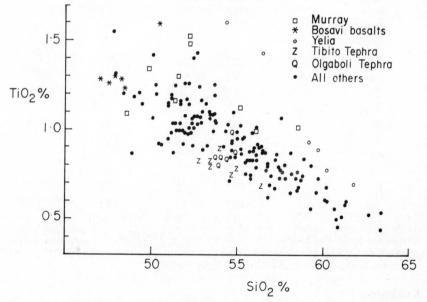

Fig. 16 TiO_2-SiO_2 data for highlands volcanoes (after MacKenzie, 1976) with Tibito and Olgaboli Tephra values

Table 4
Major element analyses* — Olgaboli Tephra
Upper Wahgi Valley

Sample No.	2	20	32	76	423	425
SiO_2	54.95	54.82	54.87	54.39	55.61	53.55
TiO_2	.99	.81	.80	.81	.84	.82
Al_2O_3	22.68	18.60	17.85	17.92	18.71	18.53
Fe_2O_3	10.05	10.97	11.19	11.55	10.53	12.94
MnO	.18	.22	.23	.23	.22	.23
MgO	2.62	3.22	3.38	3.40	3.14	3.31
CaO	5.59	7.32	7.69	7.58	7.14	7.57
Na_2O	1.66	2.25	2.55	2.44	2.35	2.39
K_2O	1.21	1.50	1.70	1.64	1.54	1.58
P_2O_5	.62	.44	.32	.49	.42	.33
Total	100.54	100.16	100.59	100.45	100.51	101.05

*Total Fe as Fe_2O_3. Samples ignited at 800°C before analysis.

Table 5
Trace element analyses* of selected tephra samples

Sample No.	11	19	7
	Tibito Tephra		Olgaboli Tephra
	ppm	ppm	ppm
Ba	245	475	455
Rb	30.0	27.0	18.6
Sr	645	510	333
Pb	10	12	15
Zr	63	85	60
Nb	—	2	1
Y	22	22	20
La	13	14	9
Ce	29	36	25
Nd	16	18	12
Sc	32	40	44
V	318	372	413
Cr	8	39	25
Ni	4	11	12
Cu	207	213	233
Zn	122	140	123
Ga	17.0	20.5	19.0

*Analysed by Dr B. Chappell, Australian National University. Mass-absorption corrections made on the assumption that the major-element chemistry of the samples is similar to that of Long Island rocks.

Krakatau

A widespread myth of a time of darkness amongst the people of the Papua New Guinea Highlands was tentatively attributed to the 1883 eruption of Krakatau by Watson (1963, 1967) and Nelson (1971). Glasse (1963, 1965) and Brookfield and Hart (1971), while confirming the widespread nature of the time of darkness legend, doubted that Krakatau was the source of the eruptive cloud. Blong (1975) showed that Krakatau (1883) could not have been the source of the legend. As a result of the researches of Verbeek (1886) and the investigations of the Royal Society Committee (1888), the 1883 eruption of Krakatau is well documented. Figure 17 indicates the commonly accepted area over which the Krakatau eruptive blasts were heard. Diego Garcia, 5000 km from Krakatau, was the most distant location to report the explosions. Mt Hagen lies some 4350 km east of Krakatau. Although no reports of the explosion are known from Papua New Guinea that does not necessarily preclude the possibility that the eruption was heard.

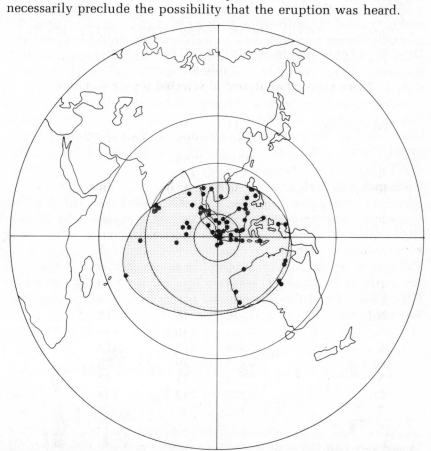

Fig. 17   Area in which sound of Krakatau 1883 eruption was heard
(after Symons, 1888)

Wexler (1951, p.48) has suggested that fine ash fell as much as 3200 km from Krakatau but there is no evidence that darkness extended further east than Bandung, only 260 km from the volcano. The only tephra from Krakatau that could have fallen over Papua New Guinea would have been the minute microscopic particles that circled the earth several times, producing optical effects such as brilliant sunsets and blue moons during the following few years. This material would have fallen unobserved as it did following other eruptions such as those of Quizapu (Chile — 1932), Agung (Bali — 1963), and Mt St Helens (USA — 1980).

Tephra from the Krakatau 1883 eruption possessed a SiO_2 content of 60-69 per cent (Judd, 1888, p.32, pp.40-1; Verbeek, 1886). It has been well described from a number of eruptions including Krakatau 1883 (Fig. 6) that the silica content of tephra increases with distance from the source as a result of the density separation of heavy crystal and lithic particles from the light frothy silica-rich pumice fragments as the tephra cloud drifts downwind (Chapter 3). Thus Krakatau tephra, if it had fallen in the Papua New Guinea area, would probably have had a silica content well above 70 per cent. In fact, tephra layers with more than about 55 per cent SiO_2 have not yet been found in the Highlands region.

Geochemical evidence and historical data lend no credence to the idea that Krakatau tephra fell on Papua New Guinea. That is not to deny, however, the possibility that optical effects and explosions were heard though lack of communication would have prevented their association with the Krakatau event.

Bismarck Sea Volcanoes

Figure 14 shows the volcanoes of the Bismarck Sea, divided into eastern and western portions and into zones as suggested by Johnson (1976). Only volcanoes of the western arc are considered here, mainly because these volcanoes are considerably closer to the Upper Wahgi Valley than are the eastern arc eruptive centres. Vokeo at the western end of the arc is some 210 km from Kuk Tea Research Station whilst Cape Gloucester at the western end of the eastern arc is more than 300 km distant.

ERUPTIVE HISTORY OF ACTIVE VOLCANOES IN PAPUA NEW GUINEA 1870 - 1977

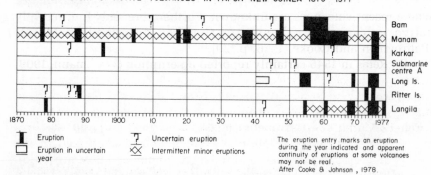

Fig. 18   Eruptive history of active volcanoes in Papua New Guinea 1870-1977

Probably all of the volcanoes shown are active with the exception of Crown Island. Bam, Manam, Karkar, Long, Ritter and Langila on Cape Gloucester have all erupted in the last 100 years and eruptive histories for this period are reasonably well known (Fig. 18). Some isolated earlier eruptions have also been recorded by passing navigators. The available data on tephra eruptions from the more important potential sources of Tibito and Olgaboli Tephra are summarised below.

Manam Island

The Manam Island volcano, reaching 1725 m asl, lies at latitude 4°06'S and longitude 145°4'E. Manam's eruptive history has been summarised by Fisher (1957) and Palfreyman and Cooke (1976). Activity of some sort seems to be continuous. Figure 18 presents a summary of post-1870 eruptions and indicates that Manam is the most active of the Bismarck Arc centres.

Stanley (1923, pp. 52-3), writing about the 11 August 1919 eruption, notes: 'When the rumbling ceased a grey-brown halo of dust encircled mountains, which gradually spread for miles over the mainland...At night, it was possible to read a newspaper 8 miles away by the reflection of the lava on the clouds.' This eruption was probably the most violent reported. Less violent tephra eruptions in 1920-1922 produced at least one period when ashfall darkened the north-west portion of the island (Palfreyman and Cooke, 1976, pp.123-4).

Pre-1870 eruptions, about which very little is known, were reported on the following dates (Palfreyman and Cooke, 1976):

1830	Morell
April 4 1700	William Dampier
April 21-22 1643	Abel Tasman
July 6-7 1616	Schouten and LeMaire
1545	de Retes.

There is some doubt about the first and last of these accounts. Morell (1832) claimed to have seen seven active volcanoes along the north coast. One volcano, he reported, was in the coast ranges, an area where recent volcanoes are unknown. Furthermore, only four recently active volcanoes are known in the area described by Morell (Palfreyman and Cooke, 1976, p.120).

De Retes in 1545 certainly reported an eruption (Wichmann, 1909) in the vicinity of the north coast but his exact location at the time of the observation is uncertain. A volcanic island is marked on a European map of 1601 (Sharp, 1968) and repeated on later maps such as that in Kircher's Mundus Subterraneus (1665).

However, the first eruption of Manam Island confirmed in the European literature was that reported by Schouten and LeMaire (1616). 'Before daybreak on the morning of the 7th we turned her head again towards the high mountain it was a burning island emitting flames and smoke from the summit, wherefore we gave it the name Vulcanus. This island was well populated and full of coker-nut trees...' (Whittaker et al., 1975, p.281).

Although the accounts of early navigators are interesting and useful, reported sightings of Manam Island are so infrequent that a continuous record only exists since 1870. Major eruptions, unreported in the European literature, could have occurred between 1616 and 1870. From Palfreyman and Cooke's (1976) summary of the eruptive history, the only definite accounts of tephra-producing eruptions are those reported for 1919 and 1920-1922. Even then it is not clear how far the tephra cloud spread, other than that the 1919 eruption spread dust 'for miles over the mainland'. Further data on major tephra eruptions from Manam must wait until tephrostratigraphic studies have been undertaken on the island.

Karkar Island

Karkar Island, located at latitude 4°18'40"S and longitude 146°15'20"E, is crowned by a double-walled caldera (Fisher, 1957; Johnson et al., 1972; McKee et al., 1976).

Relatively minor eruptions which produced ash and smoke were reported in 1885 and 1895 (Fig. 18). No further eruptions occurred until 1974. The first, and only other, recorded eruption on Karkar was reported by Abel Tasman on the night of 20 April, 1643.

The tephrostratigraphic studies undertaken so far on Karkar Island suggest that eruptions involving large-scale pyroclastic flows and major tephra falls occurred ~ 9000 years BP, ~ 2800 years BP, and twice in the period 1500-800 years BP (Johnson et al., 1972; Pain and McKee, in press). Tephra from these eruptions almost certainly reached the mainland. However, a recent analysis of wind speeds and directions indicates that it is very unlikely that Karkar volcanoes or any volcanoes to the west could deposit tephra in the Mt Hagen area (Blong, in press).

Long Island

Long or Arop Island, located at latitude 5°21'30"S, longitude 147°07'00"E is dominated by the huge collapse caldera which contains Lake Wisdom and the two extinct volcanic peaks Cerisy and Reaumur.

Motmot Island in Lake Wisdom first appeared in the eruption in 1953; its subsequent history has been described in detail by Ball and Glucksman (1975). The outline geology of Long Island has been described by Johnson et al., (1972) and Ball and Johnson (1976) while Blong et al., (1981) and Pain et al., (in press) have concentrated on the tephrostratigraphy.

The last major eruption of the island, a classic low temperature ignimbrite eruption, occurred some time between 1630 and 1800. No published eyewitness accounts of the eruption have been found. On Long Island the tephra beds resulting from this eruption have been named the Matapun beds (Blong et al., 1981). This sequence was preceded by a series of tephra beds ranging in age from more than 350 years BP to about 4000 yrs BP. The 4000 year old eruption also involved the emplacement of low temperature ignimbrites and probably the wide distribution of a tephra mantle.

Local legends about the eruption of Arop are well known. Numerous authors listed in Ball's (1981) annotated bibliography of Long Island refer to the legend. A brief description by Coultas (1933-35) taken from Ball and Johnson (1976, p.143) states:

> According to native legends Ahrup was at one time a large active volcano, much higher than Tolokiwa and with a large population. Eventually an eruption occurred which blew the cone completely out of the center of the island, throwing out hot stones and lava and killing the people, with the exception of one woman who escaped in a canoe to the mainland of New Guinea where her descendants are supposed to be living now.

Two further versions of the legend collected in 1976 are presented in Appendix 3. The legendary evidence from Long Island is supported in some respects by some of the tephrostratigraphy, particularly the Matapun beds. For example, the descriptions of fire in the legends are not bad descriptions of nuées ardentes, typical of ignimbrite eruptions. Similarly, the comment that the island is larger than it was before the eruption is demonstrably true; almost all the coastline is cliffed, exposing only Matapun beds.

Discussion of the dating of the eruption is left until later but it is worth noting here that many accounts are at variance. For example, Naval Intelligence Division (1945) states in one place that the eruption occurred 150 years ago and in another place three centuries ago (Ball, 1981).

Whenever it occurred the eruption which produced the Matapun beds was a major eruptive event and it certainly produced widespread tephra fallout. It was probably the only event on Long Island in the last thousand years to have produced tephra in amounts sufficient to leave a recognisable deposit on the mainland.

Ritter Island

Ritter or Kulkul Island lies at latitude 5°31′00″S, longitude 148°07′15″E (Fig. 14). Before the 1888 eruption the island reached a height of 782 m; now all that remains is an arcuate ridge with steep walls, representing the remnants of the east and south-east sides of the original volcano.

William Dampier reported a violent eruption of Ritter on 21 March 1700. Activity was reported again in 1793 but the volcano is known to have been inactive from 1827 to 1885 (Fisher, 1957). However, there is a more recent suggestion that Ritter was in more or less continuous activity from 1700 to 1888 (C. McKee, pers. comm.).

On 13 March 1888 shortly after dawn, most of the volcano disintegrated in a catastrophic explosion. Tsunamis up to 14 m high drowned many people on the coasts of Umboi, New Britain and the New Guinea mainland (Steinhauser. 1892; Cooke and Johnson, 1978).

The noise of the explosion was heard at Finschhafen at about 6.30 am, and tsunamis were experienced. A dirty grey ash also fell in this area (Steinhauser, 1892). No other places are known to have reported this tephra fall. A recent analysis points to the possibility of collapse of the volcano with very little actual eruption. Evidently the 1888 as well as the 1972 and 1974 events were largely the result of subsidence rather than eruption (R. Cooke, 1979, pers. comm.).

Geochemical analyses

The geochemistry of the Bismarck Sea volcanic centres has been illuminated by Johnson (1976b, 1977) though his analyses over-represent the hard rocks at the expense of the pyroclastic materials. Johnson's analyses of rocks of the western part of the arc indicating lateral changes in chemistry along the arc are interpreted as functions of differences in the rate of convergence along the Indo-Australian and South Bismarck plate boundaries (Johnson, 1977, p.108). Zonation of major element chemistry is clear on Figs. 19 and 20, the zones corresponding to those depicted on Fig. 14.

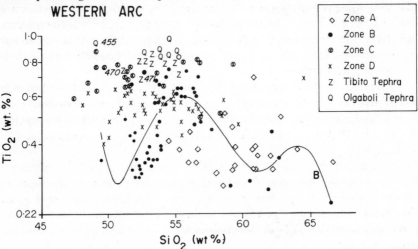

Fig. 19 *TiO₂-SiO₂ values, western Bismarck Arc volcanoes (after Johnson, 1977) with Tibito and Olgaboli Tephra data*

Values for Olgaboli and Tibito Tephra from the Upper Wahgi Valley (Tables 3 and 4) have again been superimposed on these diagrams. The high TiO_2 and P_2O_5 values for the two tephras cause them to plot in Zone C on Figs. 19 and 20. On a K_2O-SiO_2 plot the tephra values overlap Zones C and D. Three additional major element analyses on tephra samples (455 Kainantu, 470 Saidor and 471 Mugil-Karkar) are presented in Table 6 and plotted on Figs. 19 and 20. These three samples also plot in Zone C. These analyses reinforce the interpretation of the trace element data that Tibito Tephra fell at both Saidor and at Mugil-Karkar and Olgaboli Tephra at Kainantu (Chapter 3).

It seems clear from the plots and from discussions with Dr R.W.

Johnson that both Tibito Tephra and Olgaboli Tephra have major element chemistries identical with those of analysed Zone C rocks. The information conveyed on these diagrams clearly suggests that if the tephras had sources in the western arc of the Bismarck Archipelago then Zone C volcanoes are the only potential sources.

Furthermore, only two volcanoes occur within Zone C — Tolokiwa in the east, and Long Island (Fig. 14). Moreover, it seems likely that the Tolokiwa Island centre has been extinct for some time (Johnson et al., 1972).

Summary

The evidence presented above indicates that Krakatau is not a possible source for any tephra in the Papua New Guinea highlands.

There is no evidence of thickening of either Tibito Tephra or Olgaboli Tephra towards potential sources in or near the Upper Wahgi Valley. Tephrostratigraphic work suggests that the last major tephra eruption from a highland source emanated from Mt Yelia about 18,000

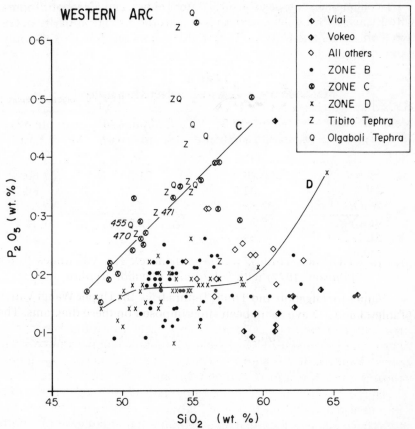

Fig. 20   P$_2$O$_5$-SiO$_2$ values, western Bismarck Arc volcanoes (after Johnson, 1977) with Tibito and Olgaboli Tephra data

years ago. However, Mt Yelia and Doma Peaks remain in a solfataric state with minor associated(?) seismic activity. Although the Doma Peaks crater lake was drained in a lahar only 600-800 years BP, no tephra was produced. The available geochemical data for highlands volcanoes is equivocal; it neither totally supports nor undeniably refutes a highland origin for the two tephras.

If Bismarck Sea volcanoes are considered as sources of the two thin tephras at Kuk, then clearly major eruptions are involved as the upper Wahgi Valley is several hundred kilometres from these volcanoes. The tephrostratigraphy of Manam Island has not yet been attempted and the only known tephra-producing eruption occurred post World War I. Tephrostratigraphic evidence from Karkar Island indicates the last major tephra was erupted 700-800 years BP. Long Island certainly produced widespread tephra sometime in the period 1630-1800 AD when the Matapun beds were erupted. The 1888 eruption of Ritter Island produced tephra that reached the mainland in only very minor amounts.

Geochemical comparison of Tibito Tephra and Olgaboli Tephra with Bismarck Sea volcanic rocks indicates the strong similarity of the two tephras to Zone C rocks. Within this zone Long Island is the only likely source.

Table 6
Major element analyses, selected samples

Major element analyses	Sample 455 Kainantu airstrip %	Sample 470 Saidor coast %	Sample 471 Mugil-Karkar %
SiO_2	50.28	51.56	52.66
TiO_2	.92	.74	.69
Al_2O_3	22.33	16.55	17.63
Fe_2O_3	15.72	12.50	11.51
MnO	.15	.25	.23
MgO	3.03	5.35	3.39
CaO	4.92	9.78	8.69
Na_2O	1.62	1.80	2.20
K_2O	.78	1.22	1.37
P_2O_5	.28	.27	.30
	100.03	100.00	100.06

5 Long Island as the tephra source

The geochemical evidence suggests strongly that Long Island is the source of both Tibito and Olgaboli tephras. This suggestion is not incompatible with the presently known distribution of Tibito Tephra as it has been found at Saidor, the closest point on the mainland to Long Island. While the known geochemically fingerprinted samples of Olgaboli Tephra cover a much smaller area remote from the coastline it is also quite possible that Long Island is the source of this material.

Tephrochronology of Long Island

The tephrostratigraphy of Long Island has been summarised by Pain et al. (in press) and Blong et al. (1981). Figure 21 presents a diagrammatic summary. Briefly, the sequence of pumice lapilli followed by a massive pyroclastic flow (or series of flows) and overlain by a series of airfall tephra with intervening palaeosols, is repeated three times. The Kiau basal pumice lapilli (Fig. 21) has been radiocarbon dated at c.16,000 years BP, and the Biliau basal pumice lapilli at c.4000 years BP. The pyroclastic flows (ignimbrites) of the Matapun sequence, which certainly followed directly after the Matapun basal pumice lapilli (cf. Sparks and Wilson, 1976), contain massive, incompletely carbonised logs which have been radiocarbon dated at 380±70 (ANU-1125), 230±75 (ANU-1126), 200±65 (ANU-1127) and 115±40 years BP (NZR-332).

Although the detailed evidence for the ages of Tibito Tephra and Olgaboli Tephra is not presented until a later chapter it was noted in Chapter 2 that the former tephra was erupted c.240 years BP and the latter some 1100-1200 years ago. Thus the Matapun beds on Long Island and Tibito Tephra are coeval. On the other hand, current evidence allows no major pyroclastic deposit on Long Island corresponding to Olgaboli Tephra. One of the airfall tephras above the Biliau pyroclastic flows could be coeval with Olgaboli Tephra but it seems unlikely that an eruption represented on the island by a relatively thin deposit (< 50cm) would have produced a tephra fall as far away as Mt Giluwe (Fig. 12).

Geochemical evidence

Major element analyses of Long Island pyroclastic flows and airfall

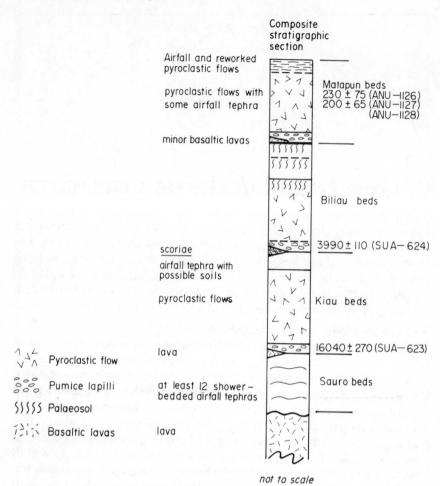

not to scale

21   *Tephrostratigraphic summary of Long Island (after Blong et al., 1981)*

tephra are presented in Table 7. Sample locations are shown on Fig. 22 and sample descriptions can be found in Appendix 1. Briefly, samples 541, 542, 543 and 548 are from the Matapun beds, 544 and 545 from the Biliau beds and 549 from the Kiau beds (Fig. 21).

The data in Table 7 can be compared with those presented in Figs. 15, 19, and 20. Like Tibito and Olgaboli Tephras, all Long Island samples plot as high-K low-Si andesites or low-Si andesites on Mackenzie and Chappell's (1972) nomenclature diagram (Fig. 15). On Fig. 19, all Long Island samples would plot within the field of Zone C rocks (as expected because Long Island is a Zone C volcano! — Fig. 14). Similarly on Fig. 20, the high P_2O_5 values of the Long Island pyroclastics place all but one analysis in the Zone C area. The K_2O values for Long Island pyroclastics plot across a range but generally within the field covered by the Long Island analyses presented by

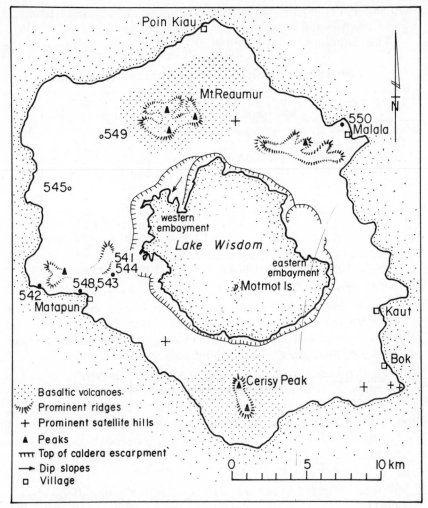

Fig. 22   Long Island sample locations

Johnson (1977). The significant point of these comparisons is that major element analyses of Long Island pyroclastic materials and Tibito and Olgaboli Tephras span identical fields.

Similarly, trace element analyses support the notion that at least Tibito Tephra was erupted from Long Island. Figure 23 shows the overlap of Long Island pyroclastics and Tibito Tephra from the upper Wahgi Valley and elsewhere in the Papua New Guinea Highlands on an Sr-Rb plot. In fact, the four Matapun bed samples (Nos. 541, 542, 543 and 548) all fall within the previously defined ellipses.

Samples 546, 547, 550 and 552 are samples of airfall Matapun tephra collected from Crown Island, some 15 km to the north-west of Long Island. The low Rb values of analyses of samples 546 and 551 reinforce a tendency noted earlier for coastal samples, but this tendency is denied by the 'normal' Rb values of the Long Island and other Crown Island samples.

The geochemical evidence presented here reinforces the

Table 7

Major element analyses* — Long Island pyroclastics

Sample No.	541	542	543	548	544	545	549
		Matapun beds			Biliau beds		Kiau beds
SiO_2	55.20	52.67	55.46	54.93	56.30	55.49	54.82
TiO_2	.77	.71	.77	.77	.82	.74	.81
Al_2O_3	16.23	16.67	16.60	15.96	16.75	17.90	16.28
Fe_2O_3	11.40	11.77	11.75	11.98	11.90	11.49	11.97
MnO	.25	.26	.25	.27	.27	.27	.25
MgO	3.09	4.22	3.46	3.48	3.34	3.33	3.52
CaO	7.98	10.06	8.40	7.72	7.12	8.07	7.89
Na_2O	2.77	2.30	2.51	2.36	2.01	1.84	2.19
K_2O	1.93	1.53	1.76	1.76	1.60	1.28	1.55
P_2O_5	.38	.31	.35	.37	.32	.24	.28
Total	100.00	100.50	100.31	99.60	100.43	100.45	99.56

*Total Fe as Fe_2O_3 — Samples ignited at 800°C before analysis.

conclusion that Tibito Tephra was erupted from Long Island. It is noteworthy that no Long Island samples plot anywhere near the Olgaboli Tephra Sr-Rb ellipse, despite the evidence from major element analyses which suggest a Long Island source for this tephra.

Tephra thickness and particle size characteristics

In the course of field investigations, the younger tephra, Tibito Tephra, has been found at many more sites than has Olgaboli Tephra, presumably because of its youthfulness, better preservation and lesser depth of burial by other sediments. Consequently much more

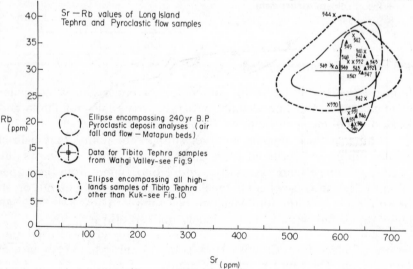

Fig. 23   Sr-Rb values – Long Island pyroclastics

information is available about Tibito Tephra than about Olgaboli Tephra.

Tibito Tephra

Figure 24 shows the thickness at known sites in millimetres. For many

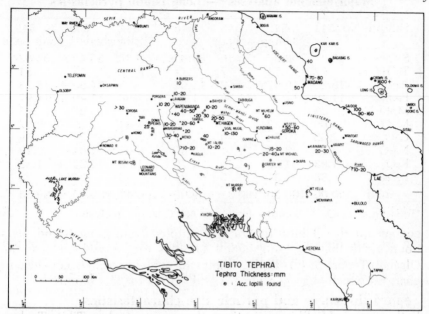

Fig. 24 Tibito Tephra: tephra thickness (mm)

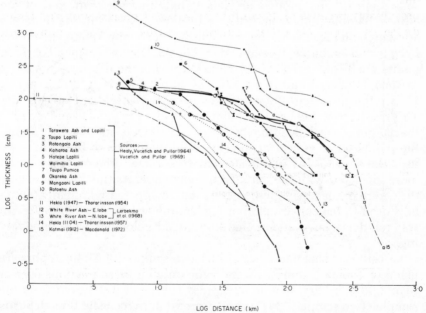

Fig. 25 Log thickness – log distance plots for 15 tephras

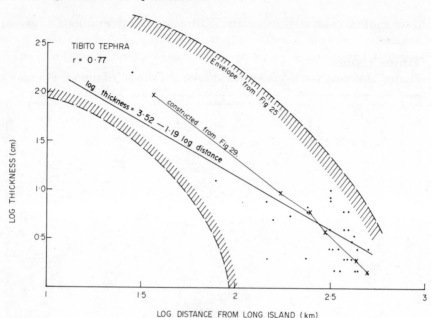

Fig. 26   *Log thickness – log distance plot assuming Long Island as the source of Tibito Tephra*

sites a range of values is given, emphasising that reworking of the tephra has occurred. The main axis of the depositional ellipse cannot be determined accurately but a general trend somewhat south of west is suggested. Relationships between tephra thickness and distance from source are usually plotted for data lying along the main axis of the ellipse. Sample plots from fifteen eruptions recorded in the literature are shown on Fig. 25. All the available data for Tibito Tephra, assuming Long Island as source, is recorded on Fig. 26. Obviously not all of these points can lie on the main axis of the ellipse but there is, nevertheless, a reasonable linear trend (r = 0.77). The slope of the best fit line on Fig. 26 is rather less than the general slope of the envelope from Fig. 25. This results from the fact that points fairly close to Long Island are near the margin of the depositional ellipse (eg. Crown Island, Saidor). If only the points on or very near the supposed main axis of the ellipse are used the slope of the line is steeper (constructed line on Fig. 26) and more in accord with the curve of the envelope. As this line plots near the centre of the envelope it is clear that, compared with many tephra falls used in the construction of Fig. 25, the eruption of Tibito Tephra was relatively large and/or that downwind velocities were relatively high.

Grain size characteristics of fifty-two samples of Tibito Tephra are given in Table 8. Analyses were made only on those fractions coarser than 4.00 ϕ by dry sieving after fines had been wet sieved from the sample. Two samples, 541 and 542, are from pyroclastic flow deposits on Long Island. Samples 543, 547, 548, 551 and 470 contain accretionary lapilli.

The relationships between mean particle size (Mϕ) and distance from Long Island are shown in Fig. 27. The curve of Mϕ illustrates nicely the decrease in mean particle size with increasing distance although the curve is surprisingly flat. It should be remembered, however, that ϕ units are a logarithmic expression of mean particle size.

The evidence presented on Figs. 26 and 27 accords well with other evidence, indicating that Long Island is indeed the source of Tibito Tephra.

Table 8
Tibito Tephra — particle size characteristics

Sample No.	Mϕ	D$_{10\phi}$	σ_ϕ	Distance from Long Island (km)
400	3.60	3.00	3.52	424
470	1.90	0.60	1.91	77
547	1.80	-0.80	1.37	28
422	3.33	2.65	3.23	315
459	3.25	2.55	3.17	235
462	3.15	2.60	3.06	193
456	3.25	2.42	3.13	193
461	3.20	2.42	3.17	235
546	.60	-1.00	0.57	28
477	3.22	2.40	3.14	238
142	3.40	2.75	3.31	318
476	3.41	2.80	3.34	238
551	-1.00	-3.40	-1.24	28
552	-1.05	-2.97	-0.06	28
543	1.75	-2.20	0.98	7
541(Flow)	-0.30	-4.00	-0.39	5
542(Flow)	0.90	-0.95	1.05	10
540	2.90	0.75	2.41	158
548	-3.65	-4.40	-3.40	7
130	3.30	2.50	3.19	389
570	3.32	2.55	3.18	357
465	3.52	2.72	3.38	389
81	3.25	-0.10	1.73	322
6	3.47	2.37	3.14	368
19	3.44	1.37	3.04	315
38	3.20	0.87	2.75	315
162	3.37	2.31	3.20	238
128	3.56	2.81	3.41	392
11	3.56	2.54	3.35	238
45	3.25	0.87	2.54	315

406	3.44	2.56	3.32	354
405	3.52	2.83	3.42	333
403	3.30	0.67	2.65	375
402	3.50	2.77	3.38	361
401	3.45	-0.05	2.78	424
164	3.63	3.00	3.46	319
172	3.75	3.06	3.56	378
417	3.40	1.81	3.17	350
242	3.35	0.21	2.70	389
243	3.50	-0.45	2.08	399
245	3.10	0.50	2.40	359
244	3.80	2.55	3.60	389
248	3.95	3.00	3.78	389
583	3.40	2.72	3.35	418
587	3.50	2.50	3.30	147
580	3.50	3.00	3.40	441
581	3.15	1.40	3.68	438
577	3.25	2.45	3.10	350
579	3.60	3.15	3.58	497
572	2.90	1.70	2.80	146
588	3.60	2.92	3.45	406
590	3.65	3.85	3.50	415

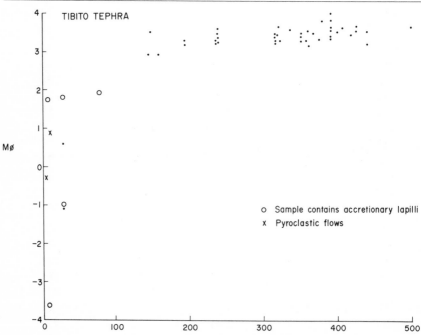

Fig. 27   *Mean particle size versus distance from Long Island – Tibito Tephra*

Table 9
Olgaboli Tephra — particle size characteristics

Sample No.	M_ϕ	$D_{10\phi}$	σ_ϕ	Distance from Long Island (km)
178	3.56	2.93	3.42	326
15 ⎫	3.05	1.69	2.85	238
15 ⎭	3.24	1.87	3.07	238
121	3.54	0.87	2.75	378
404	2.87	-1.50	1.32	373
249	4.00	-1.20	2.80	385
127	3.57	2.92	3.51	396
457	2.95	1.75	2.83	193
455	3.26	2.40	3.13	175
3	2.90	0.14	2.25	
7	3.06	0.67	2.46	
21	3.31	1.62	3.22	Upper Wahgi
28	3.44	2.40	3.40	Valley samples —
29	3.00	0.78	2.08	distance from
34	2.81	-0.08	2.00	Long Island —
39	3.37	2.00	3.29	320 km
43	3.22	1.19	2.71	
146	3.28	2.40	3.16	

Olgaboli Tephra

Too few sites with Olgaboli Tephra are known to define thickness or

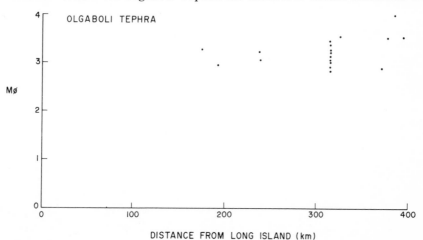

Fig. 28   *Mean particle size versus distance from Long Island –*
Olgaboli Tephra

variations in thickness, but data from the sites with good stratigraphic
control perhaps suggest a westward thinning of the tephra.

The particle size characteristics of Olgaboli Tephra are presented in Table 9 (sample locations on Fig. 12). Figure 28 suggests a westward fining of particle size but the samples from the Upper Wahgi Valley (Table 9) indicate the wide range of particle size characteristics that can occur in a limited area.

Until more sites with Olgaboli Tephra have been found no conclusions about source can be reached from the particle size evidence other than that the source does not lie within or close to the ellipse shown on Fig. 12. However, some geochemical evidence supports a Zone C source for Olgaboli Tephra.

6 Some theoretical considerations

The foregoing analysis leaves no doubt that Tibito Tephra was erupted from Long Island. This conclusion allows consideration of some theoretical aspects relating to the tephra distribution, tephra volume and the energy released by the tephra eruption, and some comparisons to be made with well known historical eruptions.

Tephra distribution and tephra volume

The area enclosed by the distributional ellipse on Fig. 11 totals about 84,000 km² (cf. Olgaboli Tephra — c.17,000 km², Fig. 12). The Tibito Tephra ellipse is based on known sites and a relatively smooth outline to the ellipse using a tephra thickness of about 1.5 cm. Thus, although Tibito Tephra has not been found in the upper Jimi River area or even nearby, a general knowledge of tephra ellipses (cf. Fig. 2) and confirmed locations in adjacent areas necessitates that the tephra did fall there.

This estimate of 84,000 km² is conservative in various ways. First the tephra must have fallen over considerable areas to the north and east of Long Island. For example, Nincovich and Heezen's (1965) distribution of Santorini tephra (c.1500 BC) shows tephra fall about 150 km upwind from the source. Lack of any data at all for the area north and east of Long Island has meant that a very conservative total has been calculated for the areal distribution of Tibito Tephra.

Secondly, a considerable area beyond the 1.5 cm isopach would also have experienced tephra fall, extending outwards to an area where only a dusting was received. For example, data published by Thorarinsson and Sigvaldason (1972) for the Hekla (1970) eruption indicate that while the total area of tephra fall was about 40,000 km², only about 6017 km² received more than .1 cm of tephra fall.

Furthermore the Hekla figures are based on uncompacted tephra thicknesses. As the Tibito Tephra data are based on compacted thicknesses we can say that about 84,000 km² was covered to a depth of about 3 cm of uncompacted tephra. If we allow a similar ratio of > 1 cm cover to total cover for Tibito Tephra as for the Hekla eruption, then the total area covered by Tibito Tephra would be of the order of 1.28 x 10⁶ km². This figure is also conservative because (1) the 1.5 cm compacted tephra isopach has been used instead of the 1 cm uncompacted tephra isopach; (2) the 1.5 cm isopach (Fig. 11) should broaden slightly westwards — not pinch inwards.

Although a true isopach map of Tibito Tephra cannot be constructed because of the paucity of data, Figs. 11 and 24 can be combined with general considerations of tephra distribution to produce Fig. 29 — a theoretical tephra distribution map.

Data from this figure have been used to calculate the areas and mean thicknesses shown in Table 10. Mean thicknesses and volumes have also been calculated to give a tephra volume of 8.58 km^3 inside the 1.5 cm isopach. If we further assume that the mean thickness of tephra outside the 1.5 cm isopach is 1 mm and that the additional area involved is 1.19 x 10^6 km^2, the total tephra volume is about 9.84 km^3. This figure is extremely conservative and it can be assumed that the actual compacted volume of Tibito Tephra is > 11-12 km^3.

Table 10
Area and volume of Tibito Tephra

Thickness (cm)	Area (km²)	Mean thickness (cm)	Volume x 10^9 m³
> 100	1570	150	2.36
10-100	6710	55	3.69
5-10	9060	7.5	.68
4-5	9500	4.5	.43
2-4	33500	3.0	1.01
1.5-2.0	23700	1.75	.41
	~84000 km²		8.58

The top half of Table 11 compares the volume of airfall tephra produced during the c. 1700 eruption of Long Island with calculations made for four very famous eruptions. This data is of great comparative value because not only are like qualities compared but also because all five of the eruptions listed are of Plinian-Peléan type; that is, an initial pumiceous airfall deposit was followed by a series of massive, pyroclastic flows or ignimbrites (see Fig. 21). In each case this part of the table lists only the volume of the airfall tephra-pumiceous lapilli deposit.

Comparisons with other well known eruptions is generally not possible because detailed tephrostratigraphic studies have not been made. However, while questioning the reliability of the data, other quoted tephra volumes have been noted in the lower half of Table 11. These volumes are considered somewhat unreliable because it is difficult to determine from the literature whether the quoted figures refer only to airfall tephra or whether they also include pyroclastic flows.

Although Howell Williams (1941, p.273) originally estimated the total volume of the Mazama eruption of Crater Lake as only 47-56 km^3,

Table 11
Comparison of airfall tephra volumes

Volcano	Year	Volume (km³)	Source
Crater Lake, Oregon	7000 BP	15	Sparks and Walker, 1977, p.338
Vesuvius (Pompeii Pumice)	79 AD	2.6	Lirer et al., 1973, p.770
Katmai-Novarupta, Alaska	1912	7.8	Curtis, 1968, pp.206-7
Santorini, Greece	~ 1500 BC	28	Watkins, et al, 1978
Long Island	~ 1700 AD	~ 11	
Krakatau	1883	13.5 18	Macdonald, 1972, p.139 Verbeek, 1886
Santa Maria, Guatemala	1902	5.5	Rittman, 1962, p.41
Quizapu, Chile	1932	16.9	Macdonald, 1972, p.139
White River tephra, Alaska	—	25	Lerbekmo et al., 1973, p.239
Bandai-san, Japan	1888	1.2	Markhinin, 1971, p.25
Gunung Agung, Indonesia	1963	1	Markhinin, 1971, p.25
Tambora, Indonesia	1815	67.5	Macdonald, 1972, p.139
Mt St Helens	1980	2.6	Volcano News (4), p.5

Sparks and Walker (1977, p.338) have recently estimated the total volume of erupted products as 54-70 km³ made up of: (1) Plinian eruption — 15 km³; (2) co-ignimbrite airfall deposit — 14-22 km³; and (3) ignimbrite — 22-33 km³. On roughly the same basis, Curtis (1968, pp.206-7) indicated that the pyroclastic flows of the Katmai-Novarupta eruption of 1912 had a total volume of 6.1 km³, nearly as great as the volume of the airfall tephra. These figures suggest that the airfall tephra represents only about a third of the total volume of products erupted during a Plinian-Peléan cycle. On this basis, the total volume of material erupted at Long Island during the eruption of Tibito Tephra was almost certainly > 30 km³ and it is this figure which should be kept in mind when comparisons are made with some of the data in the lower half of Table 11.

It is interesting to compare the Long Island eruption with the 'big' eruption of Mt St Helens on 18 May 1980. While accurate estimates for

Mt St Helens are not yet available, the total volume of all eruptive products has been estimated at about 2.6 km³, this estimate being based on a comparison with the AD 79 eruption of Vesuvius that buried Pompeii. However, the airfall tephra component of this amounted to only ~ 15 x 10⁶ m³ or 0.015 km³ (*Volcano News*, 1980 (4), p.5), 2-3 orders of magnitude less than the airfall component of the Long Island eruption.

Table 12
Duration of main eruptive phase

Volcano	Year	Duration	Source
Krakatau	1883	~ 45 hrs	Docters van Leeuwen, 1936, p.9
		~ 36 hrs	Ball, 1906, p324
Katmai-Novarupta	1912	< 20 hrs	Curtis, 1968, p182
Santa Maria	1902	~ 18 hrs	Rittman, 1962, p.41
Coseguina	1835	~ 3 days	Rittman, 1962, p.42
Tambora	1815	~ 2 days	
Vesuvius	79 AD	~ 24 hrs	Lirer *et al.*, 1973, p.768
Fogo	1563	~ 2 days	Lirer *et al.*, 1973, p.769
Asama	1783	4 days	Lirer *et al.*, 1973, p.769
Hekla	1947	1 hr	Thorarinsson, 1967
	1846	4 hrs	
	1768	5-6 hrs	
	1693	< 1 hr	
Mt St Helens	1980	~ 30 hrs	*Volcano News* (4), p.5

At first glance it might be supposed that the very large volumes of material produced during Plinian-Peléan eruptions imply a lengthy period of eruption. However, Table 12 suggests otherwise. Although eruptions such as Tambora 1815 and Krakatau 1883 were preceded by months or even years of relatively minor activity, the main Plinain pumice phase of such eruptions seems generally to last for 48 hours or less. On the basis of some of the data presented in Table 12, Bond and Sparks (1976, p.14) suggested that the Plinian pumice phase of the Minoan tephra eruption of Santorini, the biggest Plinian airfall tephra yet documented, probably only lasted about 24 hours. Thus, it can be suggested that the eruption of Tibito Tephra, the Plinian phase of the Long Island eruption, almost certainly lasted only one or two days. This does not belie the possiblility of minor tremors and eruptions in the preceding months, though there is no suggestion from the tephro-stratigraphic studies (Pain *et al.*, in press) that even minor tephra falls occurred immediately prior to the Matapun lapilli.

The extremely rapid emptying of the magma chamber during the Plinian-Peléan phases of an eruption leads to subsidence, generally to form a caldera (Smith and Bailey, 1968, p.654). Caldera collapse may occur immediately after or even during the eruption as at Krakatau or slowly over a period of decades as at Askja in Iceland (Thorarinsson, 1971) and at Ritter Island (Chapter 4), the timing of collapse presumably depending on factors such as roof thickness, rock type, the nature and extent of weaknesses and fractures, and the weight of the overlying ejected material (Vitaliano and Vitaliano, 1971, p.92).

Certainly the resulting calderas can be very large (Table 13) although, as in the case Katmai, much of the subsidence may be on a regional basis rather than in the form of a caldera (Curtis, 1968, pp.206-7). The Long Island caldera has an area of ~ 120 km² and a total volume of ~ 60 km³, much of it occupied by Lake Wisdom (Fig. 22). The margin of the caldera is scalloped, as are the margins of the Krakatau and Santorini calderas, perhaps suggesting more than one phase of collapse. It is interesting to note that the caldera volume is approximately twice the estimated volume of the eruption products. Such an apparent anomaly is not uncommon.

Table 13
Caldera areas and volumes

Volcano	Area km²	Depth m	Vol. km³	Source
Aniakchak, Alaska	78			Williams, 1941
Santorini, Greece	83.5	300-400		Marinos and Melidonis, 1971, p.278
			60	Bond and Sparks, 1976, p.15
Katmai, Alaska	3.14			Henning et al. 1976, p.31
Krakatau, Indonesia	38.5	170-280	8.7	Williams, 1941
Crater Lake, Oregon	81.5			Williams, 1941, p.269
Aira, Kyushu	379			Williams, 1941, p.277
Kikai, Kyushu	230			

Energetical and other considerations

On Sapper's (1927) scale the eruption of Tibito Tephra clearly rates as b_1 — that is, an explosive eruption involving > 1 km³ of material (Lamb, 1970, p.429). In terms of the explosivity index

$$= \frac{\text{volume of tephra}}{\text{volume of total material}}$$

the eruption that produced Tibito Tephra has an index > 99 per cent, as very little lava if any was produced during the eruption.

From the theoretical distribution (Fig. 29) and particle size data (Table 8) it is possible to make first approximation calculations of megaton yield of the eruption, the height of the eruptive cloud, and the

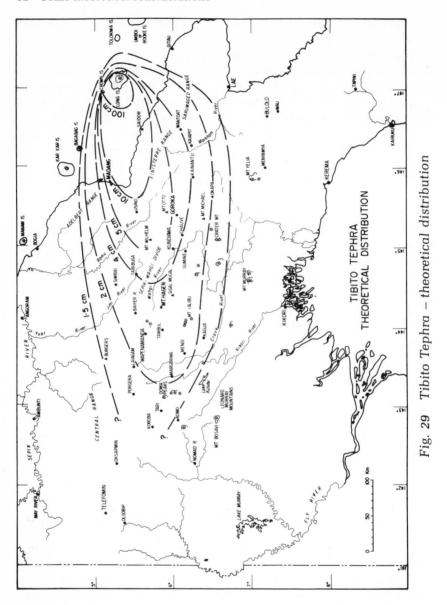

Fig. 29   Tibito Tephra – theoretical distribution

windspeed using the model derived by Knox and Short (1964) from close-in nuclear fallout studies. This model was applied to the Hekla 1947 eruption by Knox and Short and to the White River tephra by Lerbekmo *et al*. (1968), producing reasonable accuracy in each case. For the present application the more accurate fall times for rough cylindrical particles computed from tests on volcanic materials (Wilson, 1972) have been preferred to the rates of fall of smooth spherical bodies used by earlier workers.

From Fig. 29, the value of Re = 102,300 metres can be measured for the Mt Wilhelm site where Re = the radius of the stabilised tephra cloud in metres, the first approximation of which is half the breadth of the lobe. From considerations mentioned earlier it will be clear that this value of Re will be very conservative.

As Re = 15,200 W^{045}

where W = apparent yield in megatons of TNT, for the Tibito Tephra eruption W = 68.9.

With H_T = height of the top of the ash cloud in metres,
$\overline{H}$ = mean cloud height (m)
and 2Δ H = thickness of the cloud
and with the equations

H_T = 15,200 W^{07}
$\overline{H}$ = H_T-ΔH
and 2 H = 0.44 H_T

for the Tibito Tephra eruption

H_T ≡ 23.2 km
Δ H≃ 5,100 m
and H≃ 18.1 km.

Discussions with Dr L. Wilson indicate that these values for the tephra cloud height are extremely conservative and that it is likely that the top of the tephra cloud reached more than 30 km.

The eruption-magnitude (M_e) can be calculated following Héder-vári (1971) using the expression $M_e = \dfrac{\log V + 4.95}{1.59}$ where V = the volume of the magma from which the tephra originated (in m^3).

Using a rock volume of 5.1 km^3 for the production of Tibito Tephra gives an eruption magnitude of 9.22. The released (thermal) energy (E) in ergs can then be calculated using the expression

log E = 11.0 + 1.6 M_e.

For the Tibito Tephra eruption, E = 5.62 x 10^{25} ergs. However, if the volume of Tibito Tephra is assumed to be only about one-third of the total volume of the ejected material, then V = ~ 15 x 10^9 m^3, M_e = 9.51 and the total released energy E = 1.65 x 10^{26} ergs. By comparison, Hédervári's (1971) calculations for the Minoan eruption of Santorini produce a value for E of 8.02 x 10^{26} ergs and Bolt's (1976, pp.39-41) calculations on a totally different basis give an estimate of total energy release of ~ 10^{24} ergs for the 1883 eruption of Krakatau. Other calculated energy values for essentially Plinian-Peléan eruptions are given in Table 14.

Taking Bolt's figure of a 1 kiloton atomic explosion liberating a total of 4 x 10^{19} ergs, and the earlier calculation W = 68.9 as the apparent yield in megatons of TNT for the eruption of Tibito Tephra, gives a figure based on the Knox and Short (1964) model of ~ 2.8 x 10^{24} ergs. Thus the two calculations for the energy released by the eruption of Tibito Tephra give similar results but the numerous oversimpli-

Table 14
Calculated released energy values (after Bullard, 1976)

Volcano	Year	Total energy in ergs
Santorini, Greece	~ 1500 BC	1.0×10^{27}
Tambora, Indonesia	1815	8.4×10^{26}
Coseguina, Nicaragua	1835	4.8×10^{26}
Katmai, Alaska	1912	2.02×10^{26}
Krakatau, Indonesia	1833	1.0×10^{25}
Agung, Indonesia	1963	4.5×10^{24}

fications in the models inspire only limited confidence in the results.

However, further comparison with the 18 May, 1980 eruption of Mt St Helens is interesting. The energy released during this eruption has been estimated as equivalent to 10-15 megatons of TNT or $4\text{-}6 \times 10^{23}$ ergs. This very rough comparison suggests that the Long Island eruption released 7-400 times more energy than the Mt St Helens eruption. The higher figure is more likely to be correct.

Finally, it is not inappropriate to note that the Long Island eruption was not dissimilar in magnitude to the 1883 eruption of Krakatau.

A simplified model can also be utilised to calculate velocity downwind of the tephra cloud. If a particle density of 1.0 g cm^3 is assumed, a probable value for vesiculated glass, and an Mϕ value of 3.56 ϕ = 0.0084 cm for sample 11 from Mt Wilhelm (Table 8) is taken, from Wilson's (1972) Fig. 2 such particles have a fall time from 20 km of c. 4.6 hrs.

For Madang sample 570 with Mϕ = 3.22 ϕ = 0.012 cm we can estimate a downtime of 3.82 hrs. As the distance from Madang to Mt Wilhelm is c. 85 km and the difference in downtimes, 0.78 hrs, the speed of the eruptive cloud ~ 110 km/hr (~ 30 m/sec). The difference in downtime would actually be less as no allowance was made for the elevation (3500 m) of the Wilhelm site. Thus the speed of the cloud would be higher. Similarly the cloud speed from Long Island to Saidor can be approximately calculated as c. 11 m/sec, and from Long Island to Tari Gap as c. 27 m/sec.

Despite the numerous approximations and assumptions in these estimates, the cloud velocities are in accord with observed velocities recorded in the literature (Table 15) as ranging 25-100 km/hr (7-28 m/sec). Furthermore, Curtis (1968, p.183) has shown by correlating heard explosions and tephra arrival times that during the deposition of Katmai-Novarupta tephra at Kodiak in 1912 the north-west wind slowed from a velocity of 43 km/hr to ~ 7 km/hr. This decrease in wind speed recorded by this analysis probably resulted from a change in wind direction. As the tephra cloud velocities calculated for the Papua New Guinea mainland do not necessarily refer to the axis of the ellipse the variations seem reasonable.

Table 15
Velocities of selected Tephra clouds

Volcano and date of eruption	Distance (km)	Time interval (hrs)	Velocity (km/hr)	Reference
Soufrière, St Vincent 1812	160	4.5	35	Anderson and Flett, 1903, p.475
1902	160	3.5	45	Anderson and Flett, 1903, p.475
	1320		100	Bullard, 1976, p. 144
Coseguina, Nicaragua 1835	1120	24.0?	47	Caldcleugh, 1836, p. 30
Shiveluch, USSR 1964	80	1.45	55	Gorshkov and Dubik, 1970
	400	6.00	68	Gorshkov and Dubik, 1970
Mt Spurr, Alaska 1953	135	6.0-7.0	21	Wilcox, 1959, pp.420-2
Hekla, Iceland 1947			80	Thorarinsson, 1954
1970			74	Thorarinsson and Sigvaldason, 1972, p.273
Katmai, Alaska 1912	160	2.0	80	Wilcox, 1959, pp.417, 427
			30	Erskine, 1962, p27
	88	3.5	25	Erskine, 1962, p27
Quizapu, Chile 1932	2960	120.0	25-60	Francis, 1976, p.176
			65	Wilcox, 1959, p.433
Bezymianny, USSR	45	0.5	94	Gorshkov, 1959, p.86
	80	1.6	49	Gorshkov, 1959, p.87
Sakurajima, Japan 1914	560	24.0	29	Jagger, 1924, p.467
	960	48.0	20	Jagger, 1924, p.467
	9-10	1.16	9	Jagger, 1924, p.447
Taal, Philippines 1911	20	0.2	100	Martin, 1911, p.88
Askja, Iceland 1875	1800	38.0	47	Thorarinsson, 1971, p.225
Asama, Japan 1958-61	49	1.86	27	Murai & Hosoya, 1964, p.211
	224	2.25	100	Murai & Hosoya, 1964, p.211
Mt St Helens, 1980	150	1.63	92	*Volcano News*, (4), p.5
	435	5.46	80	*Volcano News*, (4), p.5

The available mean monthly wind directions at various atmospheric levels for Lae, the only radiosonde station for the north coast, are presented in Table 16. At elevations of 5-9 km winds are easterly for all months except December. At 12-16 km (200-100 mbars), mean wind directions are always easterly with mean velocities 3-13 m/sec. At still higher elevations, in the region of the equatorial jet (tropical easterly jet), wind directions and velocities are highly variable, but with strong easterly components particularly during October to February.

More general considerations presented by Mintz (1954) indicate that tropical winds are easterly during both summer and winter, with higher velocities concentrated below the tropopause, at say 18-20 km.

The quality of the data in Table 16 is rather low but the generally higher velocities at 200-100 mbars during December-March and the strong easterly components at higher elevations during October to February, together with the known distribution of Tibito Tephra and the estimated cloud height and mean velocities, perhaps suggest that the eruption occurred during the period December to February.

Conclusions

The two thin sandy tephras first identified at the Kuk prehistoric site have been shown to have a very wide distribution.

Olgaboli Tephra covered an area of at least 17,000 km^2 to a depth of more than 2 cm of compacted tephra. Although major element geochemical evidence supports a Zone C (Fig. 14) source for Olgaboli Tephra, tephrostratigraphic and trace element geochemical studies of Long Island do not support a Long Island source for this tephra. However, as the source clearly does not lie within the ellipse shown on Fig. 12, and there is no evidence of thickening of the tephra in any particular direction within this zone, it is clear that Olgaboli Tephra represents a major eruption — even the present known extent represents more than 1.0 km^3 of uncompacted tephra.

Tibito Tephra has been shown to extend across a wide area by (1) similarity of field characteristics, (2) a definite similarity in trace element geochemistry, and (3) a discernible trend in particle size characteristics and tephra thickness.

The trend in particle size characteristics and tephra thickness suggest that a volcanic centre in the Bismarck Sea was the source of Tibito Tephra. This is confirmed by tephrostratigraphic studies of Long Island and geochemical evidence based on both major and trace element analyses. There can be little doubt that Tibito Tephra was erupted from Long Island during the Plinian-Peléan eruption of the Matapun beds about 240 years BP.

The area of the ellipse encompassing Tibito Tephra (Fig. 11) totals about 84,000 km^2. As this area encompasses only those sites with compacted tephra thicknesses of more than 1.5 cm, it can be suggested by comparison with the distribution characteristics of other tephras that the total area receiving Tibito Tephra was more than 1 million km^2.

Table 16

Mean monthly wind directions and speeds, various elevations, Lae[1]

Millibars	Elevation[2] (m)	Jan 1[3]	Jan 2[4]	Feb 1	Feb 2	Mar 1	Mar 2	Apr 1	Apr 2	May 1	May 2	Jun 1	Jun 2	Jul 1	Jul 2	Aug 1	Aug 2	Sep 1	Sep 2	Oct 1	Oct 2	Nov 1	Nov 2	Dec 1	Dec 2
Surface	0	NW	3	NW	4	NW	3	NW	2	NW	1	NW		NW		NW	1	NW	1	NW	1	NW	1	W	4
850	1,500	W	3	W	5	SW	4	SE	2	SE	2	SE	2	SE	3	SE	3	SE	5	SE	2	SW	2	W	4
700	3,000	W	3	W	4	SE	2	E	1	E	4	E	5	E	5	E	5	E	7	E	3	E	3	W	3
500	5,600	E	3	NE	2	E	2	E	2	E	3	E	5	E	5	E	5	E	6	E	3	E	3	W	3
400	7,200	NE	4	E	3	E	6	E	3	E	2	E	5	E	6	E	6	E	7	E	3	E	3	W	3
300	9,200	E	3	E	5	E	9	E	3	E	2	E	3	E	3	E	6	E	7	NE	3	E	3	W	2
200	11,800	E	5	E	9	E	11	E	6		4	NE	4	E	8	E	7	E	9	N	5	SE	4	E	4
150	13,700	E	6	E	12	E	10	SW	9		5	NE	4	E	7	E	6	NE	11		5	E	5	E	7
100	16,200	E	10	E	13	E	12	W	8		4	E	3	E	6	E	3	SE	5	SE	4	E	5	E	12
70		SW	1	E	11	W	10	W	8					W	4	W	5	W	3	E	6		9	E	12
50				E	5	W	2		14					SE	9	W	9		8	E	22			E	13
30																	4								

1. Data abstracted from Dept. of Science, Bureau of Meteorology Monthly Climate data — Upper Air Australia, (1969-1973 reports).
2. From ICAO Standard Atmosphere altitude.
3. Column 1 — most common wind directions.
4. Column 2 — mean wind velocity (m/sec).
5. Blank direction columns where velocities are given indicate variable wind directions.

Reasonable assumptions indicate that the compacted tephra volume was > 11 km^3 and that the total volume of the eruption products was probably > 30 km^3. These data, together with approximate estimates of the energy involved and comparisons with well-documented eruptions, indicate that the eruption of Tibito Tephra ranks amongst the great eruptions of the last few centuries.

Given that the eruption of Long Island and the widespread fall of Tibito Tephra occurred only about 3 centuries ago it is surprising that there is no literature on the eruption. So far as is known no European navigators observed the eruption or its aftermath. Although various volcanologists have mentioned during the 1970s that there was evidence on Long Island of a major eruption only one or two centuries ago, the Plinian-Peléan character of the eruption was not appreciated until after 1976.

It would not be surprising, given the magnitude of the eruption, if survivors from Long Island or the inhabitants of neighbouring islands had passed down to successive generations accounts of the event. In fact the present inhabitants of Long Island, descendants from Tolokiwa, have such stories (Chapter 4; Appendix 3) the first of which were 'collected' by Europeans in the 1930s (Coultas, 1933-5 in Ball and Johnson, 1976). Similarly, it would not be surprising if accounts of the tephra fall and its effects were to be found on the Papua New Guinea mainland, particularly in those areas remote from recently active volcanoes and where a tephra fall would be very unusual, an interesting and perhaps hazardous event. Thus, while the eruption was unrecorded by Europeans, legends on Long Island record the event and it is possible that other groups retain memories recorded in their oral histories. Certainly numerous highland peoples in Papua New Guinea have legends about a time of darkness (Brookfield, 1961) but whether or not these refer to the fall of Tibito Tephra is a matter requiring examination.

7 The time of darkness legends

A time of darkness legend involving several days of complete darkness was known to missionaries in the Finschhafen area as early as the 1920s (Fr Bergmann, pers. comm.). In 1938-1940 Johann Gehberger published a story, collected near Wewak, which involved a time of darkness (Gehberger, 1938-40), and in 1937 S.W. Carey mentioned a story widespread in the Manus Group noting that the sun was 'not seen for many days, nor any light, and everything was covered by a thick layer of ashes'. Carey suggested rather diffidently that the source of the tephra might have been on Baluan Island, south-east of Manus, and that the event dated back perhaps a hundred years or more. In 1948 Vicedom and Tischner, in a collection of legends and myths of the Melpa (Mt Hagen) people, published the first version of a time of darkness story to be reported from the highlands (see chapter 1).

In 1961 Harold Brookfield wrote that traditional stories involving extensive falls of volcanic ash were extant in the Wabag, Mendi and Tari areas of the Papua New Guinea Highlands. Brookfield also noted that the source of these ashfalls had not been located. In 1963 J.B. Watson reported that a time of darkness story, involving a fall of sand and three to four days darkness, was extant amongst the Agarabi people of the Eastern Highlands (Chapter 1). Watson somewhat diffidently suggested that the time of darkness and ashfall stemmed from the 1883 eruption of Krakatau. R.M. Glasse (1963) replied that the bingi story was known (and important) in the Tari area, provided some of the details (see Chapter 1), and suggested that Doma Peaks, just east of Tari had probably been the eruptive centre.

On the basis of genealogical dating both Glasse and Watson placed the occurrence of the time of darkness in the 1880s. In 1971 Brookfield and Hart reported that some oral folklore implied that a time of darkness had occurred in living memory and doubted that Krakatau was the source of the darkness and tephra fall. In the same year H.E. Nelson noted the existence of the legend amongst the Kaimbi of the Nebilyer Valley and located the arrival of the sweet potato in that area as conterminous with the 1883 eruption of Krakatau. Also in the same year the volcanologist G.A.M. Taylor reported that the presence of solfataric areas on Doma Peaks was indicative of recent acitivity. He noted that anthropological evidence (i.e. Glasse's evidence) for the date of the eruption of Doma was inconclusive but he placed the event in the range of 90 to 400 years ago (Taylor, 1971).

Thus by the early 1970s it was clear that time of darkness legends were indeed widespread, occurring on the coast at Wewak, Finschhafen and on Manus and in the highlands stretching nearly 350 km from Tari to Kainantu and including Wabag, Mendi, the Nebilyer, and the Mount Hagen area.

Some versions of the legend

Three of the earliest recorded accounts of the time of darkness legends have been presented in Chapter 1. Five more versions are presented here.

The first version was told by Serave of the Kamano-Kafe near Ukarumpa (Eastern Highlands Province) to Dorothy Drew and Audrey Payne of the Summer Institute of Linguistics in 1961-62.

> I am going to tell the story of darkness. I am going to tell the story of the great darkness which appeared on this ground/area. I did not see it. People told me and so I know it.
>
> It was while they were asleep, in the night, that it was so dark on this earth, and they slept/lay for about three nights. And when they took flares and went up the hills and made signs, going with flares in the pitch blackness, they said: Can you see my flare? But the flares did not light up the place! So they said: No!
>
> This went on many times. And when they were sleepy and it should have been night they slept. And when it should have been light they woke and got up, and kept looking and looking and lit flares and went up the hills saying: Do you see my flare? And others said: Do you see? And they looked all around. But they didn't see them.
>
> They went on doing that and one time as they were going with a flare there was a little light. And they saw it and said: Ah, now it's getting light! We can see shadows! And they rejoiced greatly.
>
> It was a bit light and they were rejoicing and they could see the flares and while they went on rejoicing it became light.
>
> It became light and in the morning they looked and a lot of stuff like ash had completely 'disappeared' the gardens! It had completely covered everything and pigs, animals, rats, every creature living in the scrub and in the woods came out in the open — cassowaries and so forth, too, and they died, and in the morning the people saw them. And they smelt the stench of the creatures which were rotting. And they took the creatures which were still moving/alive, and ate them. And they call the stuff which covered everything tanoza [rubbish]. They thought: It is tano ash.*

*Tano was a harvest celebration in which an enormous fire was built, producing a lot of ash. It seems the fall of ash reminded the Kamano-Kafe of this.

They thought about the sweet potato they had left — the young sweet potato they had not dug up: I left that, I haven't dug that up, they said, and went and looked, but the leaves and stems had rotted, and the tubers were rotting, but they saw that there were some (tubers) left. And the sweet potato which sprouted from that and came up was simply white! They saw that beans which came up then were just white! Then good gardens came up and later they took and ate (the produce).

Now during that pitch blackness, because it was so dark at the time, they had many flares and so on but could not see them well. And so now, when the sun and moon turn a little bit (eclipse) they think: That thing is going to happen! And they prepared much food. They prepared firewood and so on. But it didn't happen again.* And concerning food they could eat (during the darkness), they took out and cooked and ate corn seeds. They cooked and ate wing-bean seeds. And they took out (of the containers they were stored in) cucumber seeds and pumpkin seeds and different kinds of bean seeds — whatever they had, and cooked and ate them and it became light. Then later they searched and worked in their good gardens and their food grew.

Another version of the time of darkness legend, from the Patep, near Mumeng (Morobe Province), was recorded by Karen Adams and Linda Lauck, also from the Summer Institute of Linguistics, in 1973:

One day an earthquake shook the place where the ancestors of the Pateps lived, and sand and dirt fell (from the sky). The sand fell on top of their houses, so they went and got banana leaves and covered the roofs with them. They did this so the sand would spill down onto the ground and not fall into the grass roofs and ruin their houses. There was only darkness, and no light (daytime). They lit torches of fire and went to their sweet potato gardens, but they couldn't find the sweet potatoes because the sand had covered them. The taro had the leaves broken off but the stems still stood, so they dug up taro and ate it.

After that they saw a dream which told them to kill a black dog and a black pig and then light would come from the Buang area (to the east of the Patep area). So they killed the pig and dog, and the next day they got up, and it was daylight. There was good daylight so they went to their gardens and got food. That's the end.

Several hundred km west of Mumeng, near Lake Kopiago, Dr Nick Modjeska of Macquarie University was told the following story by Duna tribesmen of the Tumbudu Valley (Southern Highlands Province).

*This refers to the total eclipse of the sun seen here on 4 February 1962, of which the Kamano-Kafe were forewarned.

Way back before there was a time when everywhere was covered with sand (yu mo) which fell from the sky along with dirt and bits of wood as if chopped by a steel axe.

Our ancestors, maybe Aiyurana and Kuiyukwoia, said this about this thing: 'When it is near, put tree bark on your roof. Kunai grass or andu hini won't be enough. Cover up your houses with tree bark. If it's an old house and the wood isn't strong, build a new house. Then bring water and firewood and kaukau inside. Mark your kaukau and bananas and everything in the gardens with strong, freshly cut sticks. Everything will be covered with sand and you won't be able to find your food otherwise. When the sand begins to fall, go inside your houses. If there are three brothers in the house, they must stay inside three days and on the fourth go out. The yu mo won't fall on them, although it will be falling in other places. If there are four brothers, then they must stay inside four days. If there are five brothers. then five days, six brothers, alright, six days. And seven brothers, seven days or eight brothers eight days. If there is just one man in the house, he can come out after one day. It will be falling all around him, but it won't fall on him. If a man comes out of his house before he should, he will die.

Later, this falling sand will finish. We don't know when. While it's been falling, it will be dry and it will spread everywhere. But when it's finished rain will come and wash it into the ground. Then everything will grow gigantically. Men will have big strong children with lots of flesh. Nut pandanus and bananas will have big fruit. Sweet potato will be big.

Before, when this happened, there were two men who were very big, born at Kuki, near Peragoia. Their names were Kuki-Muya and Kuki-Himuya. Their bones are in a rockshelter called Kuki-kuru Kananda. The ancestors said: 'When their bones are like fire ashes, then this thing will be near to happening again.'

Now, at the time when the whiteman came, the bones were powdered like ash. Everybody was expecting the fall-out to come, and when they heard the first airplane up in the sky they thought: 'What's this man coming up in the sky? It must be the yu mo'. They all waited in their gardens, but they didn't cover up their houses yet. When the whiteman came and everybody saw their axes they realised what it was: 'This is what made the wood chips. Waitman, waitman, em-yet inap pundaun'. So — the government made the yu mo. This is what everybody thought.

Another version from the Southern Highlands was recorded by Patrol Officer C.E.T. Terrell in the 1950s in the Mananda Basin, Northern Mamo area:

The third generation of old men from the time of the flood is now alive, and the infants are the sixth generation. In the first generations after the flood it started to rain one day, though not with ordinary rain, but with white stuff that was like the ground, and fell in great lumps. It rained for seven days, and all that time the sun did not come up once, but was like night even in the day time. While it was raining some of the people went outside their houses, but most stayed inside. On the eighth day the rain stopped and the sun came out again. The people went outside, and saw that all the ground was covered in white and all the trees were dead and all the sweet potatoes were rotten in the ground, as if they had been cooked, because the white stuff was very hot. However the people planted more sweet potatoes in the ground and the white stuff, when it had got cool, and they grew very quickly (from Terrell's patrol report No. 3 of 53/54 Lake Kutubu Sub-District, p.17 — information supplied by Dr Rod Lacey).

It is worthwhile repeating one final verbatim report, this time recorded from the slopes of the Markham Valley north-west of Lae, from amongst the Urii:

When the dirt was about to fall from the sky, this is what they did. First they built very large round houses with steep roofs and filled the houses with firewood. Then as the time grew near, they stored water and food. The gigisum and mangkara birds knew what was about to happen, so they came and sat under the eaves and gave warning. The pigs and chickens in the village and some other birds also came and sat under the eaves. Then it became dark and the clouds became red. When the people in their gardens saw it, they quickly ran inside their houses. The darkness kept up for a very long time, and at last, when the gigisum and mangkara birds called out, the light returned.
During the month or two that it was dark, no one could see a thing because it was so dark. The spirits who usually lived in the forest came and hid under the eaves. The people thought they were passing food to their children, but the spirits were taking it out of their hands. When they found out about that they began to hand the food to their children by the light of the fire. Therefore their own children were not left sitting there with nothing to eat.
They had to stop cooking yams, because by cooking yams they caused it to remain dark. It was dark for so long, that they would reach out from their houses and shake the bananas growing nearby to see if they were ready for cutting. When they first shook them, they heard the leaves rustle, and so they left them for a while. When they shook them again they heard the rattling sound of small young bananas. Finally when they shook them they felt a heavy feeling with no noise and then they knew that they were ready for

cutting.

When they wanted to go to the toilet, they did not go outside to the forest area at the edge of the village. No, they covered their heads with bark and went right next to the house.

All the wild pigs and cassowaries which were not under cover died. So also did all the people who just remained in ordinary houses without taking proper care. They were killed in their houses when the houses fell down. Only the smart people remained alive and safe. The steep roofs of their houses kept them safe from the dirt. It was dark so long that when they peeled the bananas they had wrapped up on the trees before it became dark, the bananas had completely ripened. They were able to peel off the skins very easily. That is how long it lasted (as told by Badidik to T. and G. Webb; McElhanon, 1976, pp.203-4).

Investigation of the legends

These five accounts differ in many aspects but each refers to a period of darkness lasting several days and a fall of material from the sky. Each account contains some reference to the physical characteristics of the tephra fall and some information about its effects.

Those experienced in the interpretation of oral folklore will detect elements of stylisation, embellishments, and a variety of other features common to oral records. On the other hand the volcanologist and tephrochronologist will notice items reminiscent of volcanic ash falls and their effects as well as some items which seem, at the least, exaggerated.

Although these versions of the time of darkness legends raise numerous issues, the present analysis is concerned very largely with the following major questions: (1) do the time of darkness legends stem from a fall of tephra?; (2) how many of the legends that arose from a fall of tephra and the accompanying darkness result from the fall of Tibito Tephra?; (3) how long ago did the time of darkness and the tephra fall occur?; (4) what were the physical characteristics of the tephra fall and the time of darkness?; (5) what were the effects of the tephra fall?; and (6) to what extent can these aspects of the legends be regarded as historically valid as judged by comparisons with the physical characteristics and the effects of other tephra falls reported in the European literature?

The inquiry then is focused on examining the relationships between the eruption of Long Island and the fall of Tibito Tephra on the one hand and the time of darkness legends and their veracity on the other. The analysis and the viewpoint presented is that of a physical scientist and not that of a social scientist, though the latter might regard much of the content as poached from their reserve.

Although the present concern is thus limited, the study of oral traditions must be founded in a wider context. Attention must be paid to the context in which the tradition is collected, whether natural (highly formal, semiformal, informal) or artificial (in that recitation or performance of the tradition was arranged by the collector). Details of external influences need also to be recorded. These might include the physical and social settings, the interactions between participants, the presence of an audience whom the performer wishes to impress, and the performance time and duration. We need to know how, when, where and from whom the informant learned the tradition, what the informant calls the tradition, how he/she classifies it, and whether the item is merely 'remembered' or is performed as part of a vital tradition. Obviously it would be useful, perhaps essential, to know something about the collector's bias, the accuracy of the transcription, and the problems of sampling (and/or homogeneity) experienced by the recorder (Goldstein, 1964; Vansina, 1965; Kuschel and Monberg, 1977).

As the present investigation also aims to examine the veracity of the time of darkness legends, Dorson's (1973, pp. 111-12) seven criteria for evaluating the historical validity of a variety of oral traditions are appropriate: (1) identifying folklore themes grafted onto historical settings; (2) allowance for personal and emotional bias slanting a tradition; (3) cross-checks of multiple traditions; (4) corroboration of a tradition from printed records; (5) corroboration of a tradition from geographical landmarks; (6) corroboration of a tradition from material culture; and (7) knowledge of the character of an informant.*

Thus rigorous methods have been established for the collection and analysis of oral folklore. However, the professional folklorist is usually concerned with only one or two cultural groups, so that the necessary cultural/ethnographic background can be attained within a few years study. In the present case the area of potential concern is much larger and cultural diversity is enormous. Eight versions of the time of darkness story have been presented ranging geographically from the Urii people of the Markham Valley to the Huli tribesmen of the Tari Basin, a distance of nearly 350 km. The area across which the legend might occur spans well over a hundred thousand square kilometres, and includes a vast number of cultural groups speaking over one hundred distinct languages. Some groups are well known ethnographically, others have been little studied. Some groups have suffered European contact for more than one hundred years, others have only been contacted since 1930. Such linguistic and cultural diversity prevents application of the rigorous methods of the oral historian to the extent that the purist might deem necessary.

For the present study a variety of data sources have been used. Some versions of the time of darkness legend have been recorded in the literature; others have been mentioned only in passing. In either case, the legend might not have been presented verbatim, some aspects might

---

*In later chapters it becomes clear that the present investigation adds to this list of criteria.

have been neglected, and/or the background context was incomplete or scattered.

However, the main information about versions of the time of darkness legends came from the circulation of a questionnaire (reproduced in Appendix 4). In summary the questionnaire is concerned with: (1) the background and location of the respondent; (2) the physical characteristics of the time of darkness; (3) the effects of the tephra fall; and (4) some minor questions relating to dating of the legend, and its context. It is clear that many of the questions are detailed and quite specific.

The quality of the data received from such a questionnaire survey is understandably variable. Some respondents had already left the field and had no opportunity to make further inquiries. Others had neither the time nor the inclination to follow up the questionnaire. But between 30 and 40 per cent of those surveyed did provide useful information, a very satisfying result as questionnaire surveys frequently yield returns of less than 20 per cent.

At first sight the use of a questionnaire might seem to transgress many of the rules of oral history. Neither the informants, their cultural background, the physical and social setting of the interview, nor indeed (in many cases) the collectors of the traditions are known to me. However, the largest group of respondents were field personnel of the Summer Institute of Linguistics and social anthropologists from various universities. Replies were also received from missionaries and patrol officers with many years' experience in Papua New Guinea.

Although the quality of data received in the questionnaire survey and culled from the literature is variable, most of the data meet many of the requirements of the oral historian. Many of my informants had lived amongst their informants for periods of up to twenty years. Many had been involved in the collection (and publication) of the oral folklore and natural history of their informants and some had heard and recorded the time of darkness legend long before the arrival of the questionnaire. By virtue of their occupations all my informants were skilled in interview techniques. Most of my informants already had detailed knowledge of the character of their informants having 'used' them on numerous prior occasions and having found by experience the best ways of extracting reliable information. In the broadest sense, many of my informants were practising oral historians.

Distribution of the time of darkness legend

Perusal of the literature, circulation of the questionnaire, requests for information published in MING (Man in New Guinea) by Dr R.J. Lacey, and in The Journal of the Polynesian Society by myself, the work of Rod Lacey's students in the Enga Research Programme, and my own inquiries in the field produced a total of about 100 separate items of information about the legend. Inquiries have been concentrated in the quadrant of Papua New Guinea south and west of Long Island although,

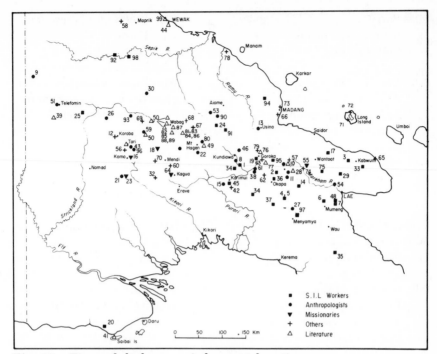

Fig. 30   Time of darkness – informant locations
as Fig. 30 indicates, some responses lie outside this area.

Three sets of information are indicated on Fig. 30: (1) the location of each item of information; (2) the type source of the items of information; (3) a number for each item, cross referenced to Table 17, which provides details of each source. It can be seen from Fig. 30 and Table 17 that the bulk of the information in the eastern part of the Highlands is derived from Summer Institute of Linguistics (SIL) field personnel. The concentration of sources around Wabag and Wapenamanda in Enga Province stems from the detailed investigation of the legend made by Paul Mai (1974, in press) as part of the Enga Research Programme. The 'others' on Fig. 30 includes information supplied by patrol officers, geographers, an oral historian and my own rather scattered and superficial inquiries. Although some information gaps occur, there is reasonable agreement between concentrations of information sources and population concentrations. The area of relatively concentrated information enclosed by Madang-Telefomin-Erave-Mumeng totals nearly 100,000 km².

Table 17
List of informants

(The name and location of each informant is given together with the name of the local language and, if applicable, the year in which the legend was first heard).

001   Barry Irwin
      9 km E of Gumine
      Salt-yui, 1977

002   Dorothy Drew and
      Audrey Payne
      16 km from Kainantu
      Kamano-Kafe, 1962

003   Mick Foster
      16 km W of Kabwum
      Timbe, 1977

004   Richard Lloyd
005   16 km N of Marawaka
      Baruya (Yipma), 1977

006   Karen Adams and
      Linda Lauck
      12 km N of Mumeng
      Patep, 1973

007   Roma Hardwick
      24 km E of Mumeng
      Mangga Buang, 1977

008   Dr Robin Hide
      10 km S of Kundiawa
      Dom, 1972

009   Dr Don Gardner
      80 km NW of Telefomin
      W Mianmin (Miyanweng),
      1977

010   Dr James B. Watson
      8 km N of Kainantu
      Agarabi, 1954

011   Dr James B. Watson
      8 km S of Aiyura
      Tairora, 1964

012   Ben Probert
      Koroba
      Huli, 1977

013   Prof. Peter Lawrence
      Usino
      Garia, 1952

014   Dorothy West
      40 km SE of Kainantu
      Ampeeli, 1966

015   Dr Roy Wagner
      26 km from Karimui
      Daribi, 1968-9

016   Fr Gabriel Lomas
      Komo
      Huli, 1976

017   John Tonson
      5 km E of Teptep
      Yupna, 1977

018   Fr Casimir and RJB
      10 km S of Kandep
      Enga, 1977

019   David Strange
      25 km W of Goroka
      Upper Asaro, 1960s?

020   Sinikka Turpeinen and
      Lillian Fleischmann
      20 km W of Daru
      Bine, 1977

021   Dr Buck Schieffelin and
      Steve Feld
      Bona near Mt Bosavi
      Kaluli, 1977

022   Dr Hal Nelson
      33 km S of Mt Hagen
      Kaimbi, 1967-8

023   Keith Briggs
      near Mt Bosavi
      Kaluli, 1977

024 Lance Woodward
16 km NW of Tabibuga
Maring, 1977

025 Marshall Lawrence
20 km W of Oksapmin
Oksapmin, 1977

026 Dr Nick Modjeska
10 km SW of Lake Kopiago
Duna, 1972

027 Dr Gilbert Herdt
near Mt Yelia
Simbari (Anga), 1975

028 Dr Brian du Toit
5 km SE of Aiyura
Gadsup, 1961

029 Edmond Fabian
50 km N of Lae
Nabak (story not known)

030 Dr Mark Dornstreich
50 km SW of Amboin
Gadio Enga (story not known)

031 Gordon Bunn
5 km from Gumine
Golin (Marigl)
(story not known)

032 Tom Na-Awi
Pimaga, L. Kutubu
(story not known)

033 Neville Southwell
20 km SE Kabwum
Komba (story not known)

034 Sam McBride
65 km SW of Okapa
Gimi (story not known)

035 Elaine Geary
Wau and Goilala
Sub-Provinces
Kunamaipa
(story not known)

036 Graham Scott
8 km NE of Okapa
Fore (story not known)

037 Dick Loving
Kainantu Sub-Province
Awa (story not known)

038 Dr Bob Smith
Lufa
Hua, 1976

040 Dr M.Y. Young (1971,
p.139)
Goodenough Island

041 Dr Wolfgang Laade
Saibai and Duan Islands,
Torres Strait

042 Dr David Trefry
S of Karimui PP
Pawaia (story not known)

043 Dr Robert Glasse
Tari
Huli, 1950s

045 George MacDonald
3 km SW of Karimui PP
Daribi (story not known)

046 Dr Paula Brown Glick
Chimbu (story not known)

047 Dr Nancy Bowers
Tambul
Kaugel, 1962

048 Bruce Hooley
     Mumeng Sub-Province
     Central Buang, 1960s

049 Vicedom and Tischner
     (1948, 3, p.50)
     Mt Hagen
     Melpa, 1930s

050 Dr Mervyn Meggitt
     Western Enga
     Enga, 1955

051 Dr Dan Jorgensen
     Telefomin (story not known)

053 Dr Georgeda Buchbinder
     W of Simbai PP
     Maring (story not known)

054 Prof. Dr Hans Fischer
     W of Lae
     Wampar/Laewomba
     (story not known)

055 Rev. Karl Holznecht
     Adzera

056 C.E.T. Turrell
     Lower Tari,
     Mananda Basin 1953

057 Pam Swadling and
     Des Oatridge
     Arona Gap area
     Binamarien, 1972

058 Dr Bryant Allen
     Dreikikir
     1973

059 Dr Paul Wohlt
     Upper Wage
     Enga, 1975

060 RJB
     15 km SE of Mendi
     1975

061 Dr John Haiman
     Lufa
     Hua, 1974

062 RJB and Dr Colin Pain
     Nupuru
     1976

063 RJB
     9 km E of Goroka
     Bena-Bena, 1975

064 Norman Ibrock
     10 km W of Kagua
     Kewa, 1975

066 Mary Mennis and Maier
     Bilbil, Madang
     1976

067 RJB
     Baiyer River
     Melpa, 1977

068 RJB
     Kompian
     Enga, 1977

069 RJB
     Timbinini near Porgera
     Ipili, 1977

070 RJB
     Nipa, 1977

073 Mary Mennis
     Kranket Island, 1976

074 Hollie Durland
     Enga, 1974

075 Toni and Gwen Webb
     Markham Valley
     Urii, 1975 (?)

076 Dr R. Skeldon and
     Dr E. Deibler
     W of Goroka
     Gahuku

077 R.J. Giddings
     Bena-Bena
     1966

078 Dr J. Z'Graggen
     Bogia coast, 1977

079 P. Munster
     Goroka
     Gahuku, 1976

080 Prof. Andrew and
     Dr Marilyn Strathern
     Mt Hagen
     Melpa, 1977

081 Paul Mai and Tipiname
     Wapenamanda
     Enga, 1974

082 Paul Mai and Saiakali Parao
     Saka Raiakam
     Enga, 1974

083 Paul Mai and Putai
     Pumakos
     Enga, 1974

084 Paul Mai and Iki Olea
     Wapenamanda
     Enga, 1974

085 Paul Mai and Wia Tabai
     Saka Raiakam
     Zumin, Markham Valley
     1976

086 Paul Mai and Katenge Paliti
     Wapendamanda
     Enga, 1974

087 Paul Mai and Wini Ponea
     Wabag
     Enga, 1974

088 Paul Mai and Buna Kaliame
     Saka
     Enga, 1974

089 Paul Mai and Tama Panao
     Saka
     Enga, 1974

090 Prof. Ralph Bulmer
     12 km from Simbai PP
     Kalam, 1960s

091 Joan Hainsworth and
     Kay Johnson
     8 km E of Tabibuga
     Narak (story not known)

092 Velma Foreman and
     Helen Marten
     30 km up river from Ambunti
     Yessan-Mayo, 1978

093 Aletta Biersack
     near Paiela
     Ipili, 1977

094 Ger Reesink
     Adelbert Ranges
     Wanuma/Usan, 1978

095 Robert Young
     Bena-Bena, 1967-68

096 Dr Stephen Frankel
     Tari
     Huli, 1976?

098 Martha Kooyers
     Ambunti
     Washkuk, 1962

097 Carl R. Whitehead
     6 km NNE of Menyamya
     Menye, 1978

099 Johann Gehberger (1938-1940)
     Wewak

Origins of the time of darkness legends

The eight traditions presented so far are clearly euhemeristic rather than etiological in character in that they seem to be based on an actual event rather than an explanation *post factum* (Vitaliano, 1973). Each of the eight accounts also refers to a fall of solid material covering the ground to varying depths, and various effects on houses, crops, animals and people.

These aspects of the tradition seem to be repeated across a very wide area although the same significance is not always attached to each aspect. An important question then arises: how many of the legends actually refer to a fall of volcanic ash as the central theme or at least as the phenomemon which gave rise to the legend? Certainly, Vicedom's and Tischner's account is entitled 'A shower of ashes', Watson (1963) believed the time of darkness legend amongst the Agarabi stemmed from the fallout of tephra from the Krakatau (1883) eruption, Glasse implied the Huli story of *bingi* arose from the fallout of a local tephra, probably from Doma Peaks, the Urii account was entitled 'when the sky rained dirt,' and Brookfield (1961) certainly attributed the origin of the legend to volcanic ash fallout. In most cases cited the evidence that the legend stems from a fall of tephra seems unequivocal; in other cases the evidence is less easy to interpret.

Some informants have produced stories which may or may not be related to a tephra fall. Some stories are strongly futuristic; these accounts generally look both forward and into the past so that it is difficult to separate the historical from the anticipated. In one such story, from amongst the Paiela (093),* the fall of ground from the sky marks the end of the earth and re-creation. Another story, from the East Sepik Province (092), tells how it first became dark — there had been no darkness before.

Skeldon (1977), in reply to Blong (1975), noted that the story extant amongst the Gahuku (076) people near Goroka was more suggestive of a hailstorm or a snowfall than a fall of volcanic ash. Similarly, Gidding's (1966) report from the Bena-Bena area is indicative of a fall of cold material. Other accounts returned with the questionnaire also suggest that in some areas the time of darkness story may refer to a fall of either hail or snow. These accounts are marked by reference to the extreme cold, the fall of heavy material, and sometimes to the presence of only

*Numbers refer to sources given on Fig. 30 and in Table 17.

wetness on the ground the following morning. Such accounts have been attributed to a hailstorm or snowstorm in the present investigation although the following points should be noted: (1) other elements in the stories parallel those in accounts which can be verified (see Chapter 8) as falls of volcanic ash; (2) one account, from amongst the Daribi (015), refers to a hailstorm immediately preceding the fall of ash from the sky; (3) falls of hail are often associated with volcanic ashfalls as the dust particles act as nuclei around which hail can condense (Vitaliano, 1973 p.258); and (4) syncretism, that is, the 'collapse' of two stories to become one, is not unknown. Furthermore, a number of informants have noted that hailstorms are sufficiently common, for example in the Tari (096) and Karimui (015) areas, that there is no possibility that even a heavy hailstorm would be confused with the events described in the legends.

Other informants have noted that the only time of darkness stories their informants know relate to the solar eclipse of 1962 (Fig. 31). On the other hand several informants first heard the time of darkness story at the time of the 1962 eclipse. For example, du Toit (1969) has written about the confusion amongst the Gadsup (028) concerning the impending solar eclipse and the earlier time of darkness.

A number of accounts refer to either the fall of material from the sky or to 'a time of darkness' but other details are insufficient to determine the source of the story. For example, the Oksapmin (025) use

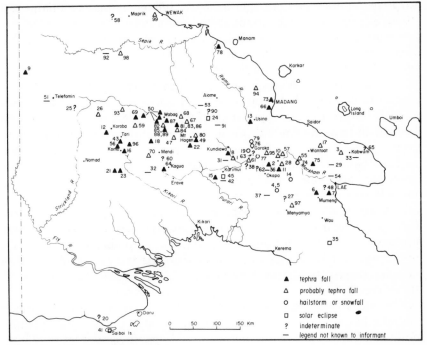

Fig. 31   Types of legend

the same term for eclipse as for the time of darkness but no informants equated the prolonged time of darkness with an eclipse. Although darkness lasted three to five days nothing fell from the sky (Marshall Lawrence, pers. comm). Accounts such as these cannot easily be placed in a particular category; the less doubtful ones with more details available have been recorded on Fig. 31 as 'probably tephra falls', whilst others have been placed in the indeterminate category. It is very likely that more information, if it becomes available, will prove some of these cases to be the product of tephra falls but a conservative stance has been adopted for the present.

One final category shown on Fig. 31 requires examination. Fifteen respondents could find no knowledge of a time of darkness story amongst their informants. Some of these respondents had never specifically asked and had left the field before the questionnaire arrived — their information can hardly be regarded as incontrovertible evidence that the story does not occur in the community which they have studied. My own observations suggest that it is not unusual for two members of similar ages and status in the one community to have quite different information about the story. On one occasion near Lufa, Eastern Highlands Province, I asked two old men ('brothers') about the story — one, who had never heard of the story, turned to the other who proceeded to give a fairly detailed outline of a more or less standard time of darkness account. The first old man continued to express surprise. A rather similar experience was related by Marshall Lawrence (025), an SIL linguist resident in the Oksapmin area since 1968. He returned the questionnaire stating that he had asked around but his informants spoke only of a 'time of darkness' that was to occur in the future. I asked him to record the details of the story anyway as I wanted to compare the 'past' accounts from other areas with this 'future' account. Some months later Marshall Lawrence replied: 'I was suddenly surprised one day when asking an older man about it, to find that he said the story relates to something that happened years ago, as well as something that will happen. Of course, after finding one person saying that a time of darkness actually occurred, it seemed that everyone I asked after that said also that it was an actual event.' These observations and rather similar experiences reported by others suggest that it is difficult to regard the absence of information as firm evidence for the non-existence of a time of darkness legend. Two cases are probably contrary to this generalisation: (1) It is probable that the story of 'a time of darkness' is not known amongst the Fore people NE of Okapa, Eastern Highlands Province, as G. Scott (036) was living with these people during the 1962 solar eclipse. Experiences relayed by du Toit (1969) and others suggest that this event led to discussion of the earlier time of darkness when ash fell from the sky. The apparent absence of such discussion amongst the Fore, suggests that they have no 'record' of the time of darkness. (2) Professor Hans Fischer (054) has recorded over 1000 oral traditions amongst the Wampar/Laewomba people of the eastern Markham Valley. He has been aware of the existence of a time of darkness story amongst the adjacent Adzera people (055) for some time, and asked specific questions of the Laewomba to no avail. It seems quite clear that a time of darkness legend does not exist amongst the Laewomba.

Thus six categories of types of legend are shown on Fig. 31: (1) tephra fall — a total of 38 cases; (2) probably tephra fall — 18 cases; (3) hailstorm or snowstorm — 8 cases; (4) solar eclipse — 4 cases; (5) indeterminate — 11 cases; (6) legend not known to informant — 12 cases. Fifty-six cases are almost certainly related to tephra fall; I would regard this proportion as conservative. Four cases have been excluded from present consideration: the two legends collected from Long Island (see Appendix 3), Young's (1971) very brief mention of ashfalls on Goodenough Island hundreds of kilometers to the east of the area under present consideration, and Carey's (1938) mention of the Manus legend.

As the fundamental concern of the present investigation involves the relationship between tephra falls and oral traditions, only those fifty-six accounts with a high probability that they stem from volcanic eruptions are considered in the following sections.

Frequency of occurrence of the time of darkness

The broad survey of the characteristics of the legends so far undertaken has eliminated from consideration all those legends not concerned with

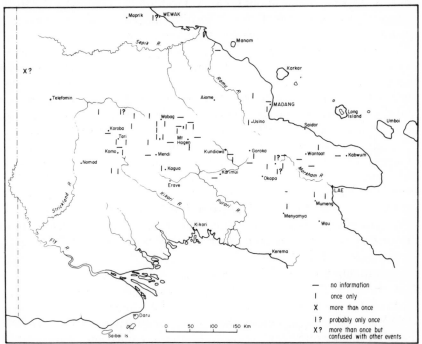

Fig. 32   *Numbers of times darkness or tephra fall has occurred*

volcanic ashfalls. However, it is not at all clear whether the remaining accounts refer to the same fall of tephra.

Figure 32 summarises the available data on the frequency of tephra fall. Clearly a time period is not specified, other than that covered by oral tradition, an interval that might vary from one community to another. Nonetheless, almost all the available evidence indicates that a time of darkness or tephra fall has occurred only once. In thirty-three accounts the informants reported unequivocally that a time of darkness or ashfall had only occurred once. For four other groups, the darkness has probably only occurred once; this is by inference in two cases (010, 011). In the case of the Mianmin (09), the most westerly group amongst whom the legend has been reported, there appears to be confusion about times of darkness caused by different phenomena including those resulting from bush and grass fires such as occurred during the drought and frost period of 1972. Anthropologist Don Gardner believes that true darkness has occurred only once. Other groups including the Waka Enga of the upper Wage Valley (059) and the Duna of the Tumbuda Valley (026) report only one time of darkness but they expect a future ashfall. Finally Robert M. Glasse in a number of papers (1963, 1965, 1973) has suggested that the Huli of the Tari area (043) have experienced bingi more than once. The tradition is certainly strong, well known, and includes attempts to induce a further ashfall in the future. 'Huli believe that bingi has occurred several times' (Glasse, 1965, p.45). Knowledge about bingi is classified as pi mana by the Huli, a category of narrative that includes supposedly historical events. Certain passages in bingi 'give practical and ritual directions for coping with recurrences. The inclusion of these prescriptions in the mana suggests that bingi has occurred more than once at Tari. Huli believe this to be true, but have no means of dating past occurrences.' (Glasse, 1973, p.5; cf. Glasse, 1963). However there is no really strong evidence that the Tari Huli have experienced bingi more than once (R.M. Glasse, pers. comm., 1978). Furthermore, the Komo Huli (016) people are adamant that the tradition originated in the Tari area before they moved to Komo. Fr Gabriel Lomas also believes that the ashfall has occurred only once, as other times of darkness seem to refer to eclipses. Ben Probert (012) interviewed Huli tribesmen around Koroba. Although no information was forthcoming from the Koroba Huli (012) on the frequency of occurrence of the bingi, Ben Probert reported that early in the interview there was some confusion with eclipses and droughts, smoke haze and dust haze.

Although the vast majority of legends included in the present analysis evidently refer to only one time of darkness or ashfall, this agreement cannot be used to suggest that all the legends refer to the one and same event. Nevertheless, there is a possibility that all the legends that refer to only one event, in fact refer to the same event. This point is considered further in Chapter 8.

Another point which is helpful in interpreting the legend involves the location of the informants at the time of the event. As already mentioned, the Huli people around Komo (016) believe they have migrated from Tari to Komo since the tephra fall. The West Mianmin (09) have migrated from the east, certainly since the time of the story, following the course of the August and Sepik Rivers. They have very likely moved some distance. The Pateps (06) lived where the Hanexs now live, when the darkness occurred; the distance to their present location is not known. The Waka Enga people (059) may also have moved from the upper Lai Valley since the ashfall. Other groups of informants have certainly moved around a little as is the wont of subsistence agriculturalists. However, with few exceptions, we can be fairly certain that the legends do refer to the specific locations shown on Fig. 31.

Finally, in order to complete the background survey of the data it is worth considering the question: 'do the informants believe the oral tradition to be a legend (an historical account) or a myth (a folktale)?' At least thirty-six of the informants believe the time of darkness or tephra fall tradition to be an historical account, a description of an actual event. Even for most of those cases where no direct information is available, there is a strong inference that the tradition concerns an event which actually occurred. Amongst the available information there is only one reply which regards the tradition as a myth — from the Huli people of the Komo area (016). Father Gabriel Lomas writes: 'They know it only as a myth or a very improbable legend — although they are willing to be convinced that it actually happened, and many say that it can be brought on again by certain, unkown rituals.'

Watson (1963, p.153) cites three lines of evidence which suggest that the account given by the Agarabi (010) has historical validity: (1) reference to the falling sands gives the account a certain concreteness; (2) the absence of stylised personages in the account; (3) reinforcement of the feeling of reality by the manner of the raconteur, in particular the absence of the hint of playfulness which usually accompanied more frankly mythological tales. However, Watson also cites evidence for truncation and stylisation of the Agarabi account.

The preliminary analysis then, has established a body of fifty-six traditions that recount the story of a time of darkness or ashfall, an event which the vast majority of informants believe to have actually occurred. The available information also establishes that most informants still live close to the sites they occupied when the event occurred, and that the majority believe the event to have occurred only once.

8 Tibito Tephra and the legends

In previous chapters some of the time of darkness legends have been described and the distribution of Tibito Tephra has been reported. Comparison of Fig. 29 and 31 indicates a considerable degree of overlap between the known tephra and the known legend distributions. Such co-occurrence, however, does not necessarily demonstrate that it was the fall of Tibito Tephra which gave rise to the time of darkness legend. The extent to which the legend results from the fall of Tibito Tephra must be demonstrated.

It seems axiomatic that legends arising as a result of tephra fall should be a product of the most recent tephra fall. To hypothesise that the penultimate tephra (or an even earlier tephra) gave rise to the legend is to invoke special pleading and perhaps to deny the evidence of the informants who almost universally maintain that the time of darkness has occurred only once. The not uncommon association of the time of darkness story with the subsequent (1962) total solar eclipse also suggests that it is unlikely that a secondary, even trifling, fall of tephra or darkness would go unnoticed or unrecorded in the legend. We can safely assume that it is the most recent tephra fall that gave rise to the legend.

The first task then is to determine which tephra is uppermost at each site.

Stratigraphic position of Tibito Tephra

Although Figs. 11 and 29 locate sites where Tibito Tephra is known to occur and demonstrate its widespread distribution, these diagrams do not supply information about the stratigraphic position of Tibito Tephra.

Certain difficulties with tephrostratigraphy of thin tephra beds in the Papua New Gunea Highlands were pointed out in Chapter 1. Intensive gardening, rapid bioturbation and annual rainfalls in excess of 2500 mm all contribute to the reworking of thin tephra beds and to the destruction of stratigraphic details. Frequently the relative ages of tephra beds in the one general area are difficult to determine because stratigraphic superposition does not occur in the available exposures. Thus, it is possible to collect a tephra sample, chemically fingerprint it, determine the source of the tephra and its physical characteristics, and still not know whether that particular tephra is the stratigraphically uppermost tephra. Such is the case with many of the collection sites located on Fig. 11.

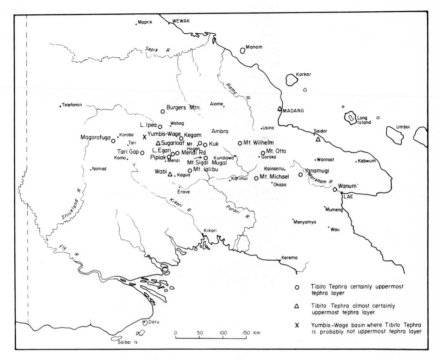

Fig. 33   Location of sites with useful tephrostratigraphy

However, in many areas relatively detailed stratigraphic investigations have been undertaken. In some sites, lengthy exposures with good preservation of tephras can be found and in others detailed palynological, geomorphological or archaeological studies have been completed. Figure 33 indicates those sites where stratigraphic investigations have been sufficiently detailed that we can be sure of the tephrostratigraphy.

With one exception Tibito Tephra is the uppermost tephra layer at every site shown on Fig. 33. On this diagram two levels of probability that Tibito Tephra is the youngest tephra in the area have been differentiated. At some sites, such as Lake Egari, Tari Gap, Mt Wilhelm and Kuk Tea Research Station there is absolutely no possiblity that any tephra younger than Tibito Tephra was deposited. This assurance can be given because exposures are good and/or investigations have been detailed. At such sites a variety of tephra beds have been examined, their relative stratigraphic positions are consistent and careful searches have been made for young tephra beds. At some sites, particularly those lake sites examined by Professor Frank Oldfield, magnetic

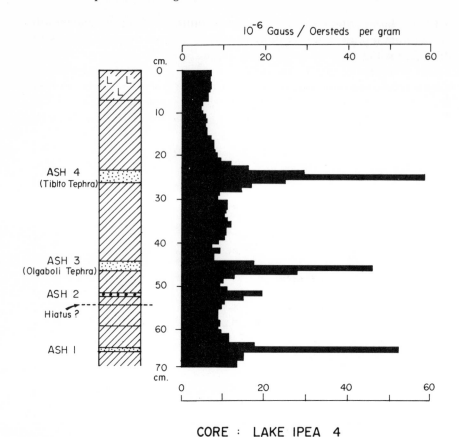

CORE : LAKE IPEA 4

Fig. 34 *Magnetic susceptibility of samples from Lake Ipea*
(after Oldfield, 1976, Fig. 9)

susceptibility measurements (Fig. 34) and other analytical techniques
have failed to reveal any tephra younger than Tibito Tephra.

At other sites differentiated on Fig. 33, for example at Madang and
Saidor, there is a high probability that Tibito Tephra is the youngest
tephra but good exposures of the stratigraphy have not been found. At
these sites lengthy searches for suitable exposures and for tephra beds
have revealed only Tibito Tephra.

At almost all those sites shown on Fig. 11 but not on Fig. 33 Tibito
Tephra is believed to be the youngest tephra present but there is little
certainty as exposures were poor or investigations hasty. At only one
site (Fig. 33; No. 400 on Fig. 11), in the upper Wage basin, has Tibito
Tephra not been the uppermost tephra. This site was found by Dr Paul
Wohlt and investigated by the author in January 1975. The stratigraphic
exposure occurs in a drainage ditch on a low angle alluvial(?) fan in the
north-eastern part of the basin. The alluvial sediments include organic
clays at depth with organic-rich sandy clays near the surface. Tibito
Tephra occurs at a depth of c. 50 cm as a series of discrete grey-green

balls, suggesting that the tephra layer was only 1-2 cm thick. The tephra layer younger than Tibito Tephra is a yellow-brown sandy clay about 2.5 cm thick varying in depth from 25-50 cm. There seems to be little doubt that the upper layer is tephra as it appears to mantle the topography, has an allophane reaction whereas the surrounding inwashed sediment does not despite the limestone lithology of the catchment, and the layer is clearly different from the surrounding sediment.

Although Sr and Rb analyses of the upper tephra (sample No. 400) indicate values close to those of Tibito Tephra (Fig. 10), Zr and Y values of 274 ppm and 40 ppm respectively indicate that this tephra layer is quite distinctive. Unfortunately insufficient sample was collected to allow major element and particle-size analyses.

Thus neither the source of this upper tephra nor its age is known, other than that it is clearly younger than Tibito Tephra. At the time of sample collection the upper tephra was assumed to have been erupted from Doma Peaks, the nearest 'active' volcano, but subsequent careful field investigations along Tari Gap (Fig. 33) and in the Doma Peaks crater clearly indicate that this volcano has not erupted since Tibito Tephra was emplaced (Blong, 1979a). Other potential sources include various vents in the Schouten Islands and Manam Island (Fig. 14). Known eruptive histories for Bam and Manam Islands are given in Fig. 18 and Chapter 4. However, as Fig. 33 shows, Oldfield's Lake Ipea site lies directly on line between the upper Wage site and the Schouten Islands and Manam volcanoes. Oldfield's investigation (1976) of Lake Ipea stratigraphy has been extremely thorough. Chemical analysis of the Lake Ipea 3 core and magnetic susceptibility analyses of Lake Ipea cores 2, 4, and 5 (Fig. 34) allow no possibility of the presence of a tephra layer younger than Oldfield's Ash 4, which has already (Chapter 3) been unequivocally identified on the basis of field and geochemical criteria as Tibito Tephra.

The post-Tibito Tephra bed in the upper Wage basin remains an enigma. It seems impossible for a north coast volcano to have deposited tephra in that area without also depositing tephra in Lake Ipea. The tephra certainly did not come from Doma Peaks. Careful field searches in the Kandep area a few km south-east of the upper Wage, the Tari Gap to the south, and Mogorofuga (near Koroba) to the south-west resulted only in the identification of Tibito Tephra and older tephras. Although re-examination of the field evidence and recollection and re-analysis of the Yumbis-Wage samples is required it seems possible that Tibito Tephra is not the youngest tephra in the area around and north-west(?) of the Yumbis-Wage basin. However, detailed stratigraphic investigations north-east, south and west of the site confirm that Tibito Tephra is the uppermost airfall tephra layer in those areas.

Figure 35 shows, superimposed, the location of the fifty-six legendary accounts stemming from a tephra fall, the 1.5 cm Tibito

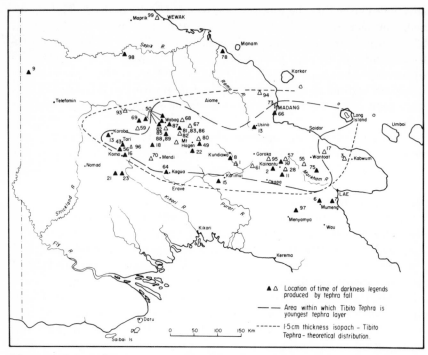

Fig. 35   *Legendary accounts resulting from tephra fall and area within which Tibito Tephra is the youngest tephra*

Tephra isopach, and the area within which Tibito Tephra is known to be the youngest tephra layer and hence the source of and inspiration for the time of darkness legend.

The 1.5 cm thickness isopach for Tibito Tephra is taken from Fig. 29. This isopach has been constructed on theoretical grounds using the actual thickness data presented on Fig. 24. As pointed out in Chapter 6, there is every reason to believe that the area enclosed by the isopach is a very conservative estimate of the total area covered with 1.5 cm of (compacted) tephra.

The area within which Tibito Tephra is known to be the youngest tephra layer has also been estimated conservatively in that the enclosing line has been drawn to lie just outside those sites where Tibito Tephra is the uppermost ashfall deposit. As there are no known active volcanoes south of the southern margin of the Tibito Tephra 1.5 cm isopach it is certain that legends extant on the northern slopes of Mt Bosavi (Nos. 021 and 023) and near Mt Karimui (No. 015) are also the product of the fall of Tibito Tephra.

Legendary accounts 06, 07 and 097 could have been the result of tephra falls stemming from the eastern part of the Bismarck Arc, New Britain, or from further east in mainland Papua New Guinea (eg. Mt Lamington). However, attempts to find tephra layers in the area immediately south of Wau were unsuccessful. As Mumeng lies only about 35 km south of Lake Wanum where c. 1 cm of Tibito Tephra has been cored from lake deposits by Dr Sam Garrett-Jones, it would be very surprising if this tephra layer did not not also cover the Mumeng area. Nonetheless we cannot attribute Accounts 06, 07 and 097 to the Long Island tephra with total certainty.

Similarly, as indicated by the location of the 1.5 cm isopach line, the areas from which Accounts 03 and 017 are drawn must have experienced the fall of Tibito Tephra. There is a possibility that these areas could also have experienced tephra fall from the 1888 eruption of Ritter Island (Chapter 4) but the analysis of Cooke and Johnson (1978) makes this a very remote possibility.

Account 078 stems from the mainland adjacent to Manam Island. Dr J. Z'Graggen, who collected this account from the Kayan people, has suggested (pers. comm., 1977) that the 1877 eruption of Manam may have been responsible for the legend. Figure 18 indicates that this eruption is one of several possibilities in the historic period. Certainly there is no basis for ascribing the Kayan legend to the fall of Tibito Tephra. Similarly we cannot be certain that Accounts 094, 098 and 099 result from Tibito Tephra.

Account 09 stems from the West Mianmin people who currently live near the Irian Jaya border. However, it seems certain that these people have migrated some considerable distance westward since the time of darkness (Chapter 7). This legendary account cannot be attributed to any specific tephra, but it is likely that it results from the fall of Tibito Tephra.

Three other accounts are shown on Fig. 25 to lie outside the area within which Tibito Tephra is the uppermost tephra layer. Professor Mervyn Meggitt's (050) account is one of these. His publication (1973) is drawn from several sources but particularly from the area north of Wabag which lies inside the ellipse. The Timbinini account (069) from the Ipili people and Paul Wohlt's account (western Enga — 059) also lie outside the ellipse. The latter site is the location where a younger tephra overlies Tibito Tephra. On the other hand, my Ipili informant (069) was insistent that the time of darkness had occurred only once.

Samples of the material that fell from the sky

Another method by which the notion that the legend is the product of the most recent tephra fall can be tested involves asking the local people if they can produce samples of the tephra that fell. Although this question was asked in the questionnaire (Appendix 4) no informants were able to produce the tephra. However, two of my own attempts to get informants to produce samples of the material that fell have been successful and four other informants, interviewed as part of the Enga Research Programme, also submitted samples.

The following six samples were obtained:
1. Informant Iki Olea from Kanakimanda near Wapenamanda, Enga Province. Analytical Numbers, 246, 402. Legendary account 084.

Date of collection 21/1/75.

2. Informant Wia Tabai from Raiakama (Tchak Valley) Enga Province. Analytical Nos. 251, 404. Legendary account 085. Date of collection 21/1/75.

3. Informants unknown. Submitted by Nita Pupu, Enga Research Programme, from Sangulapu near Wabag, Enga Province. Analytical numbers 247 and 403. No specific legendary account but Pupu's data used by Mai (in press). Sample collected January 1975.

4. Informant unknown. Submitted by Tim Pyakalya, Enga Research Programme, from near Laiagam, Enga Province. Analytical No. 410. No specific legendary account but Pyakalya's data used by Mai (in press). Sample collected January 1975.

5. Informant Pita Tambuli. Sample collected on Kondo Road south of Kandep, Enga Province. Analytical No. 588. Related to legendary account No. 018. Sample collected 12/9/77.

6. Numerous informants at Rev. Norm Imbrock's Wabi Mission, west of Kagua, Southern Highlands Province. Analytical No. 531. Legendary account No. 064. Sample collected 19/2/76.

Thus five of the six samples reputed to be material that fell from the sky during the time of darkness were collected from Enga Province. All are closely related to the time of darkness legend in that they were collected during the telling of the legend and following specific requests for information. Geochemical characteristics of the samples have been determined and the results are plotted on Fig. 10.

Field characteristics and geochemistry confirm the view that Nos. 1, 3, 4 and 5 are Tibito Tephra. No. 2 is a sample of Olgaboli Tephra some 1100 years in age but sometimes easily confused on the bases of field characteristics alone with Tibito Tephra (Chapter 2). No. 6 is quite definitely a sample of tephra but geochemical analyses and its field properties (yellow-brown clay) as well as its stratigraphic position confirmed that it is not a young tephra. Comparison with similar tephra at the Kuk site suggests that it is more then 20,000 years old. Nevertheless, the sample from Wabi is a tephra.

These experiments confirm that the material that fell from the sky during the time of darkness can still be readily identified, at least by some people in the Enga Province. Four out of five samples from Enga confirm that it was Tibito Tephra that fell most recently. The fifth Enga sample can also be interpreted as supporting that view.

The results from Wabi in the Southern Highlands are a little more difficult to interpret. The sample submitted and Tibito Tephra are quite unlike one another in field character and stratigraphic position. Nonetheless, the only relatively young tephra layer found in the Wabi area was Tibito Tephra.

Summary

Of the fifty-six legendary accounts located on Fig. 35 all but thirteen quite definitely stem from the deposition of Tibito Tephra. Of the remaining thirteen, three accounts (015, 021 and 023) cannot conceivably result from any other tephra fall even though they lie outside the area where Tibito Tephra is known to be the youngest tephra layer. It is also probable but not certain that five more accounts (03, 06, 07, 017 and 097) also result from the fall of Tibito Tephra. The north-western corner of the Tibito Tephra 1.5 cm isopach remains problematic as the younger tephra fall at site 400 (Legendary account 059) requires further investigation. There is a strong possiblity that the fall of Tibito Tephra at least contributed to the time of darkness legend but a younger tephra may also have played a part. As the west Mianmin may have migrated a considerable distance from the south-east since the time of darkness it is quite likely that they also experienced the fall of Tibito Tephra but again there is no certainty. For the areas north of the known distribution of Tibito Tephra (Fig. 35) no stratigraphic control is available. Legends 078, 094, 098 and 099 could have resulted from a tephra fall from almost any north coast volcano.

The following analysis of the legends of a time of darkness considers all fifty-six accounts plotted on Fig. 35 that are firmly believed to result from a fall of tephra but attention is focused particularly on those that clearly arose from the fall of Tibito Tephra. As the link between the time of darkness legends and the fall of Tibito Tephra has now been firmly established, two major aspects of the legends can now be examined: (1) the physical characteristics of the tephra fall as reported in the legends (Chapter 9), and (2) the effects of the tephra fall according to the legends (Chapter 10). Subsequent chapters then concentrate on examining the veracity of the legendary material related to these two aspects.

9 Physical characteristics of the tephra fall according to the legends

The physical characteristics of a tephra fall can encompass many more phenomena than just the fall of the volcanic ash. Darkness often accompanies the fall of tephra, and explosions, rain, thunder, lightning and obnoxious smells are also commonly experienced. Furthermore, easily observable characteristics such as colour, particle size and thickness of the tephra fall might be noticed and remembered in a legendary account.

Although the information recorded in the literature and in the questionnaire returns is far from complete, a great deal of information is available concerning the characteristics of the darkness and/or the tephra fall. Seven different aspects are summarised here. No verbatim material is presented here but all the available legends have been presented in full in *Oral History* (vol. 7, no. 10), published by the Institute of Papua New Guinea Studies (Blong, 1979b).

The length of time darkness remained or duration of the tephra fall

The data on which Fig. 36 is based have been extracted from the legends but in some cases the figures are based on inference or interpretation. Where more than one estimate has been provided by the one informant or group of informants a mean figure or 'best estimate' has been used on the map. The term 'several days' has been interpreted to mean three to four days; thus the figure 3.5 days appears on the map.

More than thirty of the forty-four groups of informants supplying information believe that darkness lasted less than four days (Fig. 37). However, the informant from the Urii legend (075) from the Markham Valley reported that it was dark for a month or two and Meggitt's (1973, p.54) account of the time of darkness cites 'For three months without interruption a constant drift of black dirt fell from the cloud'. One of Paul Mai's Enga informants (081) thought the darkness lasted for one hundred days but the eight other Enga informants cited by Mai all estimated durations of two or four days, many of them making comments such as: 'I really don't know how many days it happened or

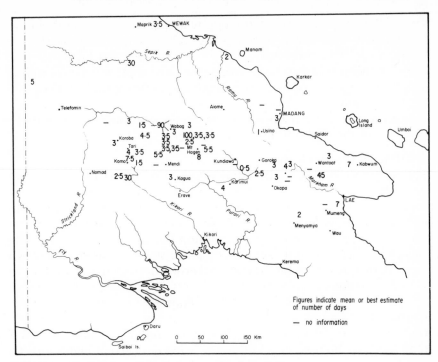

Fig. 36   Duration of darkness or tephra fall

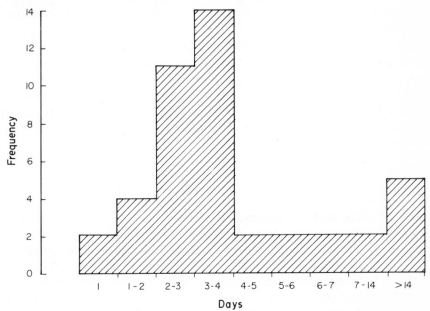

Fig. 37   Frequency distribution of darkness or tephra fall duration

how long it was dark. In those days they did not have any proper system of counting the days but I was told that it was dark for about 3-4 days . . .' (082). The only other group who mention a time of darkness lasting more than seven days are the Kaluli people (023) of the Mt Bosavi area. These tribesmen suggest that the sandfall lasted for one month. Other informants (021) who questioned another group of Kaluli people nearby received responses ranging from two to three days to two to three months.

The spatial pattern shown on Fig. 36 does not suggest any orderly variation in the duration of the darkness.

Quality of the darkness

The early accounts in the literature emphasised the darkness as one of the main features of the legend, as the common name 'time of darkness' suggests. Thus, the questionnaire contained this emphasis rather than also emphasising the actual fall of ash or sand. Figure 38 indicates that six of the accounts do not even mention the darkness (this mapping category indicates that these accounts are organised around a fall of ash or sand, that details of the legend are known in some detail, and that a period of darkness plays no part or a very minor part in the story).

On the other hand twenty of the accounts emphasise the darkness as though it had unusual quality. There are references to people carrying torches during daytime, to people afraid they would get lost if they left their houses, and to the day being dark like a night with no moon. Two further cases make reference to the daytime being 'half light' (043) or light enough to see one's way around outside during daytime (022).

Fifteen stories refer clearly to the darkness but make no reference to the quality of the darkness. This group includes all nine accounts collected by Paul Mai (1974; in press) from eastern Enga; it is a little surprising, given that the Enga apparently call the legend 'The time of darkness', to find no mention of the quality of that darkness. However, two other accounts from Enga Province state: 'The sun and the moon vanished; they did not rise' (050) and 'the sun and moon hid under the earth' (059).

It may or may not be fortuitous that four out of the six accounts in which darkness is not mentioned occur in a strip of country (Fig. 38) extending from Karimui to Usino (largely Simbu Province).

The particle size of material that fell

Figure 39 attempts to translate the descriptions of material that fell into particle sizes although this attempt is difficult because of the problems of translation. For example, the Dom (08) word *kilogebe* does not differentiate between dust and sand. Furthermore, there is no real distinction in particle size between dust and ashes; nonetheless the legends seem to make a distinction, probably indicating a difference in the feel or colour of the material. Combining the two categories, the majority of the legends for which there is information indicate that the material that fell was very fine-textured. A further thirteen accounts

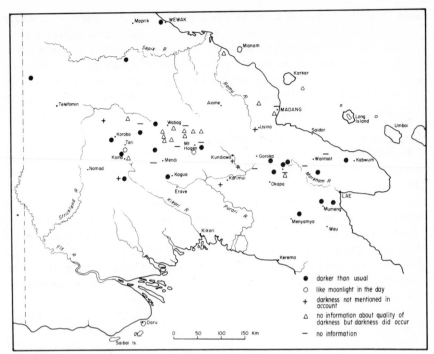

Fig. 38   Quality of the darkness

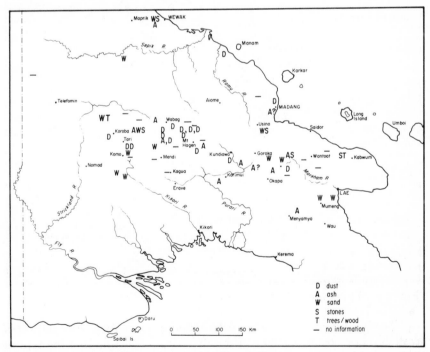

Fig. 39   Particle size of material that fell

described the material as sand-sized while four descriptions include falling stones. One of these four accounts also mentions falling trees.

As the descriptions and their subsequent translations into particle sizes can be none too accurate the mapped variations may not be very informative. However, there is some suggestion that the coarser particle sizes are concentrated at the eastern and western ends of the distribution (Fig. 39).

The thickness of fallen material

Interpreting the thickness of material that fell during the time of darkness involves problems somewhat similar to those encountered in the previous section. However, many accounts describe the covering of crops or the collapse of houses and other informants have endeavoured to indicate an actual thickness on the ground. These comments and rough indications have been translated into a six point scale: (1) a dusting; (2) material covered everything; (3) fall of material broke down trees and caused houses to collapse; (4) about 15 cm; (5) about 30 cm; (6) about 2 metres or more. The numbers given here are used on Figs. 40 and 41.

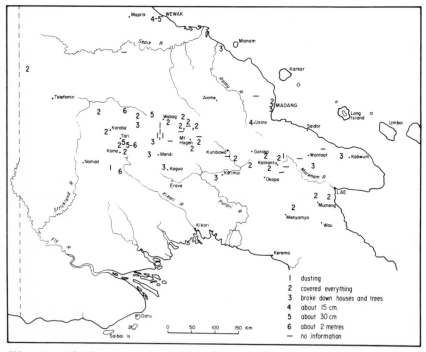

Fig. 40   Thickness of the tephra fall

Twenty-seven of the forty-three accounts for which information is available have been placed in the categories indicating that the tephra fall was either only a dusting or merely thick enough to cover gardens.

Twenty-one of the forty-three responses have been assigned to category 2 but as neither types of plants nor the amount by which the plants were covered is specified this category could obviously include a wide range of thicknesses. There is no evidence on Fig. 40 that there is any concentration in any particular area of the category 2 thickness.

If speculation could be allowed on the basis of the seven accounts which specify thicker mantles of material (categories 4, 5 and 6), it could be noted that six out of seven occur in the west. It is also interesting to note that the two accounts collected from Kaluli tribesmen (021 and 023) are in marked disagreement concerning the thickness of the fallen material. Account 021 (Dr E.L. Schieffelin, pers. comm.) specifies that the fallen sand did not even form a layer but just filled the interstices of leaves, while Account 023 suggested the thickest covering specified in the accounts — 'Up to the eaves on houses 6 feet off the ground'.

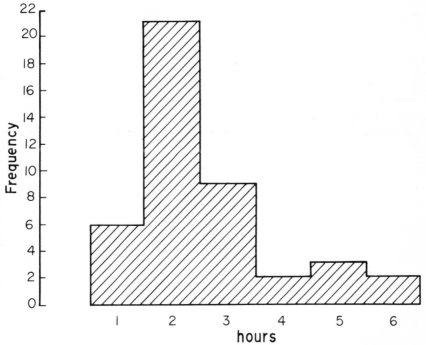

Fig. 41   Frequency distribution of tephra thicknesses reported in legends

Colour of the fallen material

A wide range of colours have been given by informants to describe the fallen material (Fig. 42). It should be noted that 'ash-like' is used as a colour in this section and that it was used earlier as a particle size description; where it has not been possible to decide whether the informant used 'ash' to describe colour or particle size 'no information' has been recorded.

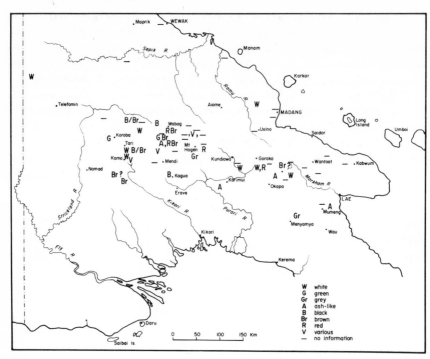

Fig. 42   Reported colour of the tephra

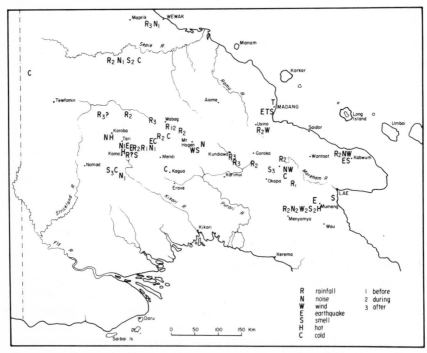

Fig. 43   Physical effects accompanying the tephra fall

The most interesting aspect of the colour question is the wide range in colours reported. Thus in eastern Enga where all nine of Mai's (1974) informants (081-089) live, although there is good agreement on the particle size of the fallen material (Fig. 39), a very wide range of colours is reported. Given the relatively small area in which they live, and the agreement of eight out of nine informants that the ashfall has only occurred once, the variation is rather surprising. Other Enga informants (018, 059 and 050) give the colour as black (twice), red, and white.

Physical effects accompanying tephra fall

Additional physical effects which accompanied the ashfall are indicated on Fig. 43. These effects include rainfalls (R), noises (N), wind (W), earthquakes (E), tsunamis (T), odours (S), and temperature changes (H or C). Three time periods are recognised: (1) preceeding the tephra fall, (2) at the same time as the fall of ash, and (3) following the tephra fall. The time period is indicated by a subscript numeral (Fig. 43): 1, before; 2, during; and 3, after the tephra fall.

In the continually wet highland environment, it is difficult to attach much significance to a rainfall following the ashfall as no time period is specified. If the ashfall occurred in the wet season we might expect rainfall before and during the two to four days of ashfall, as well as subsequent to the event.

No obvious pattern of spatial variation emerges. All types of

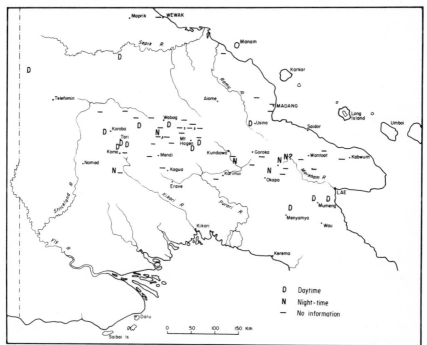

Fig. 44   Daytime or nighttime when tephra fall began

associated effects are reported towards both the east and west ends of the distribution except tsunamis (obviously restricted to the coastal sites). Very few informants have recounted physical effects associated with the tephra fall despite a number of specific questions in the questionnaire (see Appendix 4).

The time of day when darkness began

Some direct information reported in legends, questionnaire replies and inferences have allowed the construction of Fig. 44 showing whether it was day or night-time when darkness or ashfall began.

The available data, and they are far from complete, suggest that when the darkness or tephra fall began it was daytime in the area south of Lae, nighttime in Eastern Highlands Province, and probably daytime in the Western and Southern Highlands Provinces. There seem to be only one or two exceptions to this pattern.

Summary

Although most informants believed the darkness lasted two to four days, some believed darkness lasted up to 100 days. There is no order to the spatial pattern. About one-third of the accounts emphasise the quality of the darkness as being darker than usual, while six accounts do not even mention an accompanying darkness. Four of these six occur in the Karimui-Usino area. Of the thirty-nine informants with data about the particle size of the tephra fall, twenty-eight suggest that it was dust or ash-sized material that fell. There is some suggestion on Fig. 39 that coarser particle sizes are concentrated on the east and west ends of the distribution. The most common reference to the thickness of the tephra is that it covered everything. Interestingly the two Kaluli versions span the complete range of thicknesses. Despite such variations there is a tendency for the thicker mantles to occur in the west. There is a marked variation in the colour descriptions. Although the nine Eastern Enga accounts agreed well on the particle size, numerous colours are reported. Effects accompanying the tephra fall, such as noises, thunder and smells, are only occasionally reported; all types of associated effects are reported from both east and west. Two out of the three coastal informants report tsunamis accompanying the event. That few informants mentioned associated effects indicates either (a) they did not occur, (b) they are not recorded in the legend, or (c) they were not associated by those who experienced the tephra fall as being part of it. Data on the time when darkness or tephra fall first began suggest daytime south of Lae, nighttime in the Eastern Highlands, and probably daytime in the Western and Southern Highlands. This agreement in spatial variations is good, despite the missing information, compared with the patterns of variations for the other physical characteristics.

10 The effects of the tephra fall according to the legend

One might surmise that while the colour and the particle size of the material that fell from the sky might be forgotten or misrepresented after several generations, the effects that the tephra fall produced would be more memorable. If that is the case the data dealt with in this chapter can be regarded as superior in quality to those concerned with the physical effects of the tephra fall. This hypothesis can also be stated in an alternative fashion; it does not seem possible to draw any inference from the absence of information about colour, thickness or particle size. The absence of such data from the account or failure to produce such information during questioning does not lead one to conclude that the fallen material had no thickness and was colourless. On the other hand it seems probable that effects of the time of the darkness on material culture would be better remembered. Thus a stronger case can be made in the present section for the interpretation of information gaps. It seems likely that the absence of a reported effect probably means that there was no effect. However, the distinction between 'no effects' and 'no information' is maintained on the following maps.

A general consideration of the effects of tephra falls on people and their possessions (Blong, in press) and a general knowledge of Papua New Guinean subsistence economies, indicate that the following effects should be considered: (1) on houses, (2) on vegetation including crops, (3) on animals, (4) on drinking water and streams, and (5) on people. Accordingly, this section considers each of these aspects. The more esoteric question, 'Was the darkness/tephra fall harmful or beneficial?' is also investigated.

Effects on houses

As is to be expected the data on the effects on houses are of variable quality and specificity but several groups of effects can be recognised: (1) houses collapsed; some attempt was made to indicate, from the general sense of the account, whether this was a common or unusual event by subscripts on Fig. 45: viz. C_1 (many houses collapsed), and C_2 (a few houses collapsed). Where this differentiation is not possible the symbol 'C' alone is used. (2) Roofs were deformed or fell in during the tephra fall. In practice there may be no difference between this category and the first one and the distinction made here might be an artefact of translation or expression. On the other hand the difference might be real, the first category representing a more complete state of destruction. (3) Occupants of the houses took avoiding action; this usually involved strengthening the roofs, climbing on the roof to remove the dust/sand, or 'bumping' the roof from the inside to remove the tephra. The essentially verbatim material from which these three categories were derived is presented in Table 18. These data and two additional categories are also shown on Fig. 45. (4) The legends positively state that houses were unaffected by the tephra fall or associated events. (5) No information available.

Figure 45 indicates that both house collapse and avoiding action were widespread. However, there is a paucity of information in eastern Enga Province where no accounts mention effects on houses. Given the intensive investigation, recording and documentation of the legend in this area it seems quite likely that houses did not collapse there.

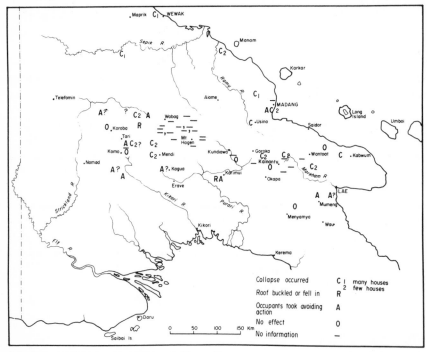

Fig. 45   *Effects of tephra fall on houses*

The event seems to have produced little record of adverse effects on houses in the Eastern Highlands as only two accounts (057 and 095) refer to the collapse of houses.

A number of the accounts contain futuristic elements. For

Table 18
Effects on houses

(See Fig. 45 for key to symbols.)

Legend No.	Map Symbol	
03	C	Houses knocked down by trees (trees fell from sky).
06	A	No effect mentioned but story says '...sand fell on top of their houses, so they went and got banana leaves and covered the roofs with them. They did this so the sand would spill down onto ground and not fall into the grass roofs and ruin their houses'.
07	A?	No houses collapsed but some people feared that they would if the sand continued to fall.
013	C	Some big stones broke houses, shattered them — and killed men, women, children, pigs, dogs, etc.
015	RA	Broke in house roofs (sago roofing) '...they pulled up bark flooring and bark partitions from walls and put bark inside sago roofing and then they tied kanda sticks to the big roof poles and tucked the lower parts under the eaves'.
018	C_2	Old houses collapsed — new ones okay.
021	A	No houses collapsed but people hit roof of longhouse with sticks from inside and heard sand roll down sides of roof.
023	A	None collapsed because old whiskery man prophesied that no one would die.
026	A?	In future — cover up house with tree bark — if it's old house, build a new one.
043	A	Ash cleared from house tops which threatened to buckle (1973); (new communal houses built beforehand; 1963).
050	A	Men regularly climbed onto the rooftops to clear away the heavy deposits of dirt that threatened to break through the thatch.
057	C_2	Big stones fell, some of which broke houses.
059	R	Fell like marbles and ruined the houses especially the roofs — will make bark roofs next time. Said that people used to make roof of bark or pit pit because of stones falling. Since stones did not fall again, people began to use pandanus leaves as they do now.
064	A?	Next time it happens will make pandanus roofs so that material will run off — will bump roof up and down to knock it off.

066	AC_2	Had to sweep ash off house roofs, some houses collapsed.
069	C_2	Old houses but not new houses collapsed — killed some men and children.
070	C_2	Some houses collapsed.
075	C_2	Some people built new round houses with steep roofs beforehand — people who didn't build new houses killed.
078	C_2	Old houses collapsed but newer and stronger ones survived.
093	?	All the houses were/will be buried and lost. Were/would be all created again in new ground epoch.
094	C_1	Skyfruits (the brokenup sky) fell clear through the roofs, and demolished the houses.
095	C_2	Houses collapsed in earthquake.
096	C_2?	Special houses not damaged — roofed with hardwood and not thatch.
097	O	No houses collapsed because of the slope of the roofs.
098	C_1	All the houses fell down and all the people went into the spirit houses.
099	C_1	All the houses except the especially built house had been destroyed by the stones which came down first.

example, Accounts 064 (west of Kagua), 026 (near Lake Kopiago), and 059 (Upper Wage) all refer to avoidance actions that will be taken next time a tephra fall or time of darkness occurs.

Effects on trees and crops

The more or less verbatim comments concerning effects on trees and crops are presented in Table 19. Only deleterious effects are listed. Apart from the general category of gardens ruined or destroyed (R on Fig. 46) in which little specific information is provided, three less general categories can be defined: B — leaves burnt or spoiled; S — leaves stripped; and T — tubers rotted. Obviously, some informants have reported more than one of these effects. A fifth category — W — where the food (crops?) was all washed away was cited only once, by the Timbe people near Kabwum (03).

Because subsistence cropping is so central to the whole highland economy, the absence of any mention of adverse effects on garden plants probably suggests that there were no such deleterious effects (discussion in this section excludes references to the covering of plants by the sand/ash/dust as such notifications have been recorded in Chapter 9). Six accounts (Fig. 46) specifically mention no serious effects.

Thirty-six accounts mention adverse effects on crops but quite a number of these contain no specific information. For example, most of the Enga informants (Table 19) mentioned only that the gardens were ruined, without reference to why or how the plants were destroyed. The accounts from the Kamano-Kafe (02) and from the Huli at Koroba (012) stand in sharp contrast.

Table 19
Effects on trees and crops

(See Fig. 46 for key to symbols.)

Legend No.	Map Symbol	
02	BT	No effect on trees; on crops spoiled leaves, but sweet potato sent runners again; beans and sweet potatoes which sprouted were white; 'leaves and stems had rotted, and the tubers were rotting, but they saw that there were some left'.
03	W?	On flat lands all the food washed away.
06	S	Taro had leaves broken off, but stems still stood, so they dug up taro and ate it (during darkness); sweet potato covered.
08	B	Vegetables and trees dried up/burnt.
09	B?	Said by some — denied by others — that dry trees caught fire.
012	BST	All leaves on trees dried (burnt?) and fell off — no permanent damage. Leaves on sweet potato, sugar cane, bananas, pit pit (Phragmites spp.), kunai etc. were burnt brown. Not possible to eat sweet potato because of taste — famine.
013	SB	Dust and stones stripped trees of leaves and burnt kunai; all crops destroyed.
017	B?	Crops dried out and were ruined.
018	SB?	Broke branches off trees; sweet potato leaves died but tubers alright.
022	B	Killed all tree leaves and taro leaves.
023	S	Sand falling took all the leaves off trees and crops leaving only central shoots of things like bananas.
026	R?	Gardens may have been ruined but emphasis on spectacular recovery.
043	SR	Destroys unprotected crops — many trees lose foliage (1963); many gardens destroyed — those which survived had bare meagre crops.
049	RT	Gardens had all been destroyed — food was covered and rotted.
050	R?	Only a few remaining shoots of sweet potatoes, taro and greens.
056	TR?	All the trees were dead and all the sweet potato were rotten in the ground.

Legend No.	Map Symbol	
059	RS?	Leaves fell from trees. Ruined crops by covering with ash.
064	SB	Smashed down trees — roots and leaves of sweet potato died but tubers came up again.
066	RB?	Gardens ruined but taro came up later — grass and leaves of trees killed.
067	R	Gardens ruined.
068	R	Crops killed.
069	B?R?	Big trees in forest, pandanus and bamboo killed; crops covered (and killed?).
073	R	All crops killed.
078	R	Plants destroyed.
081	R	Gardens ruined.
082	R	Damaged all the gardens.
085	R	Dust spoiled vegetable gardens and sweet potato gardens.
086	R	Caused much damage to gardens in particular.
088	R	Ruined gardens.
089	R	Ruined the gardens.
093	R	All vegetation died (sweet potato mentioned specifically).
094	T?	Covered all gardens so that food began to stink.
095	RB	Sweet potato buried and spoiled.
097	RS	Branches of trees and pandanus broken by stones and all gardens were destroyed.
098	RS	Tree branches were broken off and the sago trees were killed and didn't grow up again. Just destroyed everything and no one went to the gardens.
099	R?	Crops covered.

Effects on animals and birds

There is considerable diversity in the legends concerning the effects on animals, partly because of the diversity of animals involved. Some respondents report, as we would expect, that pigs and dogs were relatively unaffected, because they were inside houses with the people. Some accounts report the slaughtering of these animals as the human occupants became hungry and as the darkness continued (e.g. 050 — western Enga). Quite a number of groups report the ritual killing of an animal to bring about the end of the darkness (e.g. 006 — the Patep near Mumeng: 009 — the Mianmin north-west of Telefomin: 010 — the Agarabi near Kainantu). Very few accounts report the death by misadventure of domesticated animals. A number of accounts, in fact, make a distinction between the effects on animals in the houses and animals left to their own devices. This section is concerned more

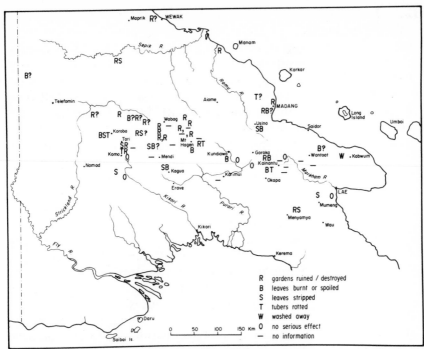

Fig. 46   *Effects of tephra fall on trees and crops*

particularly with the latter.

More or less verbatim accounts of adverse effects on animals are presented in Table 20. It has proved difficult to categorise these effects; only two general categories, death and discomfiture, are presented on Fig. 47, though each category is subdivided. The details in Table 20 are more informative than the map categories suggest.

Many accounts indicate that animals were bewildered. Wild animals are frequently reported coming into the open and in eastern Enga, into the houses. There are several reports of animals or birds being sufficiently bewildered or stunned, or, in the cases of cassowaries and other birds, so loaded down with ash that they were easily caught, killed and eaten. Rarely are all the animals reported as dying, although the Kaluli people on the northern slopes of Mt Bosavi (021 and 023) state that the white UWA:S bird disappeared at the time never to return.

Table 20
Effects on animals

(See Fig. 47 for key to symbols.)

Legend No.	Map Symbol	
02	K₁	'Pigs, animals, rats, every creature living in the scrub and in the woods came out in the open — cassowaries and so forth too, and they died, and in the morning the people saw them. And they smelt

Legend No.	Map Symbol	
		the stench of the creatures which were rotting. And they took the creatures which were still moving/alive and ate them.'
03	K_1	Some animals washed away and some killed by falling trees; some birds killed by falling trees.
07	K_2	Sick birds died.
013	K_1D_1	Mai (dust) killed many wild and domesticated animals. Others were just bewildered and deranged. Birds and cassowaries were killed.
015	D_1	Domestic and wild pigs as well as cassowaries had their bristles and feathers so full of ash that they couldn't move; wild pigs couldn't run away, because they were too heavy and men killed many of them. Pigs and cassowaries that slept under fallen trees or in holes escaped.
018	K_1	Birds died, some cassowaries died, wild pigs died; tame pigs stopped in houses.
021	K_2D_1	One species of colonial nesting birds (starlings) became extinct. Cassowaries easy to hunt because they were weighted down.
023	K_1	All animals except those in houses died because sand covered their food; many birds died but others hid under logs and overhanging limbs. Cassowaries also hid and some survived. The white bird UWA:S disappeared at the time never to return.
028	D_1	Pigs became vicious and large wild pigs came out of forests.
043	K_2	Birds and animals died.
057	D_1	Animals reported to have been stunned and easily caught because they were blinded by the ash.
059	K_1	All birds and animals died. People ate them afterwards.
061	K_2	No effects on dogs and pigs (in houses?) but rats, marsupials and birds got ash in their eyes and died.
064	K_1	Animals outside died everywhere; those in houses alright and didn't die when they let them out. One bird (alumba) found up inside banana flower — let it go after washing it and it flew away.
066	K_1	Some pigs and birds died.
067	K_1	Rats, marsupials and birds all died.
068	K_1	Rats, marsupials and birds killed, particularly young ones.

075	K₁	*Gigisum* and *Mangkara* birds and other birds came and sat under eaves; also pigs and chickens. All wild pigs and cassowaries which were not under cover died.
078	K₂	Animals were destroyed.
081	D₂	Animals and birds came into the houses and pet animals like pigs stayed inside the houses.
083	D₂	Rats, birds came into the houses.
084	D₂	Animals and birds came into their houses and people caught them and provided food for themselves.
086	D₂	Birds, rats came into the houses where people were staying.
089	D₂	Birds, rats and wild cats came to people's houses as tamed animals and birds.
093	K₁	All pigs died — all animals were outside. Everything died. People remained inside houses.
094	D₂	Animals and wild pigs ran into houses.
095	D₂	Wild animals left the bush and were either stunned or tame.
096	D₂	Forest animals, marsupials, snakes and birds came into and under houses.
097	K₁	Many animals, fish, pigs, cassowaries killed.
098	K₁D₁	Birds, pigs, snakes, cassowaries, crocodile and turtles were all afraid and went into the Spirit houses. All the animals in the bush were killed.
099	D₁	Pigs, cassowaries, wallabies, tree birds and opossums all covered in ash and easy to catch.

Although the eastern Enga accounts (081-089) of Mai (1974) make no references to animals and birds being killed directly by the tephra fall, Mai's (in press) account, based on a wider sample, mentions (p.12) such deaths. This later account also notes that snakes as well as rats and birds came into the houses. 'The people killed them and threw away the nonedibles such as snakes, otherwise they were cooked and eaten by the people' (Mai, in press, p.9).

Figure 47 indicates that both death and discomfiture for animals was widespread, although death was more common, or more commonly reported. Only two groups (01 — the Salt-yui in Simbu Province) and (09 — the Mianmin near the Irian Jaya border) specifically reported no effects on animals.

Effects on streams and drinking water

There is very little information in the available accounts on the effects of the sand/dust/ash fall on streams and/or drinking water. All but twelve of the fifty-six accounts fail to mention drinking water* or effects on streams (Fig. 48). Four of the remaining ten mention that there was no effect or allow that this is a reasonable inference. In fact the Huli

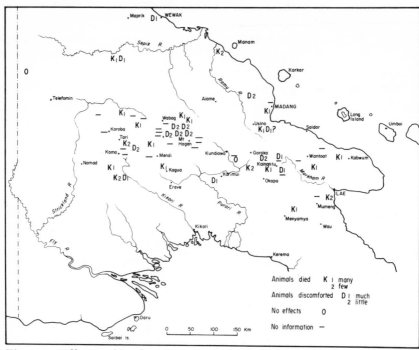

Fig. 47   *Effects of tephra fall on animals*

men at Koroba (012) interviewed by Ben Probert noted that drinking water was not mentioned in the account and suggested that 'water unaffected because water is important and would have been included in that case'.

Of the eight accounts reporting adverse effects, two mention muddying of streams, and two mention that streams were choked with mud. A fifth account (016 — Huli at Komo) indicates that most streams turned red. This is interesting; as mentioned earlier the Huli people at Komo are believed to have migrated to Komo from Tari since the ashfall. The Huli account from Tari (043), reported by Dr R. M. Glasse (1973), mentions only that streams were blocked by ash and stopped flowing. A sixth reference, from amongst the Paiela (093), is couched in very general terms: 'Everything becomes "bad" so, yes, the drinking water would become undrinkable'. The diversity of replies is further illustrated by reference to the Kaluli people north of Mt Bosavi (see 021 and 023; Fig. 48).

As some accounts report that streams were choked with ash or mud, a related question arises: was erosional removal of the ash or mud from the hill slopes and gardens a problem or of any significance? Although such questions were included in the questionnaire

---

*Some accounts do mention a shortage of drinking water inside the houses while darkness lasted. This aspect is not considered here.

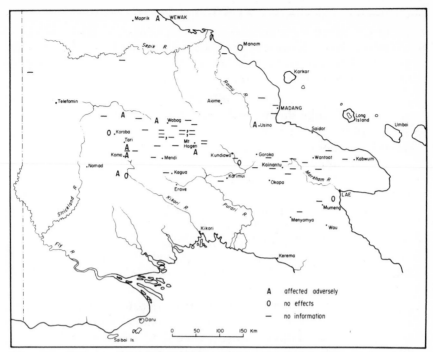

Fig. 48   *Effects of tephra fall on streams and drinking water*

(Appendix 4) only two groups provided any information; interestingly enough neither account was obtained by questionnaire.

The Hewa people at Wabia (064 — near Kagua) reported that the effects of the ashfall were not so bad in the gardens on slopes, but gardens on flats were very adversely affected. Meggitt's (1973) account of the time of darkness amongst the western Enga (050) reports more fully: 'The hilltops and higher slopes were less seriously affected by the dirt, which moved down to the rivers and creeks in great drifts. On the steeper and less stable slopes, such as those in the Ambumu Valley, the dirt set off landslips and choked many of the tributary valleys. Indeed it even dammed the headwaters of the Laigapu River' (Meggitt, 1973, p.55). Heavy rain then washed the dirt from the slopes and opened blocked streams.

Deaths during and after the tephra fall

As pointed out earlier in this chapter, it is the direct effects of the 'darkness' on humans and their activities that we might expect to be best recorded in the legends. It is in this subsection, above all others, that we might expect 'no information', to mean 'no deaths'. Slightly more than half (29) of the fifty-six accounts considered here neglect to provide any information on this point. A further eleven cases report specifically that no human deaths occurred. Thus only fifteen accounts are represented in Table 21. Broadly, these can be divided into categories where either many (meaning a significant proportion of the population) or few people died. A further subdivision can be made in terms of whether those who died succumbed during or after the tephra fall. Table 21 indicates that at least some of those who died during the event were killed in collapsing houses; those who died subsequently suffered mainly from starvation.

Table 21
Deaths during and after darkness/ashfall
(See Fig. 49 for key to symbols.)

Legend No.	Map Symbol	
03	M_1	Many by many ways during darkness.
012	S_2	Tradition has all 'bad' men, trouble makers, people with bad thoughts, thieves etc. die during *bingi*. Dust burnt the eyes.
013	$S_{1,2}$	People killed by falling stones and by hunger.
017	S_2	Afterwards, through lack of food.
018	S_1	People died in house collapses.
022	S_2	Starvation.
049	M_2	After one month the people died in large numbers. Only a few people remained and survived this famine. Most people died at this time.
059	M_1	Allegedly only three survivors.
069	$S_{1,2}?$	Some men and children killed in house collapse; big famine afterwards.
075	M_1	Many (?) killed when houses fell down.
093	$M_1?$	Implication that everyone will die, but contradiction in that people will leave houses on different days.
094	M_2	Referring to future event story says people would be so hungry that they would eat their children, their bark clothes, their breech cloths, even pull their hair out and eat that.
096	O	Those people who did not obey *mana*, who harmed the animals, or did not remain celibate, they would have died. But all obeyed.
097	M_1	Smell killed people. Dead bodies were put in a ditch — when it was full buried dead in a hole near the door. Survivors had to marry their own sisters.
098	$M_1 S_2$	Cold, hunger, sores. Inside the spirit house many people and animals died but the people couldn't bury them so they were just thrown outside and a terrible stench was all over.

The information collected by Dr Stephen Frankel from the Huli at Tari (096) bears some similarity to the material sent by Ben Probert of

Koroba (012). The former account notes that those who did not obey
mana would die while the latter account indicates that 'bad men' die
during the tephra fall (Table 21).

The mapped occurrence of the reports indicates some notable
variations (Fig. 49). For example, the 1948 Vicedom and Tischner
account (049) from amongst the Mt Hagen Melpa, and the less complete
account from amongst the Waka-Enga of the Upper Wage (059) both
indicate that few survived the tephra fall and its aftermath. On the other
hand, the intervening populations, particularly the eastern Enga
(broadly the Mae Enga and the Raiapu Enga) record no information
about human fatalities during or after the darkness.

Was the darkness/ashfall harmful or beneficial?

Although only fifteen of the fifty-six accounts report deaths of humans
during and in the aftermath of the tephra fall, earlier sections have
indicated that destruction of gardens and animals was widespread. It
might seem fatuous then to ask the question: was the tephra fall
regarded as harmful or beneficial?

A surprisingly large number of direct answers to this question are
available and some further answers can be inferred. The available
information is collated in Table 22 — only those cases where a
relatively clear answer can be provided are plotted with the appropriate
symbols on Fig. 50.

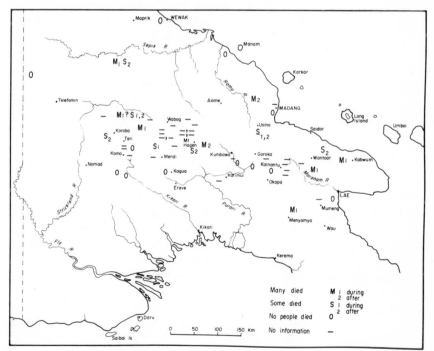

Fig. 49   *Deaths during and after tephra fall*

Table 22
Darkness/ashfall harmful or beneficial

(H = harmful, B = beneficial)

Legend No.	Map Symbol	
02	H	Bad thing because food disappeared. When forewarned of eclipse in 1961 they built special big houses to live together, got in stocks of food and firewood.
07	H?	It was something sent to them because they were angry with each other.
09	H	Harmful because taro only grows well when the sun makes it strong.
011	H	'The darkness made everything cold — all of our ground, our gardens, our animals, ourselves. After that it was cold and we were cold. Before it had always been hot, but now we were a cold people.' Reference to 'cold' is at least in part if not wholly to strength and capability rather than to climate.
012	B	Beneficial — followed by time of plenty, good crops — all pigs, sons etc. will be bigger and better after a bingi. Later on all crops were excellent, like a 'medicine' to the soil; flatter gardens better still. Tradition has all 'bad men,' trouble makers, people with bad thoughts, thieves etc. die at time of bingi.
013	H	It was very harmful, it killed people.
015	B?	'I have a general sense that they see it in terms of an abundance of meat. "Many pigs and cassowaries were killed at this time, and people ate as if it were a pig feast."'
016	B	Very beneficial — resulted in a very fertile land — good crops of everything, but especially sweet potato afterwards.
017	H	Harmful.
018	B	Beneficial — sweet potato came up very strong after darkness. Ash used as 'medicine' on sores.
021	?	Strange occurence but never discussed as either beneficial or harmful.
022	H	Was harmful — caused much starvation; some say locals traded bird feathers for food.
023	H	It was unpleasant and harmful in itself at the time and because it killed so many animals it was bad. They don't seem to think it had any beneficial effects.

Legend No.	Map Symbol	
026	B	*In future* — then everything will grow gigantically. Men will have big strong children with lots of flesh, nut pandanus and bananas will have big fruit, sweet potato will be big. Despite these perceived benefits Duna don't want it to happen again.
028	H	Harmful.
043	B	For a time food is short but people quickly replant their crops and these flourish in the enriched soil. Each *bingi* foreshadows a remarkable increase in soil fertility. They hope *bingi* will recur and the aim of one of their most complex rituals, *Dindi gamu* (Earth magic) is to secure a repetition (1963). A fallout of *bingi* ushers in a period of plenty (1965).
049	H	Harmful (inference).
050	?	'To everyone's surprise, the plants grew at a great rate and gave unheard of yields of food. Nevertheless, the members of each clan parish made placatory offerings to their ancestors in the hope of ensuring that such untoward events would not recur — and indeed nothing like this has happened again.'
056	?	Sweet potatoes grew very quickly.
059	H?	Harmful, at least in that it killed 'everyone', but sweet potatoes after the event grew huge.
061	H	Harmful.
064	B?	Had good crops year after ashfall (same as after frost of 1972).
068	B?	Everything grew better after event.
081-9	B?	No mention in Mai's 1974 interviews account. However, Mai (in press, p.4) writes 'Some informants from Lagaip, Wabag, and Wapenamanda clearly stated that there was economic prosperity particularly in crop production where food crops had higher yields and different kinds of food were more abundant than ever before'. There were also developments in culture, language and the *Mena Tee* (pig exchange ceremony). Crops that were affected by the ashfall died out and took a very long time to recover. The ash itself was used for curing sores — the ash is useful.
093	B	If the tephra falls again, people will go on living,

Legend No.	Map Symbol	
		and if it doesn't fall again, people will die.
094	H	Harmful.
096	B	After *Dapindu* (the material that fell) there was a time of plenty, numerous pigs and numerous healthy children. *Dindi gamu* performed with aim of bringing return of *bingi*.
097	H	Harmful.
098	H	Harmful.

Quite a number of the informants, some of them noted in Chapter 7, made preparations for the 1962 solar eclipse. These preparations usually involved the collection of food from gardens, and firewood, the herding of pigs, and, sometimes, the building of new (communal) houses. However, it is not possible to determine whether these preparations suggest a positive or negative attitude to an assumed recurrence of the time of darkness.

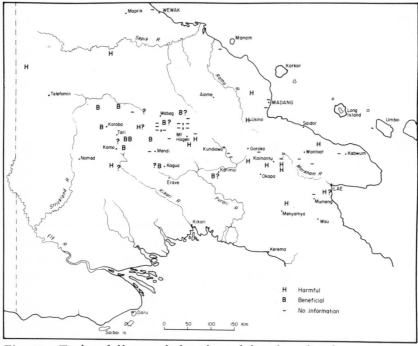

Fig. 50   Tephra fall regarded as harmful or beneficial

Fig. 50 indicates that fifteen groups regarded the occurrence as harmful and a further eleven groups thought the event was beneficial. However, as shown in Table 22, Mai's (in press) report suggests that the eastern Enga people believe major cultural achievements stem from that period. This provides an interesting contrast with the attitude expressed by the Tairora people of the Eastern Highlands (011).

A notable feature of Fig. 50 is that the groups regarding the occurrence as beneficial are, with one exception, located in the Western and Southern Highlands. For the one exception, the Daribi south-west of Mt Karamui (015), the beneficial aspect stems from the ready availability of meat after the tephra fall.

Correlations

It seems reasonable to expect that there might be strong correlations between some of the variables discussed in Chapters 9 and 10. For example, we might expect to find that those groups who reported the heaviest/thickest falls of tephra also experienced the darkest darkness or the longest darkness. We might also expect the same groups to have suffered the most damage to crops and houses. On the other hand it is more difficult to decide whether those who regarded the ashfall as beneficial received the heaviest or the lightest fall. Each map (each variable) can be compared with every other map individually or maps can be prepared in combinations. A formidable number of combinations is possible.

The following points of interest arise from comparison of the maps:
(1) There is some tendency for groups reporting darkness greater than usual to also report longer durations of the darkness.
(2) Although groups which report darkness greater than usual report the whole range of ash thicknesses, there is a tendency for the thicker ashfalls to be associated with the deepest darknesses. There is also a general, though not particularly strong tendency, for reports of lengthy darknesses to be matched with the thicker ashfalls.
(3) There is no readily evident connection between particle size of the fallen material and the quality of the darkness; those places reporting darkness greater than usual also report the complete range of particle sizes.
(4) The association is not striking but those places reporting the most drastic effects on trees frequently report the most dramatic effects on animals. Exceptions exist, however, at least at three locations reporting no effects on trees and crops, but the death of animals.
(5) Positive connections between effects on houses and effects on trees and crops are weak. Although some locations reporting rotted tubers (the most serious effect on crops) also report collapsed houses, at other places where, reputedly, houses were adversely affected, no effects on vegetation were recorded. The visual inspection technique and the paucity of data do not allow very positive statements to be made, but it cannot be argued that damage of all kinds is confined to a few specific locations.
(6) The comments made in (5) are, not surprisingly, also true of the association between damage to houses and death or discomfiture of animals.
(7) As we would expect the correlation between effects on houses and human deaths is quite good because deaths during the darkness are

generally attributed to house collapse. There seems to be some connection between human fatalities and serious effects on crops. This is not unexpected given that fatalities after the darkness are reported as being due to starvation. The connection is also encouraging in that groups reporting 'no effects' in relation to the two questions also show considerable overlap.

(8) There is almost no correlation between human fatalities and animal deaths. This remains true even if only human deaths during the darkness are compared with animal deaths.

(9) On the whole those groups reporting human fatalities regard the darkness as harmful. For many cases where accounts report the darkness to be beneficial, no information about fatalities is available.

(10) Connections between the darkness as harmful or beneficial and the effects on vegetation are interesting. Fig. 50 gives a general sense that the event was regarded as harmful in the east and beneficial in the west although there is much missing data. On the other hand, the subjective impression is that the effects on plants were greater in the west, while the proportion of 'no effects' and 'no information' records were much higher east of Kundiawa.

(11) There is no obvious connection between quality of darkness and house collapse. There is a similar lack of correlation with length of darkness. There is some connection between house collapse and ash thickness as we would logically expect, but it is not the correlation of two independent variables, as one criterion for determining ash thickness was house collapse. There also seems to be little correlation between effects on houses and particle size.

(12) All degrees of effects on vegetation are associated with the greatest darkness. Those accounts reporting that darkness is not mentioned similarly show a range of effects though generally lacking in severity. There is no obvious connection between the length of darkness and the effects on vegetation. There is probably a real positive association between the thickness of the ash and the reported severity of effects on vegetation.

(13) A moderately good correlation exists between effects on animals and quality of darkness in that areas experiencing the greatest darkness also record many animals killed. However, a number of sites with unusual darkness provide no information on animal fatalities. There seems to be relatively little relationship between the length of darkness and animal fatalities, although once again a lot of data points record no information. On the other hand the reported effects on animals and the thickness of the tephra fall do seem to be correlated.

(14) Deaths during and after the tephra fall seem to be poorly correlated with quality of the darkness as the category of greatest darkness is associated with 'many deaths', 'no effects' and 'no information'. Similarly, lengths of darkness categories seem to be associated with all categories of deaths during and after darkness/tephra fall. There is also

a poor correlation between fatalities and thickness of the ashfall.

(15) There seems to be no correlation between quality of darkness and whether or not the darkness was regarded as harmful or beneficial. Finally there is a similar lack of correlation between the latter variable and either length of darkness or thickness of the ash.

It is relatively easy for the reader to think of those pairs of variables between which we might expect to find logical positive (or negative) associations. The rather cursory analysis undertaken above indicates, however, that there are rather fewer strong (either positive or negative) connections than we might expect.

Summary

Although it seems rather unlikely that effects on houses, crops, animals and people would be unrecorded in the accounts, if they were serious, and thus missing information could possibly regarded as 'no effects', the temptation to interpret the data this way has been resisted. Collapse of houses is only reported in fourteen areas. Thirteen of the fifty-six accounts neglect to mention adverse effects on trees and crops. These are concentrated in Eastern Enga, though the Eastern Highlands and Simbu Provinces have a number of similar reports as well as a number specifically mentioning no effects. Dogs and pigs, the domesticated animals, were evidently little affected, but other animals were more commonly reported killed rather than merely discomforted. Only eight of the fifty-six respondents reported adverse effects on drinking water and streams, a fact that may be significant in suggesting that few sources of drinking water were affected. Similarly only fourteen cases of fatalities resulting from the time of darkness are reported but these are scattered across the whole area. Finally only eleven informants reported that the time of darkness was generally regarded as beneficial, while fifteen noted it as mainly harmful. However, the Eastern Enga seem to relate major cultural developments to the time of the tephra fall. In general those who regarded the time of darkness as harmful are concentrated towards the east, those with a more favourable view, toward the west.

The problems of absent data are particularly manifest in attempts to correlate distributions of physical characteristics and the effects of the event. It is clear that few strong correlations exist and some of those are partly spurious as the variables are interlocked. While the quality of darkness seems to be slightly associated with longer durations of darkness and the thickness of the fallen material, there are no close connections between damage to houses, crops and animals, but there is some between darkness quality and thickness and effects on animals. Thickness of fallen material and effects on vegetation also appear to be connected but this may be spurious and the covering of gardens was one of the chosen thickness attributes. Finally, there seems to be some relationship between human fatalities on the one hand, and effects on crops and the harmfulness of the event on the other.

11 Issues arising from analysis of the legends

Variations in the legendary accounts

It is evident that there is considerable variation in the total amount of information contained in the various accounts. Clearly, this results in part from variations in the depth and quality of investigation from area to area. Furthermore it is obvious that some accounts provide information about certain topics and ignore others. For example, although the Melpa (049) and Urii (075) stories are both fairly lengthy (see Chapter 7), neither contain much detail about the physical characteristics of the event.

Other types of variation are also interesting, Two accounts collected from two groups of Kaluli people north of Mt Bosavi (021 and 023) reveal major differences (discrepancies) on many aspects of the physical characteristics of the event (eg. quality of darkness, thickness of the ashfall and associated effects) although there is considerable agreement as to the particle size of the ash and its colour. Some differences do occur in their two versions of the effects of the event but these are less serious, falling more in the category of what has or has not been recounted by the informant, rather than fundamental differences of opinion. The location from which the two versions were collected were very close together and the communities knew each other, suggesting that there has been strong cultural interference with some of the material (Dr E. L. Schieffelin, pers. comm. 1978).

There are also significant differences in the accounts relayed by the various Huli groups (012, 016, 043, and 096), though these differences are perhaps more expectable given the widely scattered locations of the Huli (Fig. 30), the different modes of collection (012 and 016 by questionnaire; 043 during ethnographic fieldwork completed before this survey began), and the differing periods of collection (043 — Glasse's fieldwork was undertaken during the middle 1950s). Nonetheless, the account collected at Komo (016) purports to be a Tari legend originating in the Wabia area (Fr Gabriel Lomas, pers. comm., 1977), and we might expect more similarity to the Tari accounts (043 and 096). Instead, a glance at the various maps and tables indicates that the characteristics of the event and its effects are described differently. Furthermore, the Komo account seems to refer to just the one event while the Tari account was believed by Dr R. M. Glasse to refer to several past events; it also has a decidedly futuristic outlook, some at least of the story being directed toward future occurrences (a characteristic not shared by Ben Probert's story from Koroba (012)).

We can also recognise great diversity amongst the accounts collected from the Enga people (018, 050, 059, 067, 068, and 081-089). It is easy to recognise close resemblances between the accounts (081-089) described by Mai (1974); all of these were collected at the same time from the Wabag-Wapenamanda area and perhaps the relatively rigid framework of this inquiry produced somewhat stereotyped responses. There is quite good agreement in evidence on the maps between the reports of the physical characteristics and the effects of the event. There is less agreement with Meggitt's published account from the Wabag-Ambumu Valley area, an account in which he reports 'local variants of this story are remarkably consistent'. (1973, p.29). In fact the emphases of the Mai and Meggitt versions are quite different. Meggitt's account has people scouring the hillsides for food during the darkness and eating their pigs when no more garden produce could be found. There is also an emphasis in the story on what has happened to the hillslopes and gardens and rivers during the darkness. On the other hand, Mai's nine accounts emphasise the migration of wild animals into the houses (where they were eaten), the songs made to remember and describe the darkness, and the timing or dating of the darkness. There are also differences between Meggitt's account and that collected by Dr Paul Wohlt from the Waka-Enga of the Upper Wage (059). The Waka-Enga account resembles in some items, particularly its rather futuristic view, the Huli account of Dr Bob Glasse and the Duna account of Dr Nick Modjeska. This is not surprising as Wohlt's informants lived on the eastern margin of the Upper Wage basin, the western edge of which is peopled by Huli; most of his informants were bilingual.

The diversity among the Enga accounts might also be explained in part by the cultural diversity of the Enga people themselves, as has been amply documented by Meggitt (e.g. 1973). It is also clear from Meggitt's paper that considerable cultural change was under way even in 1955-56 when Meggitt undertook his field work and collected his version of the legend. That change can only have increased during the following twenty years. Conceivably the differences between the Mai and Meggitt versions are due to changes in Enga society during that 20-year period, as well as the result of established cultural differences and the other factors already mentioned.

The examples given here, drawn from multiple accounts collected from amongst the Kululi, the Huli and the Enga peoples, indicate that details of the event recorded in the legend evidently vary within the one ethnic/cultural group. Such variations might arise from differences in time and method of collection, from cultural variation and from differences in memory. An interesting point here is that there is a usual assumption in much of the anthropological literature that grandparents are alive and able to pass on stories to grandchildren. However, Barth (1975, pp.270-3) shows that among the Baktaman of the Olsobip area the overwhelming majority of children have no grandparents alive. Dr Robin Hide (pers. comm.) reports that a similar but less marked situation exists among the Nimai of Simbu Province. This situation might help explain the patchy knowledge of the time of darkness legend alluded to in Chapter 7 and some of the variations found within quite small areas.

Another potential source of variation in the accounts lies in variations in the material equipment of the many cultures. Not all the people included in the survey are highlanders, with sturdy houses sitting flat on packed earth floors and with thick roofs of kunai thatch. Some informants in the Madang area are coastal people with houses perched on short stilts and of an altogether different construction. Others on the southern fringe of Simbu Province make roofs with sago fronds. Within the highlands themselves there are enormous variations in roof size and shape, weight per support, and roof slope. To what extent the variations in reported effects on houses are the product of variation in dwelling fashion is not known but it is evident that it could be important. It is also possible that the house styles in use at the time of darkness may not have been the same as those in use now. There is some evidence from amongst the Duna, for example, that men and women shared larger communal houses at some time in the past and it seems plausible that houses raised on poles (as among the neighbouring Hewa) may have been in use before the present wooden slab-walled and pandanus or kunai thatched style was adoped (Dr Nick Modjeska, pers. comm., 1978). In a similar vein Dr Paul Wohlt reports that the Enga of the Upper Wage basin (059) made roofs of pit pit (Phragmites spp.) or bark after the time of darkness but as the stones and ash did not fall again, people began to use pandanus leaves as they do now (pers. comm., 1978).

Variations in the reported effects of the time of darkness could also have arisen because different groups have different basic crops, the highlanders relying primarily on the sweet potato staple, the people of Morobe Province south of Lae indulging in a more mixed cropping, with perhaps a bias toward taro as the staple, while some informants live in important sago-producing areas. Different cultivation practices might also influence the destructiveness of the tephra fall. For example, although the Hagen and Enga people share a sweet potato dominated economy, the former group usually plant in flat rectangular beds, the latter in enormous raised and steep-sided mounds. Gardens are constructed on a variety of slopes but in a general sense the Hageners occupy less steeply sloping ground than do either the Chimbu or the Enga. Similarly there is an enormous variation in altitude and in seasonal rhythm. Plant susceptibility to tephra fall may vary not only from one species to another but also during each stage of growth.

It is clear then that an accurate and detailed assessment of the spatial variability in the legendary accounts analysed here requires not only the sort of cultural background material desired by Goldstein, Vansina and others alluded to in Chapter 7 but also detailed information about the physical environment and the material culture of each group. However, even with this data it is doubtful that a totally meaningful analysis could be completed. Furthermore, such detailed investigation and assessment is clearly beyond the scope of the present study.

Embellishment and stylisation

Informants who completed the questionnaire were asked whether they believed religious or other embellishment of the legend occurred. Of the twenty-three responses available only five of the informants believed that religious embellishment had occurred.

Dr Paul Wohlt (059) thought that he detected confusion of the legend with Christian teachings in that the Waka-Enga legend reported that all the people had been killed in a holocaust. Father Gabriel Lomas suggested that the Tari story at Komo (016) was embellished by reference to Noah and the Flood but it seems quite likely that the flood story is a separate Huli legend (Blong, 1979a) that has certain parallels with the Biblical flood.

Stylisation of the Huli version of the time of darkness legend collected at Koroba by Ben Probert (012) has also occurred in that the tradition has it that all 'bad men', trouble makers, people with bad thoughts, thieves etcetera die during bingi. The Tari version collected by Dr Stephen Frankel (096) is similar in that those people who did not obey Mana (instructions), who harmed the animals, or did not remain celibate, would have died, but all obeyed.

More subtle embellishments or modifications have also occurred. Dr J.B. Watson (1963), for example, refers to the stylisation of the Agarabi account (010), noting the common occurrence in their stories of a sequence involving three unresolved repetitions of the same occurrence followed by a final episode. The Agarabi time of darkness story has darkness lasting three days with light reappearing on the fourth day.

Watson also notes that the killing of a pig or pigs is reported on many occasions of great omen amongst the Agarabi. It is interesting to note then that ritual slaying of animals is reported in the time of darkness legend, not only by the Agarabi, but also by the Salt-yui (01), the Patep (06), the Mangga Buang (07) and the Mianmin (09).

Watson's comments on the killing of a white-skinned pig on the third day, and the lifting of the darkness on the fourth day (see account in Chapter 7) are worth repeating:

> The three — days — of — darkness — with — resolution — on —
> the fourth I consider a cultural — specifically folkloristic —
> pattern, as I have tried to indicate by punctuation. I suppose it is
> possible that the real events occurred with that duration and
> sequence, but I assume they did not. We need not doubt that a pig
> was killed, nor that a white one was. Indeed, quite possibly
> several pigs were done away with before the curtain of darkness
> lifted. Whether or not all were white is of course entirely
> conjectural. Perhaps the decision to try a white one followed upon
> unsuccessful attempts with dark pigs — or a white one had to be
> sent for, not being immediately at hand. It is conceivable that the
> people permitted three days to elapse before trying pigs — or any
> other measures; but this seriously strains one's belief. I assume the
> sequence and duration may have differed substantially from this
> narrative quatrain. I make this assumption, moreover, because
> there are in other Agarabi stories — indeed in the tales of various
> peoples in this area — sequences involving three unresolved
> repetitions of the same occurrence with a final episode, typically
> after an appropriate step by one of the actors, following on the
> fourth. The casting of events into this pattern, therefore, was a
> measure of how far stylisation had proceeded in the span of years
> between the actual date of the darkness and 1954. Projecting a
> further uninterruped career for this story, other changes might
> presumably take place. This was simply the first one — or at any
> rate one of the first, if other processes have been overlooked by me
> through my ignorance of the original version. (Watson, 1963,
> p.153).

Another stylisation in the length of time the darkness remained can
be found amongst the Duna, the Paiela and the Huli versions of the
legend. In response to the question 'how many hours or days did
darkness last' Dr Aletta Biersack's Paiela informants replied: 'The first
born child would leave the house on the second day, the second born
child would leave the house on the third day, and so on'. One
informant said the darkness would last three days and one or two
others said they did not know (A. Biersack, pers. comm. 1978). A
similar ritualisation can be found among some Tari Huli informants, as
some accounts imply that each person's bingi lasts as many days as
they have sons. 'Some people have said four days as the time of
darkness, but that too is as likely as not to be a stylisation, as groups of
four always recur in Huli religious ideas' (Dr Stephen Frankel, pers.
comm., 1978). Dr Nick Modjeska (pers. comm., 1978) also noted a
ritualistic formula amongst the Duna by which the length of time
people should stay in their houses was related to the number of their
siblings. It is interesting to note that the three groups known to have

stylised the length of darkness in this way are essentially adjacent to one another (Fig. 30), suggesting diffusion or cross-fertilisation of the legend across linguistic boundaries.

The processes and extent of embellishment, stylisation and cross-fertilisation of the legends are of obvious relevance to the present investigation but in most cases we do not have the necessary information to determine the extent to which each has taken place.

Logical inconsistencies

Although there seem to be only a few obvious logical inconsistencies in the legendary accounts, some at least are worthy of mention. For example, an Enga informant (089) stated that 'birds, rats and wild cats came to people's houses as tamed animals and birds'. It seems inconceivable that feral cats could have been present in the Wabag area before 1950 yet the informant maintained, on the basis of genealogical evidence, that the time of darkness occurred in the mid-nineteenth century.

There also seem to be inconsistencies in legends which mention long periods of darkness (050 — 3 months; 081 — 100 days; 075 — 1-2 months; and 023 — one month) in that there is no reference to the psychological condition of the villagers, their feelings of despair and deprivation, not to mention starvation and death. Although Meggitt's account (050) does mention the conditions in the gardens, the others do not even mention events or conditions after the end of the darkness. The periods of darkness mentioned would be more than sufficient to kill much of the vegetation. Yet there is no sense of inconsistency evident in any of these accounts. It is interesting to note that Watson (1963) suggested, because of the absence of information about despair and deprivation, that the Agarabi account of the time of darkness had been truncated. The Agarabi believed that the darkness lasted about three days and three nights. An alternative view is that even this length of darkness is exaggerated and the lack of reference to despair and deprivation occurs because neither arose.

There also seems to be a logical inconsistency in the Kaluli account (023) which describes the ashfall as being so thick that it came up to the eaves of houses 6 feet off the ground. However, no houses collapsed because an old whiskery man prophesied that no one would die. There is a similar inconsistency in the Paiela account (093) in that one informant describes ashfall as about twice the height of a house yet the people sit in darkness in a pit pit house. 'The implication is that people will die, since the people of the next ground epoch are not borne by the people of the previous ground epoch . . . But the death of the people in the house is contradicted by the instruction that the first-born should leave the house the second day . . . and so on' (Dr Aletta Biersack, pers. comm., 1978).

A number of accounts (including 02 — Kamano-Kafe; 043 and 096 — Tari Huli; 075 — the Urii; and 093 — the Paiela) refer to the building of new (sometimes communal) houses at the first sign of approaching darkness. Other preparations have also been related, but the building of houses suggests a warning of the approaching darkness of at least three or four days, a very unlikely occurrence (see Chapter 12) except for those actually living near the source of tephra fall.

Significance of the event

A theoretical measure of the significance of the time of darkness story to any group would be some estimate of the proportion of people in the group who know the story. Such estimates are not available but information from a total of twenty-three communities suggests that about half of these regard the time of darkness as an important event or story. However, it seems likely that the story is unimportant for most of the other groups. Young people seem generally unaware of the story and truncation of the story has probably occurred progressively, as Watson (1963) has suggested for the Agarabi version. It is also difficult to discern any evidence that the most complete, logical, integrated or consistent accounts belong to the groups professing the importance of the legend.

Presumably those groups which believe that the time of darkness will occur again in the future regard the legend as important. Such groups include the Kaluli (021, 023), the Kewa at Wabi (064), the Waka-Enga (059), the Duna (026), the Tari Huli (043, 096) and the Paiela (093), all living in or on the fringe of the Southern Highlands Province. The Huli at Tari seem to have the strongest belief that the *bingi* will return. R.M. Glasse (1965) writes:

> In the last two generations they have made two major attempts to secure a recurrence of *bingi*. About fifty years ago they undertook without success a traditional pig-killing rite called *Ega Wandari gamu*, which parish after parish performed in a customary sequence. A generation later they adapted a rite (*Dindi gamu*) from the Dugube people, which was also unsuccessful. The Huli attribute the failure of the *Dindi gamu* to an excess of enthusiasm. The finger of a red-skinned Duna child was to be pricked, his blood mixed with the blood of a pig and the mixture sprinkled in areas of poor fertility. But, instead of pricking the child's finger, the Huli butchered him and scattered the dismembered body in their gardens, a fatal deviation from the *mana* instructions. In 1955 several earth tremors led the Huli to believe that a recurrence of *bingi* was imminent. Remembering their earlier behaviour, the men who had killed the child hastily paid compensation to his relatives in Duna, fearing that *bingi* would otherwise prove catastrophic. *Bingi* is outside the range of ordinary experience, and Huli beliefs do not adequately explain it for them. Thus, they are ambivalent about its possible recurrence. On the one hand, they are eager for the putative increase in garden fertility; on the

other, they view *bingi* as a dangerous threat which could lead to complete devastation (Glasse, 1965, p.46).

Dr E.L. Schieffelin (pers. comm., 1978) has made the interesting point that the Huli and the Kaluli had fairly extensive trading connections in pre-contact times. The Huli *Dindi gamu* ceremony seems to be a Huli transformation/inversion of the 'men's ceremonial hunting lodge' of the plateau people which has nothing to do with the tephra fall. Schieffelin raises the possibility that the Kaluli may not have even experienced the tephra fall but that the story was traded (or diffused) from the north via the Dugube people. Certainly there is not yet any firm physical evidence that Tibito Tephra did fall around Mt Bosavi, although theoretical considerations (Figs. 26 and 29) suggest that it did. Whether or not the *Dindi gamu* ceremony amongst the Huli provides evidence of trading of the time of darkness story, the futuristic element to the story in the Southern Highlands area suggests widespread discussion of the event. Dr Nick Modjeska (pers. comm., 1978) has suggested that the widespread futuristic element in this region is in part relateable to a general tendency to integrate traditional lore with post-contact materials. He also points out that there are elements in time of darkness stories from the Eastern Highlands which imply 'in case the time of darkness occurs again' and that it is only one further step to 'when it occurs again'.

The tephra fall also assumes major importance in the Paiela (093) cycle of destruction and recreation. Dr Aletta Biersack (pers. comm., 1978) has indicated that the Paiela believe 'if it comes then the ground will be good: stay; If it doesn't come then the ground will be bad: die; if the tephra falls again people will go on living, and if it doesn't fall again, people will die. The fall of tephra will make bad the present 'ground' so as to initiate the next 'ground' (or world epoch).' The Duna also see an apocalyptic end but the tephra fall seems not to be associated with this end. The Huli (Dr Stephen Frankel, pers. comm.) also recognise epochs, *bingi* occurring only once in the present epoch.

The time of darkness legend is of major significance to the Huli and perhaps also to the Paiela. It seems doubtful that any other groups are as intent on a recurrence of the time of darkness.

However, the Enga believe that the time of darkness was associated with the onset of their economic and cultural prosperity. According to Mai's (in press) analysis the Enga stated that after the event food crops had higher yields and different kinds of food were more abundant than ever before. The Enga, particularly the Mae Enga, also believe 'that cultural developments such as language expressions and expansion, composing of complex songs, the complexity of tribal or group dances and technological developments such as building fences and housing styles, all improved after the event had occurred' (Mai, in press, p. 4). Furthermore, the *Mena Tee* (pig exchange ceremony) spread more widely, the accumulation of wealth was on a greater scale, and population expansion (leading to land disputes and tribal wars) all occurred after the time of darkness. It is not clear whether these benefits are causally or merely temporally associated with the occurrence of the time of darkness, but either way the legend gains in significance amongst the Enga. Despite the benefits which the Mae Enga believe stem from the tephra fall they make 'placatory offerings to their ancestors in the hope of ensuring that such untoward events would not recur . . .' (Meggitt, 1973, p.125).

Temporal associations of the tephra fall and other events have been noted, including amongst the Enga. Paul Mai recorded the arrival of a plant and a bird in Enga around the time of darkness. The Tairora (011) associate the arrival of the economically important *Casuarina oligodon* in the Kainantu area with the event (Watson, 1967). On the other hand the Kaluli associate the disappearance of the white bird (UWA:S) with the tephra fall. Nelson (1971) believed the sweet potato arrived in the Nebilyer Valley at about the time of darkness and the Menye near Menyamya say that everyone had scabies when the ashfall stopped (Carl Whitehead, pers. comm., 1978). In a general sense the event which created the legend provides a time plane prior to the most common time plane, the arrival of Europeans. Thus the Tari at Komo (016), the West Mianmin (09) and the Waka-Enga (059) all place their migrations to their current locations as occurring since the time of darkness.

Significance can also be attached to the legend in another way. On 4 February 1962 a total solar eclipse was experienced, lasting approximately 2 minutes 30 seconds at 140° longitude (Tom Morgan, Sydney Observatory, pers. comm.). The Adminstration went to great lengths to warn the people not to look directly at the sun as eye damage could occur. Du Toit (1969), in an interesting paper entitled 'Misconstruction and problems in communication', has set out the effects of the government warning and his own innocent actions on the people of Akuna village, (028), Eastern Highland Province:

> The *Kiap* had called all the village headmen from the subdistrict to the administrative headquarters and had warned them of two things. The first and foremost was that there was to be a solar eclipse on the fourth of February and that they should not be affected by any teachings people might express. 'In two weeks, the fourth of February, the sun will disappear for five minutes', the Kiap said. The lululai returned to Akuna and told his people and me, 'The Kiap says that on the fourth day of February the sun will disappear for two weeks.' The second warning was that when the sun disappeared, the people should not look into the sky unless they had sunglasses to protect their eyes. (du Toit, 1969, p.47). During the following week the radio reported shortages of

kerosene and sunglasses throughout New Guinea because the natives were preparing for the darkness by seeking the magical powers the sunglasses would give them. A missionary allegedly was telling his converts that the whites were not afraid of the impending darkness because they wore neckties. From a friendly old lady in Boston he had received a large number of old wide ties, which he sold to his 'congregation' (du Toit, 1969, p.47).

Although du Toit's Akuna people did not build special communal houses for the event, other Gadsups, the nearby Kamano-Kafe (02) and Binamarien (057) did. The Kamano-Kafe near Kainantu built large houses so they could live together and stored in huge amounts of firewood and food. The local store sold out of all small lamps and kerosene — despite the fact that the local Summer Institute of Linguistics personnel explained the eclipse with diagrams and the Kamano-Kafe said that they understood (Audrey Payne and Dorothy Drew, pers. comm., 1978). Dr Nancy Bowers (pers. comm., 1978) noted that at Okapa (Eastern Highlands) in October 1961 people in some areas were buying up supplies like tinned food and lanterns but that at a later date there was little reaction amongst the Kaugels (Western Highlands — 047) and that she was the only one who made any preparations.

At a village near to Akuna, du Toit was told by the headman about the ancestors and what had happened when his father was young:

> Once during those years it had grown dark, he explained, and the earth was covered by white powder . . . when he was asked what that had to do with the house they were building, he explained that they would all gather in there — the entire village — and that the people were already gathering large supplies of firewood, food, and water in bamboo containers. They feared, he said, that the long period of darkness would result in a repetition of the earlier situation . . . they also expected the ancestors to return, and they were all going to be waiting for them in a central ceremonial structure (du Toit, 1969, p.48).

Du Toit goes on to recount the explanations he was forced to make to the village elders concerning his just executed fortnightly visit for stores, and the passage of the eclipse with he and his family standing in the village square and almost all the villagers remaining in their houses.

Extreme responses to the impending solar eclipse seem to have been largely restricted to the Eastern Highlands. They seem to result from warnings issued by the Administration, perhaps enhanced by diffusion of various beliefs, but it is clear that such warnings struck a responsive chord, and promoted a response engendered by the earlier time of darkness.

Another millenarian cult, earlier than the 1962 eclipse, also owes a little to the time of darkness legend. Meggitt (1973) has set out in some detail his account of the 'Sun and the Shakers' and its transformations during the early 1940s. There is no need to detail here the beginnings of the cult amongst the Taro Enga, and the subsequent modifications that occurred as the cult spread through the Enga district and to the Ipili people of the Porgera Valley. Meggitt's account (1973, p.28) of the cult among the Ipili includes the following: 'Within a few months massive discharges of lightning would signal the coming of a great darkness that would cover the land for days or weeks, during which time the local people must shelter within the cult house and intone the spells that would invoke the help of the sun to disperse the cloud of darkness.' As Meggitt also notes, the expectation of the coming darkness is probably connected to the earlier time of darkness (p.29).*

An eclipse of the sun and a fall of volcanic ash also appear in a Yabob (south of Madang) version of the Kilibob-Manup myth (Lawrence, 1964, p.22). In this version Kilibob invented useful arts while Manup was responsible for lore magic, sorcery and warfare. The reconciliation between the brothers was prophesied for the future:

> They would return to Madang, heralded by portents; Kilibob by the discovery of a Siasi wooden plate at sea to the south, and Manup by the arrival of a canoe from the north. There would be an eclipse of the sun, and a volcanic eruption and fall of ash that would destroy the gardens and lead to war and cannibalism. The crisis would end only when the brothers settled their dispute (Lawrence, 1964, p.22).

It is perhaps instructive to consider the character of the events related here if the tephra fall and the time of darkness had not occurred. In the absence of the tephra fall, the Ipili millenarian cult and the Yabob version of the Kilibob-Manup myth would each have been different in one (unimportant?) detail, the 1962 solar eclipse would not have involved the Eastern Highlanders in intensive preparations, the Huli would be without an important part of their elaborate ritual, and the Paiela cycle of 'ground' epochs would probably be different.

Conclusions

Although it is usually possible to group accounts in terms of physical character and/or in terms of reported effects for each of the individual variables considered, few meaningful spatial patterns emerge and few accounts can be grouped as similar (except Paul Mai's Enga stories — 081-089) when all or even most analysed variables are considered together. These poor connections result not only from the high proportion of missing data but also from the concentration of many

---

*The Sun and the Shakers cult died out very quickly in the mid-late 1940s. It would be interesting to know whether there was a resurgence amongst the Ipili during 1962. A 4 minute solar eclipse is due in 1983 in the Papua New Guinea Highlands. Again it will be interesting to know if there is a renewed interest in the time of darkness legend.

accounts on just a few aspects of the event and the exclusion of other aspects.

It is not difficult to imagine ways in which specific items have been diffused and various accounts truncated, stylised or embellished, but it is difficult to demonstrate that such assumptions about individual cases are correct. One can see the necessity for the scientific approach of the oral historian and the virtue of the functionalist approach even though it is doubtful that even this rigour would provide sufficient information about the physical environment to make complete analysis possible. One can also see that even if the desirable background information was available the magnitude of the task would make it well nigh impossible.

However, contemplation of such difficulties seems unduly pessimistic. The analysis, after all, does demonstrate that a legend about a tephra fall and a time of darkness extends across an area of nearly 100,000 km^2 and that a remarkable number of details of the event have been recorded. While the accounts may have, on some issues, little spatial consistency in that neighbouring accounts sometimes disagree on the physical characteristics or the magnitude of the effects, there is a large measure of consistency in the fact that across a vast area the accounts report the same sorts of effects and the same sorts of characteristics. Although the rather poor spatial consistency of the various legends leads one to wonder whether or not they all refer to the one tephra fall, the analysis completed in Chapter 8 indicates quite conclusively that almost all the highlands legends at least stem from the fall of Tibito Tephra (Fig. 35).

Despite the variations in the details, I am left with a general sense of a westward decline in the severity of the experience from the Eastern Highlands (and further east) toward Simbu Province and then a strengthening of the effects into the western part of the Southern Highlands. These trends are reinforced to some extent by the general notion that the eastern part of the distribution, so far as data are available, regarded the time of darkness as harmful, while the western part, broadly speaking, saw the event as beneficial. Perhaps at this level of generality there is consistency in the accounts.

It is also true that there are remarkably few obvious logical inconsistencies in the accounts and those that have been identified are rather trivial. The very dearth of inconsistencies lends credence to the legend. This does not deny that modifications to the accounts have occurred in a variety of ways, even to the extent that we can regard them only as having an historical basis and not as strictly historical accounts. The philosopher-historian might well argue that that is as true of written history as it is of this example of oral history.

Although few logical inconsistencies have been found, each legend makes claims about a variety of physical characteristics of the tephra fall and the effects produced. Could six feet of tephra have fallen on the

Kaluli? Could Enga gardens have been ruined? Could animals have been blinded and weighed down by the ash? Could house roofs have collapsed, the ash been green or red, the explosion heard, darkness in the daytime been pitch black? And so on. Are such items embellishments moving the legend toward the fabulous, or do they lend credence to its historicity? To what extent is the legend a folktale?

We can arrive at partial answers to such questions by examining the evidence provided in the world-wide literature detailing the physical characteristics of tephra falls and their effects on dwellings, vegetation, animals and people.

12 The legends and reality: the physical characteristics of the tephra fall

Changes in tephra layers following deposition

With relatively thin tephra layers (< 20 cm) such as we are concerned with here the nature of the surface onto which the tephra is deposited can exert important influences on the subsequent character of the tephra layer. For example, field experience with Tibito Tephra, especially in the Tari Gap area (Fig. 35), where long continuous exposures are available, suggests that a continuous stratigraphic layer of tephra is much more likely to be preserved when the vegetation is grassland. In this area, deposition of Tibito Tephra onto forest vegetation has resulted in very poor preservation; quite lengthy exposures frequently reveal no tephra layers. Observations of experimental plots made eight months after deposition of an 'artificial' tephra on a variety of grass and bare (garden) surfaces suggest that disturbance of the thin layer is greater on garden surfaces than on tall (20-30 cm) grass surfaces. Similarly, disturbance of the layer is less on short, close-cropped grass surfaces than it is under the tall grasses.

On bare ground, mixing of the tephra with the underlying organic topsoil by bioturbation ensures that the tephra takes on some of the colour of the surface onto which it is deposited. Thus the initially dark yellowish-grey colour of Tibito Tephra can darken further as a result of mixing. Weathering of the tephra, particularly where the deposited layer is thick and coarse-textured, frequently imparts reddish iron oxide stains to the surfaces of structure faces and root channels. Because the fine fraction of Tibito Tephra is lighter-coloured than the coarse fraction (Chapter 2) selective erosion of the tephra with winnowing of the fines or concentration of the coarse fraction, can also produce some variation in colour of the layer.

Three important points arise from this brief discussion: (1) colour of the one tephra layer can vary within reasonable limits even across a small area; (2) thickness of the deposit can vary from absence (probably because vegetation character prevented deposition of a layer and because of bioturbation), to enhanced accumulation of tephra (as a result of redeposition following erosion from surrounding sites); (3) selective erosion, deposition and mixing can produce significant variations in particle sizes within small areas.

It is evident then that the physical characteristics of a tephra layer can vary within small areas. Even without taking account of such variations we might expect changes as a result of downwind transport and winnowing of the eruptive cloud. The former effect could mean that descriptions of the present day character of Tibito Tephra may be different from descriptions produced at the time of the eruption. Although Fig. 24 indicates the details of tephra thickness at individual sites, the theoretical distribution (Fig. 29), which 'smoothes' these data, gives results more suitable for our present purposes.

Important as these variations in physical characteristics may be, they are of limited significance compared with the changes that occur in the bulk density of tephra following deposition. Obviously the bulk density of Tibito Tephra at the time of deposition is not known but data available from various sources provide a basis for comparison.

Some of the available evidence is collected in Table 23. Bulk density ranges from 0.23 to 1.23 gm cm ^{3}. However, it is not known how long after emplacement these measurements of bulk density were made although numerous passing references suggest that tephra compacts fairly rapidly. Values in the range of 0.6-0.8 gm cm ^{3} are probably most appropriate to the bulk density of freshly fallen Tibito Tephra.

Bulk densities for compacted tephra of 1.3 gm cm^{-3} and 1.7 gm cm^{-3} have been given by Moore (1967, p.19) and Duncan and Vucetich (1970), respectively. Measurements of the bulk density of Tibito Tephra made at Kuk Tea Research Station by Dr P. Hughes give values of $\sim$ 1.5 gm cm^{-3}. Furthermore, Gorshkov and Dubik (1970, p.283) have indicated the compaction of layers of freshly fallen tephra 10-15 cm thick down to a compacted layer 4-5 cm thick. Similarly, Aramaki (1956, p.200) indicates that the tephra from the 1783 eruption of Asama was 120 cm thick 13 km SW of the crater immediately after the eruption, rapidly compacted to 105 cm, and is now only 65 cm thick. Unpublished results from seven experimental plots in the Papua New Guinea Highlands using an artificial tephra made from the c. 13,000 year old Ep Tephra hand-crushed to pass through a 2.00 mm sieve, with approximately half the material passing through a 1.00 mm sieve, indicate compaction to about half the initial thickness, almost all the decrease in volume occurring in the first two weeks.

All of these compaction measurements suggest a decrease in thickness from the freshly-fallen to the compacted state by a factor of 0.4-0.6. We can reasonably assume that the initial thickness of freshly fallen Tibito Tephra (Fig. 51) was about twice its present thickness. This assumption is also in accord with that made by Watkins et al. (1978) for Minoan tephra from Santorini.

Table 23
Bulk density of freshly-fallen tephra

Thickness of tephra	Weight of tephra	Area	Bulk density gm/cm³	Reference
1.5 in	1.75 lb	1 ft²	0.23	Anderson and Flett, 1903, p.475
1-12 in	1.45 lb	1 ft²	0.25	Anderson and Flett, 1903, p.475
0.375-0.5 in	17.58 tons	1 acre	0.35-0.47	HMSO, 1903, p.33
3 cm	28 kg	1 m²	0.93	Gorshkov and Dubik, 1970, p.268
2.5 cm	2 kg	1 m²	0.80	Gorshkov and Dubik, 1970, p.269
20 mm	24.5 kg	1 m²	1.23	Gorshkov, 1959, p.86
20 mm	22.3 kg	1 m²	1.12	Gorshkov, 1959, p.87
6 mm	3.5 kg	1 m²	0.58	Gorshkov, 1959, p.80
16.6 mm	10.9 kg	1 m²	0.66	Gorshkov, 1959, p.81
25 mm	16.kg	1 m²	0.64	Gorshkov, 1959
5 mm	40 tonnes	1 ha	0.6-0.8	Thorarinsson and Sigvaldason,
			0.7-0.92	1972, p.273

Physical characteristics: Tibito Tephra versus the legends

All of the available evidence for the characteristics of the Tibito Tephra fall stems from the properties of the tephra itself; viz, thickness, particle size, and colour. The uncompacted thickness of the tephra (Fig. 51) is by far the most important property at least as far as comparison with the legendary accounts is concerned. The uncompacted thickness values can be directly compared with the thicknesses reported in the legends, and with amounts of tephra fall and durations of darkness reported in the volcanological literature to arrive at estimates of the duration of darkness which occurred during the fall of Tibito Tephra. This type of analysis also provides some additional information about the quality of darkness.

The particle sizes reported in the legends can be compared with the actual particle sizes of the tephra. The present colours of the tephra can also be compared with the reported colours although the considerable variation in actual colours even in small areas makes interpretation of the comparison difficult. Other properties of the tephra fall and legends that can be compared include those described in Chapter 10 as associated effects. Earthquakes, optical effects, noises,

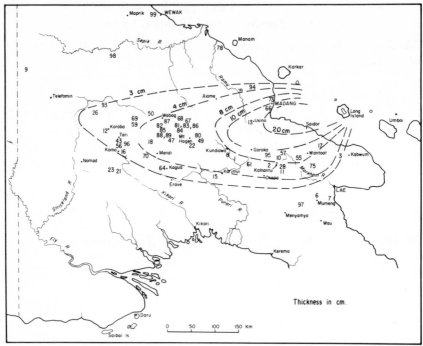

Fig. 51   *Uncompacted thicknesses of Tibito Tephra, informant locations and identifying numbers*

odours, winds, etc. are included in this group. As no physical evidence for any such effects remains we can only examine the possibilities or even probabilities that such effects were observed by comparing the Tibito Tephra eruption with eruption effects recorded in the literature.

The thickness of the tephra fall

Fig. 51 indicates the uncompacted thicknesses of Tibito Tephra based on field determinations of tephra thickness (Fig. 24), theoretical distributions of tephra, and compaction considerations. Fig. 51 also indicates the locations of the fifty-six legend sources of which possibly fifty-one are believed to be associated with the fall of Tibito Tephra.

Fig. 52 compares the uncompacted thicknesses of Tibito Tephra with those reported in the legends. Where a legendary account lies at some distance from a tephra isopach on Fig. 51, uncompacted thickness has been estimated by linear interpolation (or, in a few cases, extrapolation). The thicknesses reported in the legends have been determined by the following procedure: (1) the comments on tephra thickness culled from the legends were examined; (2) these comments were grouped into six thickness categories (Fig. 40) on the basis of (a) interpretation, (b) actual comments about thickness made by informants, and (c) comparison with reported effects in the literature — see for example Blong (in press); (3) the thickness groups shown on Fig. 40 were interpreted as actual uncompacted thicknesses, viz.

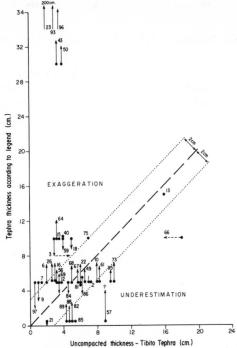

Fig. 52   Uncompacted thickness of Tibito Tephra versus tephra
thicknesses reported in versions of the legend

Group 1	5 mm	4	c. 15 cm
2	5 cm	5	c. 30 cm
3	5-10 cm	6	200 cm or more;

(4) Each point was then plotted on Fig. 52. (5) Arrows were drawn
following further interpretation of evidence in the legends which might
indicate reported thicknesses greater or smaller than the group values
chosen. The length of individual arrows is proportional to the possible
changes, the arrowheads indicating the best estimates of the reported
thicknesses. Two points (3 and 66) also have horizontal arrows,
indicating that the location of these points is in areas of the isopach
distribution where the thickness gradient is steep and incorrect
estimates are possible. Two further points (78 and 99) were not plotted
because they are almost certainly unrelated to the fall of Tibito Tephra.

The dashed line on Fig. 52 indicates equal reported thicknesses
and field thicknesses of uncompacted tephra. The dotted lines 2 cm
each side of the dashed line indicate, rather arbitrarily, a reasonable
margin of error. Thus, points (or, more accurately, arrowheads) located
between the parallel dotted lines represent accurate estimates in the
legend of the actual tephra fall thicknesses. Points falling outside this
zone represent exaggerations or underestimations. Only three or four
points plot as underestimates whereas fifteen plot as overestimates. In
five cases (23, 43, 50, 93, 96) the overestimation is extreme. More

importantly, twenty-three estimates (more than 50 per cent), seem to be accurate to within 2 cm or so.

Duration of the tephra fall and quality of the darkness

Thorarinsson (1971) believes that the airborne equivalent of 0.5 cm of tephra will produce total darkness (Vitaliano and Vitaliano, 1971, p.92). However, a fairly detailed investigation of the volcanological literature has revealed only a few sets of data which allow comparison of the thickness of tephra falls and the duration of the accompanying darkness (Table 24). These data are also shown in graphical form in Figs. 53 and 54. The mean number of hours of darkness per cm of tephra fall is shown as a dashed line on the logarithmic plot (Fig. 53). It is necessary to remember that the data are average values, and that there may have been periods when tephra fell at a diminished rate; Erskine (1962, p.58-60), for example, indicates such a lull during the fall of

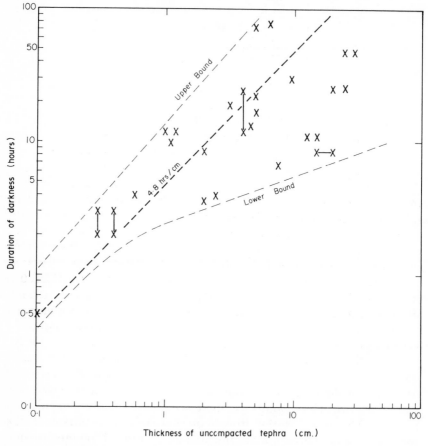

Fig. 53   Thickness of uncompacted tephra versus duration of
the accompanying darkness – examples from the
literature

Katmai-Novarupta tephra at Kodiak (Table 24). The upper and lower bounds on Fig. 53 are drawn to just enclose the available data; they indicate a considerable spread in values particularly for longer durations and/or greater thicknesses.

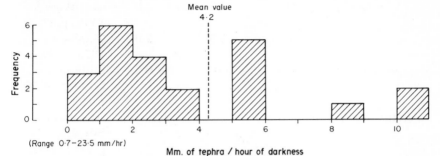

Fig. 54   *Frequency distribution of estimates of rate of tephra fall/hour of darkness derived from the literature*

Table 24
Tephra thicknesses and the duration of accompanying darkness — examples from the literature

Volcano and date of eruption	Distance from volcano (km)	Duration of darkness (hrs)*	Thickness of uncompacted tephra (cm)	Reference
Tambora, 1815	65	29-30	9.5	Anon, 1816, p.254
	460?	22	5.0	Ibid.
	380	19*	3.2	Ibid.
	400	25*	20.0	Raffles, 1830
	400-500	72*	5.0+	Neumann Van Padang, 1971
	600	712	5.0	Ross, 1816; Raffles, 1830
Taal, 1911	20	0.5	0.1	Martin, 1911
Soufrière, 1902	20	4.0?	2.5	Anderson and Flett, 1903
Coseguina, 1835	80	28*+48	6.5	Caldcleugh, 1836
	40	5*+1.5	7.5	Caldcleugh, 1836
Askja, 1875	60	7*+1.5	15.20	Thorarinsson, 1971, p.225
Soufrière, 1812	160	4.5*+7.5	4.0	Anderson and Flett, 1903, p.466-73
Ulawun, 1967	10-12	12.0	1.0-1.2	Johnson, 1970,

Table 24 (contd)

				p.23
Bezymianny, 1955	45	10.0?	1.2	Gorshkov, 1959, p.87
	80	8.5	2.0	Gorshkov, 1959, p.87
	45	3.5	2.0	Gorshkov, 1959, p.86
Mt Spurr, 1953	135	4.0*?	0.6	Juhle and Coulter, 1955, p.199
Vesuvius, 1906	5-6	48*	25.0-30.0	Anderson and Bonney, 1917, p.11; Hobbs, 1906, p.652; de Lorenzo, 1906, p.479
Mayon, 1871	10-12	2.0-3.0	0.4	Faustino, 1929, p.19
Mayon, 1887	10-12	2.0-3.0?	0.3	Faustino, 1929, p.20
Katmai, 1912	160	11*	12.5-15.0	Erskine, 1962, p.58
		26*	25.0	Erskine, 1962, p.60

*An asterisk indicates total darkness.

Fig. 55 presents available data from Papua New Guinea using the boundaries and mean values from Fig. 53, the uncompacted thicknesses from Fig. 51, and the data on darkness duration from Fig. 36. Standard deviations from the mean value (4.8 cm/hr) are also plotted. Vertical and horizontal lines extending from some data points indicate the bounds of interpretation resulting from a range of estimates for the duration of darkness and (in only two cases) possible variations in tephra thickness.

Only three data points fall below the mean value representing relationships reported in the literature. Only five points fall within one standard deviation of this value and only thirteen points within two standard deviations. Seventeen points lie below the Upper Bound, leaving twenty-three points (nearly 60 per cent of cases) as quite definite exaggerations of darkness duration.

Figure 55 also indicates the quality of the darkness as recorded on Fig. 38. It is interesting to note that no version of the legend which mentioned unusual darkness occurs within one standard deviation of the mean value, and only four such versions (out of seventeen) occur within two standard deviations. The distribution on Fig. 55 suggests that it is those people who experienced (or reported) unusual darkness

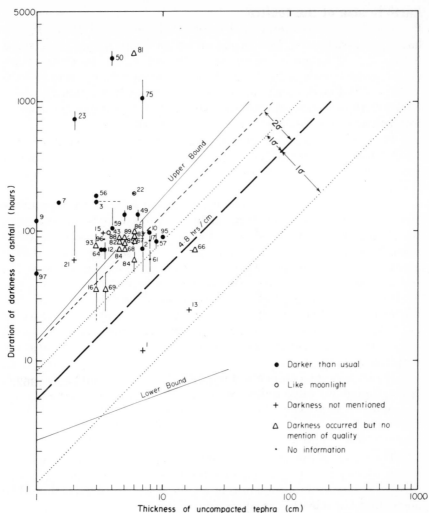

Fig. 55   *Thickness of uncompacted tephra versus darkness durations reported in versions of the legend*

who are most likely to dramatically overestimate the duration of the event.

Some of the comments listed in Chapter 9 concerning the quality of the darkness may seem extreme but in fact they are quite typical of those found in European accounts of tephra falls. Comments such as 'like a night with no moon', 'impenetrable blackness', 'couldn't see my hand at arm's length', 'couldn't see a lighted candle across the room', 'pitch blackness', 'like night even in daytime', 'an almost palpable blackness' and so on, can be found in many of the references given in Table 24. In fact, the high frequency of such references in the European literature on tephra falls perhaps makes the lack of reference in some of the legendary accounts surprising.

Particle size of the tephra

Particle size analyses for a large number of samples of Tibito Tephra have been presented in Table 8 and related to distance from Long Island in Fig. 27. Although a variety of scales are in use in sedimentary petrology, materials with mean phi-unit values ranging from -0.75 ϕ (2.00 mm) to 4.00 ϕ (0.062 mm) are usually regarded as sands. Pettijohn (1957, p.19) indicates that pyroclastic materials are usually divided into coarse tephra (0.25-4.00 mm) and fine ash (< 0.25 mm).

With these two scales all of the tephra samples further away from Long Island than about 100 km would be ranked as either sand or coarse ash. This zone includes all sites near to the sources of versions of the time of darkness legend.

However, two points need to be recognised. First, the mean particle size values were calculated from sieved samples of tephra, a technique which precludes from analysis all material finer than 4.00 ϕ (0.062 mm). Thus a considerable fine fraction of the sample is lost during analysis. The technique clearly overestimates mean particle size and indicates that many samples could have a significant fine fraction; this is also indicated by the fact that 50 per cent of the sample is finer than the mean size value. Thus it is certain that many samples do have a dust (< 0.062 mm) component. Descriptions of tephra fallout, which frequently include penetration of fine dust into closed rooms and so on, emphasise this fact.

Second, Table 8 indicates there is a coarser fraction to the tephra ($D_{10\phi}$), though the table indicates that for the area in which the legends are reported, 90 per cent of each sample would be finer than -0.50 ϕ (1.4 mm). The biggest particles in the tephra cloud over mainland Papua New Guinea would still be classed as medium to coarse sand.

The slopes of the curve of distance versus mean particle size (M ϕ) is remarkably flat, indicating that there is practically no change in particle size within the area of interest (Fig. 27). However, it should be noted that particle size analyses only extend as far west as Koroba. Some locations of interest lie further west or further from the axis of the tephra ellipse.

These observations indicate that the particle size descriptions in the legends should be similar to one another, that a fine dusty phase has not been included in the analysis, and that there was no component of the tephra fallout coarser in texture than coarse sand.

Accepting these points, it is clear that those versions of the legend which report essentially sand-sized tephra are accurate, those reporting finer particle sizes such as dust and ash contain at the very least an element of truth, while those which report the fall of material coarser than sand are clearly exaggerations. It is evident then that almost all of the versions located on Fig. 39 are at least partially accurate.

Only five accounts (03, 026, 057, 059 and 097) appear to indicate significant exaggeration of particle size. Four of these accounts refer to the fall of stones. This seems quite unlikely but two possibilites can be suggested: (1) Accretionary lapilli, rounded accumulations of layered volcanic fallout, frequently form when tephra clouds are flushed by rainfall. Such lapilli are found in Tibito Tephra on Long Island, Crown Island and SE of Saidor. Such deposits could have formed elsewhere. However, lapilli were not found in the Upper Wage deposits of Tibito Tephra (or in the putative younger tephra) found at this site. Although Tibito Tephra has not been found close to the source of Account 057, north-east of Kainantu, any accretionary lapilli found there would almost certainly be only a few mm in diameter. At the 03 site near Kabwum the fall of accretionary lapilli seems quite likely. (2) Skeldon's (1977) analysis of some time of darkness legends from the Eastern Highlands Province promotes the view that some legends stem from hailstorms. In fact, Skeldon cites Pamela Swadling's (057) account as evidence contributing to his thesis. Certainly, as pointed out in Chapter 8, some accounts not included in the present analysis support Skeldon's argument. Furthermore, the possibility of syncretism cannot be ignored, in that two or more separate events may have been collapsed to form the one legend. In the four cases considered here it is not improbable that the fall of stones refers to a hailstorm despite the fact that other aspects of the accounts refer to tephra falls.

Two legendary accounts refer to the fall of wood or trees (03 and 026). I have no explanation to offer concerning the reference to bits of 'wood as if chopped by a steel axe' referred to in the Duna account. However, it should be pointed out that this account is unusual in a number of ways in that it is at least partly futuristic. Account No. 03 contains references to earthquakes as well as to falling trees and it is likely that the former is a cause of the latter.

Tephra colour

It has been mentioned already that tephra colour can vary considerably as a result of selective concentration of particle sizes and as the thin tephra layer takes on the colour of the surrounding sediment or soil. Nevertheless, Tibito Tephra has a basically grey-green colour, a colour that may become dark grey where the fines have been removed. In some cases weathering and release of oxides may give some structure faces a reddish-brown tinge. When fine fractions of the tephra are dry and dusty the colour may appear as a very light green (Chapter 2). Thus Tibito Tephra can be reasonably described at the present time by a variety of colours. However, the range of accurate descriptions at the time of deposition and for a few years thereafter would probably have been more limited; for example, changes due to weathering would hardly have begun.

Approximately fifteen of the twenty-eight colour descriptions listed on Fig. 42 can be regarded as reasonably accurate. A further two or three are also appropriate in some circumstances. Other descriptions may also be appropriate but insufficient details are available. For example, the Salt-yui (01) word for white can also mean light-coloured or grey. Grey-coloured can be an appropriate description for Tibito Tephra but white certainly is not. Similar linguistic and/or semantic problems may occur with descriptions included in other versions.

Nonetheless, it seems that the colour of Tibito Tephra is less accurately or consistently described in the legend than are particle size and tephra thickness.

Associated physical effects

Physical effects associated with the tephra fall include earthquakes, tsunamis, odours, noises, rainfall, and temperature fluctuations. No field evidence can be found to substantiate the occurrence of any of these phenomena in association with the tephra, although it is conceivable that detailed archaeological investigations in some sites could provide evidence for associated earthquakes. Instead, the testimony must rely on the volcanological literature and the determination of what is and what is not possible. Each of the possible associated phenomena is considered independently but briefly; substantive details, culled from the literature, are presented by Blong (in press).

Table 25
Distances from volcanic eruptions at which earthquakes have been experienced

Volcano and year of eruption	Distance km	Reference
Shiveluch, 1964	430	Gorshkov and Dubik, 1970, p.281
Tarawera, 1886	250	Grayland and Grayland, 1971, p.135
Bandaisan, 1888	80	Sekiya and Kikuchi, 1889, p.170
Soufrière, 1902	130	Anderson and Flett, 1903, p.406
Coseguina, 1835	90	Williams, 1952, p.32

Earthquakes

Earthquakes in association with volcanic eruptions are not uncommon, although such earthquakes are usually of shallow focus and thus the area over which they are experienced is usually limited (Shimozuru, 1972). However, during the 1815 eruption of Tambora, probably the greatest tephra eruption of the millenium, houses shook 780 km away in East Java* (Raffles, 1830). The distances at which earthquakes have been experienced during some other volcanic eruptions are presented

*It is possible that East Java experienced atmospheric shock waves similar to those noted during the 1883 eruptions of Krakatau and not earthquakes.

in Table 26. While some eruptions are preceded by long series of premonitory earthquakes (e.g. Mt Lamington, 1951; Taylor, 1958, pp.18-19) others present no premonitory warning of any kind (e.g. Asama (1783) — Aramaki, 1956, p.195; Lassen Peak (1914) — Day and Allen, 1925, pp.5-6).

Earthquakes of moderate magnitude that are not associated with volcanic eruptions are commonly experienced across much of Papua New Guinea (Denham, 1969; Johnson et al., 1971). Thus it is quite possible that earthquakes independent of the eruption of Long Island could have occurred at about the same time, and by the association of events, or even by syncretism, have become part of the time of darkness legend. Certainly Papua New Guineans have frequently experienced earthquakes; it seems likely that only exceptionally severe earthquakes, or those closely associated in time with the tephra fall, would rate a mention in the legend.

Table 26
Distances at which volcanic explosions have been heard

Eruption and date	Distance from source (km)	Reference
Soufrière, 1812	1280	Heilprin, 1903, p.240
Tambora, 1815	1775	Neumann van Padang 1971, p.54-5
Coseguina, 1835	430	Williams, 1952, p.33
Mt Pelée, 1902	1280	Perret, 1937, p.87
Asama, 1911	400	Murai and Hosoya, 1964, p.24
Katmai, 1912	660	Griggs, 1922, p.23
	1440	Erskine, 1962, p.52
Santa Maria, 1902	850	Rose, 1972, p.31
Taal, 1911	240	Pratt, 1911, pp.66-7
Hekla, 1947	280	Thorarinsson, 1970, p.25
Mt St Helens, 1980	425	Volcano News, (4), p.4

In fact Fig. 43 indicates that only six versions of the legend mention associated earthquakes, three in the Southern Highlands (018, 043 and 096), one near Madang (066), one near Mumeng (06) and one on the Huon Peninsula (03). Three of these accounts indicate that the earthquake preceded the tephra fall. Earthquakes in the other three areas evidently occurred during the time of darkness (Fig. 43).

Thus earthquakes associated with the tephra fall are reported by only a few informants but at distances of up to 500 km (Tari) from the eruptive centre. Such a distance is beyond that at which volcano related earthquakes are usually felt but it must be remembered that Tibito Tephra was the product of a particularly big eruption. However, shallow focus earthquakes are not uncommon in the Tari area. Local seismic activity and syncretism would seem to be more probable explanations than eruption-related quakes in the case of the reports from Tari and Kandep. The other three reports are more likely to be volcano-related, particularly in the case of the Kabwum and Madang accounts.

Tsunamis

Tsunamis or seismic sea waves are generally associated with volcanic eruptions only when caldera collapse occurs and the sea has access to the crater. The most commonly quoted example of this phenomenon occurred during the cataclysmic eruption of Krakatau in 1883. Most of the 36,000 or so people who died along the shores of the Sunda Straits during this eruption were killed not by the fall of tephra but by the tsunamis consequent upon caldera collapse (Furneaux, 1965). The collapse of Santorini volcano and the consequent tsunamis c. 1500 BC is also believed by many to have been an important influence in the decline of Minoan Crete (Galanopoulos and Bacon, 1969).

The Long Island caldera, Lake Wisdom, is a large body of fresh water clearly isolated from the sea and there is no evidence to support the view that caldera collapse during or subsequent to the eruption of Tibito Tephra allowed ingress of the sea and tsunami formation. However, the eminent Dutch geologist Rein van Bemmelen has recently suggested that tsunamis can be generated during major volcanic eruptions by the mechanism of elastic compression of the crust. If van Bemmelen's (1971) thesis is believed, the Long Island eruption of c. AD 1700 could have generated tsunamis. It is interesting to note that van Bemmelen's argument was developed with reference to the Minoan eruption of Santorini, an eruption identical in some ways to the Long Island event with which we are concerned.

As only two of the 56 versions of the legend under consideration are from coastal sites, only two versions can be expected to contain information about the occurrence of tsunamis. Both versions (066 and 073), from the Madang coast, do in fact mention the occurrence of unusual waves.

Thus the physical evidence indicates that tsunamis could have occurred during or shortly after the time of darkness but the evidence does not demonstrate that tsunamis did occur. Moreover, on the Madang-Rai coast tsunamis may not be uncommon. Mikloucho-Maclay (Sentinella, 1975, p.237) reported the occurrence of a massive tsunami along the Rai Coast in the mid-nineteenth century, probably about 1855-56. His informants told him of numerous deaths and the abandonment of coastal districts by the survivors. The destruction of Ritter Island in 1888 caused massive tsunamis on the Huon Coast, and on the coast of New Britain and Umboi Island (Steinhause, 1892; Fisher, 1957; Cooke and Johnson, 1978). Evidence of one or other of these events still survives in that on at least some parts of the coast (for example, around Saidor) the local people state that they are recent immigrants from the hinterland. They have little knowledge of fishing or canoe building.

One other point is of interest in connection with the possible occurrence of tsunamis during the time of darkness. Account No. 03 from near Kabwum is a rather strange version of the legend. Although details are sketchy, the legend refers to the destruction of houses by falling trees and stones, the death of many people in many ways, and to the washing away of trees and crops. The emphasis on destruction in this particular account is perhaps consistent with the occurrence of a tsunami rather than just a tephra fall. It seems quite likely (Mick Foster, pers. comm. 1978) that these Timbe people, now living inland, are survivors from the coast.

The available evidence does not confirm or deny the possibility that tsunamis occurred during the volcanic eruption which led to the time of darkness legend.

Atmospheric sound waves

Atmospheric sound waves have frequently been referred to in the volcanological literature. Once again the most famous example is probably that stemming from the 1883 eruption of Krakatau when the noise of the explosion was heard as far away as Rodriquez, 4930 km from source (Fig. 17). Table 26 indicates the distances at which a number of other volcanic explosions have been heard.

Noises accompanying volcanic explosions are frequently described as sounding like the continuous firing of heavy cannon (Heilprin, 1903, p.239), the explosion of dynamite in the nearby hills (Erskine, 1962, p.52), or like someone banging an iron tank (Pond and Smith, 1886, p.351). The most interesting description comes from Williams (1952, p.33) concerning the 1835 eruption of Coseguina and at a distance of c. 300 km from the volcano: 'Colonel Galindo, who was then camped on the banks of the Rio Polochic, in eastern Guatemala, heard noises like those of artillery, which led him to suppose that the commandant at the port of Izabel was "in some sort of extraordinary inebriation" celebrating his birthday by the discharge of guns.'

A commonly reported feature of atmospheric sound waves is that they are reported from great distances but are not heard close to the source. Near the volcano the progress of the eruption is recorded as a continuous loud noise with no distinctive explosions while at greater distances individual explosions are clearly heard. This 'not uncommon anomaly' (Taylor, 1958, p.25) has been noted during the eruptions of Tambora (1815), Krakatau (1883), Tarawera (1886), Soufrière (1902), Katmai (1912), Lamington (1951), Asama (1958) and Kelut (1966). Bolt (1976, p.15) explains that the velocity of sound in the atmosphere first decreases and then increases with altitude so that at some distances the sound may focus, like rays of light through a lens.

At short range, the zone of silence is disturbed only by weak sound waves diffracted along the ground . . . At ranges of 50 kilometres or more, jet streams may duct the sound waves considerably. In the U.S. tests at the Nevada proving grounds, as much as fifteen-fold amplification in sound pressure compared with normal has been observed 65 kilometres from the explosion. (Bolt, 1976, p.15).

During the Hekla 1947 eruption, for example, explosions were heard at distances up to 280 km but there was a fairly broad belt at about 70 km from the volcano in which little noise was heard (Thorarinsson, 1970, p.25).

Experience at other eruptions suggests that it is very probable that explosions would have been heard over much of the area from which legends have been recorded during the time of darkness origin. It is perhaps surprising to find that only ten of the 56 versions refer to the occurrence of atmospheric noises. These have usually been described as thunder and some or all of them may actually refer to thunder rather than to the passage of atmospheric sound waves. The report closest to Long Island is from near Kabwum (03) at a distance of about 80 km. The most distant reports come from near Koroba and north of Mt Bosavi, over 500 km from Long Island (Fig. 43).

The data concerning sounds accompanying the fall of tephra presented in the legendary accounts are certainly in accord with those found in historical accounts of major eruptions. However, it is perhaps a little surprising that more versions do not refer to accompanying thunder or similar loud noises. This possible discrepancy might be explained by the arrival of sound waves, travelling at the speed of sound, some hours before the tephra cloud moving at a velocity of less than 100 km hour (Chapter 6).

Gases and acidic rains

The effects produced by acidic rains and gases during volcanic eruptions range from the barely noticeable and mildly irritating to death for plants, animals and humans. Some large eruptions such as Tambora (1815) and Krakatau (1883) produced only minor effects, at least for survivors beyond the zone of almost total destruction. For example, at Macassar, 370 km from Tambora, the 1815 tephra 'was perfectly tasteless and did not affect the eyes with painful sensation, had a faint burnt smell, but nothing like sulphur' (Anon, 1816, p.253). On the other hand, the 1912 eruption of Katmai seems to have been particularly sulphurous. At Kodiak 160 km distant, sulphur fumes made throats raw and eating almost impossible (Erskine, 1962, p.46), burning drops of combined gas and water tasted like vinegar but left large blisters on lips (p.65). At Latouche 480 km NE of Katmai tender annual garden plants were completely destroyed and the leaves of many native perennials were so burnt by acid rains that they dropped (Griggs, 1922, p.25). Even before the cataclysmic eruption of Mt Pelée on 8 May 1902, fumes of sulphur were so strong in the streets of St

Pierre that horses fell down and died and people wore wet handkerchiefs over their mouths (Heilprin, 1903, pp.39, 62). The 'burning' of leaves of a variety of plants around Mayon volcano in 1928 was attributed to the fall of volcanic dust coated with films of hydrochloric acid (Faustino, 1929, p.39). At other eruptions, notably Hekla 1947 and Heimaey 1973, CO_2 collected in depressions near the volcano, and caused the death of numerous animals (Kjartansson, 1957; Bolt et al., 1975, p.113).

These examples demonstrate that acidic rains and gases are quite commonly produced during volcanic eruptions and that although the effects are usually felt near to the volcano, transport of fumes and acid rains can occur over hundreds of kilometres. However, some major eruptions have been relatively free of these effects.

Terrible smells are reported in eight versions of the legend, but two of these (02 and 023) seem to refer specifically to the stench of dead animals after the tephra fall. The other six accounts are less specific although one (07) mentions a smell 'like rotten rubbish'. The distance at which smells during the darkness are noted range from near Kabwum (03) to Komo (016).*

The evidence of terrible smells presented in the legends is quite consistent with evidence from other eruptions presented in the historical literature. Only a small percentage of versions reports this phenomenon, and it is not clear from the literature whether sporadic or patchy distribution of gaseous effects is characteristic. We do not know, therefore, whether gaseous effects would have been widespread or localised.

Other associated effects

The other associated effects reported in Chapter 9 include rainfalls, winds and temperature changes. Each of these needs to be considered only very briefly.

Little can be said about associated rainfalls. A not very convincing analysis in Chapter 6 indicated that a preliminary analysis of upper atmosphere wind patterns suggested that the eruption might have occurred in the period December to February. As this period is the wet season in much of the highlands, rainfalls can be expected every day. Even during the dry season in much of this area rainfalls can be expected on many afternoons. Therefore, statements in versions of the legend that rainfall occurred before or after the tephra fall are hardly surprising. However, Account No. 015 states that 'Hailstones the size of tree fruits fell' before the tephra fall. While this may be evidence of either syncretism of two temporally separated events or an example of a purely fortuitous occurrence, Dr Roy Wagner (pers. comm., 1978) believes that hailstorms are sufficiently common for hailstones not to be mentioned unless a fall had actually occurred.

Four accounts note that it was raining during the tephra fall

*The Komo people lived near Tari during the time of darkness (see Chapter 8).

(Accounts 03, 013, 096 and 097). Under this circumstance, which is quite likely because the fine tephra particles form condensation nuclei for raindrops, we might expect the formation of accretionary lapilli, usually regarded as the result of rain flushing of the eruptive cloud. As it happens, no accretionary lapilli have been found in Tibito Tephra further from Long Island than Saidor (about 80 km) but tephra samples from close to the sources of the four accounts have not been examined. Certainly accretionary lapilli occur in other tephras found in the highlands. Another factor compounding the already severe difficulties in interpretation is that it is not at all certain that accretionary lapilli will definitely form if rain flushing occurs. No conclusion can be reached.

References in the legends to winds associated with the tephra fall are no less problematical. Three accounts (Nos. 013, 022 and 028) contain references to wind, presumably abnormally strong winds (Fig. 43).

During Plinian eruptions, with eruption velocities of up to 200 m/sec and temperatures above 600°C, the gas thrust phase of the eruption and the subsequent convective thrust phase of the rising tephra cloud can be expected to incorporate large quantities of air, the entrainment and expansion of this air eventually driving the cloud to heights of up to 50 km (Wilson, 1976). During this phase of the eruption there is a strong movement of air towards the eruption column. During the 1906 eruption of Vesuvius the inward rushing air had sufficient velocity to alter the trajectory of falling volcanic bombs at Ottaviano so that windows facing away from the mountain were broken (Hobbs, 1906). Similar inward movements of air were reported during the 1902 eruptions of Soufrière (Huggins, 1902, p.16) and Mt Pelée. However, these accounts relate to distances of 20 km or less from the eruptive centre.

Around Long Island such winds might possibly have extended as far as Kabwum (03) and Usino (013). Certainly, winds experienced in the Nebilyer Valley (022) and in the Eastern Highlands (028) must have some other origin which cannot be accounted for volcanologically.

Several versions of the legend also contain references to the temperature during the tephra fall. Such references are often confused with contradictory information from related sources (Fig. 43). Six versions suggest that it was cold (09, 011, 018, 023, 064, 089). One of these accounts (064) indicates that it will be hot during the next time of darkness. Two other accounts (013, 016) suggest that it was partly hot and partly cold. References to cold could stem from occasions when hail or snow fell in some areas (cf. Skeldon, 1978; Giddings, 1966) but such references may also stem from the chilling caused by the non-appearance of the sun. Such a suggestion has been made by the West Mianmin (09) and, in the literature, by Vitaliano (1973, p.196).

Only three accounts (012, 056 and 097) indicate that it was hot during the time of darkness. One of these (056), stemming from the western part of the legend distribution, refers to the 'white stuff that fell' being very hot. However, this seems quite impossible. Transport through the atmosphere cools the tephra very rapidly so that thermal equilibrium is usually achieved within a few kilometres. Even on Crown Island only 13-20 km from Long Island there is no evidence that the tephra fall was hot. However, during the Katmai-Novarupta 1912 tephra fall, the captain of the *Dora*, steaming north-east from Kodiak on the first night of the tephra fall, reported that the heat on board rose and everyone felt as though they were in the tropics (Erskine, 1962, p.175).

Another account (012) refers to the tephra being too hot to walk on. Given that the tephra layer was 3-4 cm thick near Koroba and dark in colour, a warm day with absorption of solar radiation by the essentially black body could heat the tephra in much the same way as a black beach sand becomes too hot to walk on barefooted on a sunny day. However, this is probably a very Euro-centric viewpoint and it is possible that thick-skinned indigenous feet would not notice this heat.

Optical effects have not been reported in any versions of the legend. This is perhaps surprising given the well-known optical effects associated with the Krakatau 1883 eruption, and the descriptions of 'sun-days' at Kodiak in 1912 (Erskine, 1962, p.36). However, most available descriptions seem to be from relatively high latitudes and

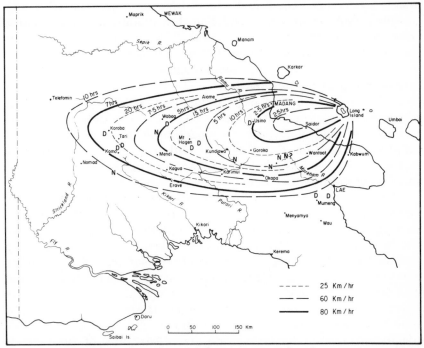

Fig. 56   *Positions of margin of the eruptive cloud assuming various constant cloud velocities*

such phenomena may not be observed where the sun is overhead and, in the case of Papua New Guinea, where afternoon cloud usually obscures the setting of the sun.

Daytime or nighttime when tephra fall began

The available information gleaned from the legends concerning the time of day when tephra fall first occurred has been presented in Fig. 44.

From Table 15, mean velocities of eruptive clouds vary from about 10-100 km/hr with values commonly in the range 50-60 km/hr. Using the shapes of the tephra isopachs as a guide and three different mean velocities, the position of the leading margin of the tephra cloud after various time intervals can be mapped (Fig. 56). The shape of the isochrons on this diagram indicate quite good agreement with the pattern of day and night shown by the legend data. However, it is clear that good agreement between advance of the margin of the tephra cloud and the day-night pattern of the legends can only be obtained if cloud velocities of as little as 12 km/hr are used (velocities other than those illustrated can be easily calculated by halving or doubling time values on the isochrons). If the development of the Plinian eruption cloud is assumed to have occurred at about midnight then good agreement is found.

Although a mean velocity of 12 km/hr is possible, comparison with recorded velocities shown in Table 15 indicates that it is rather low. However, Table 15 also indicates that the velocity of the one tephra cloud can be quite variable (for example, the data presented for the Sakurazima and Asama eruptions). Thus the pattern of day and night occurrences shown on Fig. 55 may be quite accurate.

Forewarning of the tephra fall

Perusal of the various legends indicates that there are numerous references to forewarning of the event. Some accounts refer to the collection of food and water, the covering of crops in the gardens, protection of roofs, herding of animals, and, in some cases, the building of new homes. It is thus worthwhile examining just how much advance warning was available.

Those groups of people who possibly lived within sight of Long Island (e.g. 03, 017, 066, 073 and possibly 013) may have had some warning of the impending cataclysmic eruption in that they could have seen the initial stages of the event with small tephra columns and steam clouds rising. These people might also have seen reflections from the crater on the night sky, felt the preliminary earthquake tremors, and even heard violent explosions. Such warning signs could have preceded the major eruption by as much as several months. If the import of these warning signs was known and heeded substantial preparations could have been made. As at least three of these groups believe that the time of darkness has only occurred once (Fig. 32) it seems unlikely that any lengthy preparations could have been made on the basis of experience.

All of the other groups from whom versions of the legend have been collected are sheltered from Long Island by mountain ranges including the Finisterres, the Saruwageds, and the Sepik-Wahgi divide. Furthermore, such groups are almost certainly beyond the range of shallow focus volcanically-induced earthquakes. Hence the earliest warning sign available to Highland people would seem to be the noise of the eruption itself (or perhaps, as was the case around Krakatau, the preliminary explosions).

However, the stratigraphic evidence from Long Island itself indicates that the eruption sequence began with a Plinian phase which produced Tibito Tephra (Chapter 5). Thus the longest warning period for any group would seem to be the difference in arrival times for the explosions and the tephra. With the sound waves travelling at about 340 m/sec and the tephra cloud moving westward at a minimum speed of about 10 km/hr the maximum possible warning would be $\sim$ 18 hrs at Kainantu and $\sim$ 50 hrs at Koroba. This period of warning assumes immediate recognition of the significance of the sound waves and an extremely slow rate of movement of the tephra cloud.

As only a few groups even mention the explosions it seems unlikely that their significance was widely recognised. As only one or two groups suggest that the time of darkness had occurred more than once there would seem to be no basis for attaching any significance to the explosions even if they were heard. Even then, the sort of evidence presented by Meggitt (1957) suggests that two days is not long enough to build a house.

On the other hand it is possible that the dark, heavy, ominous tephra cloud, probably shot through with lightning, was observed on the horizon by those groups with some view to the east. If so, one or two, or even three hours, warning in which to make some preparations could have been available even if the character of the event to come was unknown. However, for other groups the tephra cloud evidently arrived at night. For still other populations low cloud could have obscured the tephra cloud from view. With the exception of the few groups living along the Madang-Rai-Huon coast, it seems improbable that more than one or two hours warning of the tephra fall was received.

13 The legends and reality: the effects of the tephra fall

Obviously no direct information is available concerning the effects of the fall of Tibito Tephra so an examination of the historical validity of the legend can only be made by comparing details of the legends with details of tephra falls that have been well documented. As was the case with the physical characteristics of the tephra fall, the most important link between legend and reality lies in the uncompacted thickness of Tibito Tephra.

A great deal of the volcanological literature seems almost totally concerned with the character of the eruption or the chemistry and petrology of the erupted materials, with barely a mention of the effects of the tephra fall on houses and vegetation or the trials and tribulations of the populace. Although there are a great number of isolated references in the literature to the effects of tephra fall on dwellings and vegetation, only a few of these records mention the associated thickness of the fallen tephra. Follow up studies indicating the effects of the eruption on people and their activities some months after the event are almost never published even in the popular press. Thus, examples chosen here to illustrate the effects of tephra fall are often isolated and chosen from a variety of little known sources. As the maximum uncompacted thickness of Tibito Tephra with which we are concerned here is only 16 cm or so, details taken from the literature are limited to examples with tephra falls of less than 16 cm except where occasional examples of greater thicknesses provide useful illustrations.

There is a considerable bias in the literature toward mayhem and destruction and against survival and escape. For example, almost every popular book on volcanoes since the early nineteenth century classic geology texts has contained an account of the AD 79 eruption of Vesuvius, usually with a verbatim version of Pliny the Younger's letter to Tacitus detailing the death of his uncle and his own flight, and often completed with accounts of the destruction of buildings and the deaths (usually horrible, agonising or just painful) of some 2000 citizens. Most accounts fail to mention that about 90 per cent of the populace of

Pompeii escaped and survived, having taken a lot of their valuables with them. During other eruptions, reports which mention the collapse of buildings under 10 cm of tephra usually fail to mention that more than 90 per cent of buildings survived the same tephra fall.

It is these sorts of biases in the available information which must be remembered. Comments made by Lt. Colonel Delmé-Radcliffe in a report to His Britannic Majesty's Government concerning the 1906 eruption of Vesuvius are worth recalling:

> I have thought it worthwhile, in view of the exaggerated, absurd, and hysterical statements that have appeared in many papers, to make a sober estimate, as close as the facts and figures at my disposal permit, of the actual damage caused by the eruption. A certain amount of excuse must be made for those who have lived through what must have seemed a cataclysm, with its dangers of unknown extent, the darkness, the contagious terror and natural discomfort, but viewed in the cold light of day the area affected is really small, the permanent damage only at Boscotrecase and Ottajano [Ottaviano] and the number requiring organised help no more than such a rich neighbourhood, assisted by the generous contributions already poured in from all directions, can easily afford to a class of people so frugal and easily satisfied in the matter of the necessities of life (Delmé-Radcliffe, 1906, p.5).

Effects of tephra falls on houses

Tephra fall damage to buildings is caused mainly by the weight of the tephra and by the impact of volcanic bombs. Only the former influence is of concern here as the mainland of Papua New Guinea is beyond the range of bombs ejected from Long Island.

Table 27 lists some of the occurrences of tephra fall which have produced damage to buildings and the thickness of such tephras.

House roofs in tropical countries often tend to be rather flimsy and often have only a gentle pitch. On the other hand roofs built to shed snow loads are stronger and usually steeply pitched. It is noteworthy that only minor damage to (European) house roofs was done in Kodiak in 1912 even though c. 35 cm of Katmai tephra fell (Griggs, 1922; Wilcox, 1959, p.447). At Heimaey in Iceland in 1973, some houses at least survived relatively intact a fall of 4-5 m of pumice although most house roofs were cleaned periodically during the tephra fall. Jagger (1956, p.105) observed with reference to the 1914 eruption of Sakurazima that on the island 'village roofs were bent down, crushed and half-buried under a heavy snowfall of ash and it was notable that flat-roofed cottages were crushed, whereas those with steeper roofs were less damaged'. Perret (1950, p.115) noted that, around Vesuvius in 1906, 10 cm of tephra fall was usually quite sufficient to cause the collapse of flat roofs. Clearly, wet tephra is heavier than dry tephra; thus, even small amounts of wet tephra could cause roof collapse.

Table 27
Effects of tephra fall on buildings

Eruption	Uncompacted tephra thickness (cm)	Damage	Distance from source (km)	Reference
Tambora, 1815	9.5	roofs collapsed	65	Anon, 1816, p.254
Soufrière, 1812	1.5-2.5	roofs collapsed	—	Anderson and Flett, 1903, p.468
Vesuvius, 1906	2.5	roofs of market in Naples collapsed plus some house roofs.	—	Hobbs, 1906, p.640
Ulawun, 1967	1.0-1.2	minor (unspecified) damage.	11	Johnson, 1970, p.23
Santa Maria, 1902	20	houses & farm buildings crushed.	—	Coleman, 1946, p.65
Fuego, 1971	30 cm incl. 5 cm bombs	10% of houses caved in by weight of tephra.	8	SICSLP, 1971, p.114

Data culled from the literature illustrate three points that are very important with respect to the effects of Tibito Tephra on houses: (1) tephra fall of only a few cm can cause roof collapse; (2) the slope of the roof is important; and (3) usually only a relatively small proportion of buildings are affected.

With these points in mind, an examination of the data presented in Table 18 indicates that the effects of the tephra fall on houses described in versions of the legend are indeed plausible. Some accounts refer to the collapse only of older houses, some refer to the buckling of house roofs and attempts to clear the tephra or to strengthen the roofs, while still other versions mention that next time a tephra fall occurs kunai roofs will be protected with coverings of bark or pandanus or banana leaves. All such references and actions seem sensible and reasonable except that there will probably be as little warning next time as there was when Tibito Tephra fell (see Chapter 12).

Some other accounts such as 057 and 059 make improbable claims in that they include references to the fall of stones, an event judged earlier (Chapter 12) to be not part of the fall of Tibito Tephra. Such accounts could arise from the associated fall of hailstones or from a hailstorm on some other occasion, both events giving rise to the collapse of some houses, and the consequent syncretism of the two occurrences.

In terms of the available literature and knowledge of the uncompacted thicknesses of Tibito Tephra, almost all claims made in the legends concerning the actual effects on houses are quite probably true. However, references to the construction of new houses following warning of the forthcoming tephra fall are certainly incorrect, perhaps arising only from the purely fortuituous completion of new houses just before the tephra fall. Given the almost continuous cycle of new house construction described by Meggitt (1957), this fortuituous occurrence seems not at all unlikely.

As mentioned earlier in Chapter 11 there are obvious major differences in housing construction style across the area from which the legends are drawn. Differences such as roof style, shape, slope and construction material could be of major importance in terms of strength under a static load of tephra. If in fact such differences do exist they are not obvious in the available legend data.

Effects of tephra fall on vegetation

Four obvious causes for the death or decline of vegetation influenced by tephra fall have been suggested by Rees (1970, p.17): (1) complete burial of the plant; (2) partial burial restricting root access to oxygen; (3) defoliation and prolonged absence of leaves; and (4) ash covering foliage surfaces, clogging stomata and blocking out sunlight.

Certainly the most widespread effects of tephra fall are on vegetation. While it is clear that remarkably small amounts of tephra are capable of causing significant damage to plants it is also clear that in some cases reported damage is due to acid coatings on mineral grains rather than to the tephra per se. Table 28 provides examples of the effects of tephra fall on vegetation.

From the data presented in this table together with a consideration of the examples presented by Blong (in press), the following general comments can be made: (1) Falls of tephra of only a few cm can affect plants in a number of ways: (a) physically beat plants down and break branches; (b) blight leaves; (c) cause fruit to drop; and/or (d) prevent pollination; (2) snow-adapted plants are probably less affected by the weight of tephra than are tropical plant species; (3) differing plant species are adversely affected to differing degrees by the one tephra fall (see, for example, Eggler, 1948); (4) the one plant species is affected to differing degrees and in different ways according to the stage of plant growth. For example around Paricutin, 1943-45, pines with basal diameters ranging from 10-30 cm diameter survived best because their stems were strong enough to resist excessive bending yet sufficiently flexible to dump part of the ash load and avoid breakage (Eggler, 1963); (5) the season of tephra fall can influence survival. Thorarinsson (1971, p.230) points out that a thin layer of tephra deposited during the growing season can do more harm than a thicker layer deposited at some other season.

Table 28
Effects of tephra fall on vegetation

Eruption	Thickness (cm)	Damage	Distance (km)	Reference
Tambora, 1815	3.2	plants beaten down	380	Anon, 1816, p.254
	5.0	crops somewhat injured	740	Raffles, 1830
	20	paddy totally destroyed plantations injured	400	Raffles, 1830
Coseguina, 1835	10	branches of trees broken	100	Williams, 1952
Ambrym, 1894	2.5	trees drooping; much of undergrowth broken down		Purey-Cust, 1895, p.9
Soufrière, 1902	1.2	tender plants blighted and yellowed; breadfruit dropped	21	Anderson and Flett, 1903
	2.5-3.0	damage to sweet potatoes, yams, tannias and sugar cane	17	HMSO, 1903, pp.65-7
	5.0	crops burnt up roasted by sand forced ripening spoiled food	17	HMSO, 1903, pp.65-7
Taal, 1911	1.0	bananas and other delicate vegetation killed	15	Pratt, 1911
1965	10.0	palm fronds broken	c.10	Moore et al., 1966
	5.0	banana trees damaged	c.10	Moore et al., 1966
Paricutin, 1943-45	10 cm	fine ash prevented pollination of avocado flowers	20?	Rees, 1970, p.13
Sakurazima, 1974	2.0	mandarin oranges, vegetables and mulberry trees crops considerably damaged	—	SICSLP, 1972

These generalisations indicate how difficult it is to make further generalisations. However, with tephra falls 50 cm or more in thickness, damage to vegetation is probably very severe. Around Katmai, 1912, where more than 50 cm of tephra fell, most trees were killed (Griggs,

1919 in Thorarinsson, 1971, p.231) while around Paricutin similar thicknesses broke large tree branches (Rees, 1970, p.13). Falls of only 20 cm at Rabaul, 1937, broke down tropical trees and shrubs (Jagger, 1945, p.389; Cilento, 1937, p.47).

Two further examples illustrating the effects of very minor tephra falls are also worth mentioning. Although the thickness of the tephra fall is not mentioned, dust caused the leaves of the abaca plants 10-15 km from Mayon volcano (1928) to wilt and turn brown with black spots forming later. Acacia, santol and pilli trees lost most of their leaves while cogon and other grasses including bamboo turned burnt brown. In some cases only those portions of the plants facing into the wind were damaged. Chemical analysis indicated that hydrochloric acid films on the dust caused the damage described (Faustino, 1929, pp.30, 38-9). During the 7 May eruption of the Soufrière in 1902:

> pebbles and globular drops of mud fell so thickly that clouds of leaves were struck from the trees and the larger foliage was perforated in many places. The writer counted 205 perforations in a breadnut leaf taken haphazard, and 14 in a hiberian coffee nut but neither of these leaves had been touched by the larger-sized pebbles (Huggins 1902, p.13).

The few examples mentioned here illustrate the wide variety of effects on vegetation produced by relatively minor tephra falls and perhaps demonstrate that it is difficult if not impossible to separate the effects of tephra fall *per se* and the effects of associated acid rains (in reality, acid aerosols attached to the mineral grains).

A comparison of the reported information, the uncompacted tephra thicknesses shown on Fig. 51 and the effects reported in the legends (Table 19, Fig. 46) indicate that most of the effects mentioned quite possibly did occur. Almost all of the recorded effects are in accord with historical evidence. It is also interesting to note that even the rather non-specific effects such as 'gardens ruined' mentioned in the legends are paralleled in the historical data by comments such as 'plants blighted', 'delicate vegetation killed', and 'plantations injured'. Even the references to the vegetation being 'burnt' would seem to be substantiated by the historical comparisons. Moreover, it is clear from Table 28 that effects reported in the legends have been recorded elsewhere with even smaller amounts of uncompacted tephra.

With few exceptions we can regard the effects mentioned in the legend as accurate historical reports. However, a few comments are necessary with respect to specific accounts:

> 09; dry trees could not have caught fire except after a long period of drying following the tephra fall. Self-combustion is not possible.
> 013 and 097; stones almost certainly did not fall.
> 056; it seems unlikely that more than a relatively small percentage

of trees were killed.

064; unlikely that trees were smashed down but branches may have been.

069, 093 and 098; probably only some of the vegetation died.

While a great deal of data suggest wholesale destruction of vegetation and crops by small amounts of tephra fall it must be remembered that such effects may have been short-lived. This possibility is considered later.

Effects on animals

A wealth of evidence elucidating the effects of tephra fall on birds, animals, fish and insects has been presented by Blong (in press).

The 30-35 cm of tephra that fell around Kodiak during the 1912 eruption of Katmai-Novarupta was sufficient to kill large numbers of birds. Small birds were gassed, while large birds flew around in panic until they hit something (Erskine, 1962, p.65). Birds were smothered and buried in the tephra, tangled in trees, and drowned at sea. During the 1886 eruption of Tarawera, in areas where about 20 cm or less of tephra fell, pigeons, ducks and sparrows were exterminated in large numbers. Pheasants had so much mud in their feathers that they were unable to fly and sparrows were found temporarily blinded with their eyelids gummed together by falling mud. Pheasants and quail came almost to house doors searching for food (Grayland and Grayland, 1971, p.102-3). Somewhat similar effects have been reported 400 km north of Tambora in 1815 where only 3 cm of tephra fell and on Barbados where only a few cm of tephra was recorded during the 1812 eruption of Soufrière, 160 km away (Anon, 1816, p.253; Anderson and Flett, 1903, p.397).

Animals were also adversely affected by the fall of tephra at Kodiak. Cattle survived 35 cm of tephra despite a shortage of food and water. They obtained water from rain and ice, some food from shoots that poked through on steep slopes, and salt from kelp beds on the shore. The cattle also suffered severe nasal infections and running eyes (Erskine, 1962, pp.154, 209). Similarly, around Tarawera in 1886, 8 cm and more of tephra caused cattle with parched tongues, bloodshot eyes and noses filled with mud to moan piteously with hunger (Grayland and Grayland, 1971, pp.102-3). At Banjuwangi, 400 km west of Tambora, in 1815, 126 horses and 86 cattle perished following a 20 cm tephra fall, 'chiefly for want of forage, during a month from the time of the eruption' (Raffles, 1830).

The available literature suggests that smaller animals have suffered more than the larger beasts. At Kodiak the smaller animals such as marmots and ermine were almost totally annihilated but foxes survived, coming to the edge of town in search of food two weeks after the tephra fall (Erskine, 1962, pp.205, 210). At Tarawera, rats and mice 'made bold by hunger' were seen hunting for food in the ruined buildings (Grayland and Grayland, 1971, pp.102-3). A cat survived burial for several days and a breeding sow reportedly dug its way out after three weeks of burial. Around Paricutin, 1943-45, where tephra fall was long-continued, post mortem examinations revealed that sheep and goats' lungs were infested with an ash-mucous coating that interfered with respiration (Rees, 1970, p.13). Herbivores have also suffered from the grinding away of teeth surfaces as a result of eating tephra-laden vegetation (Bolt et al., 1975, p.79).

Some tephra layers, particularly in Iceland, have produced fluorine poisoning in animals. In such cases even falls of 1 mm can prove lethal, particularly to close-grazing animals such as sheep. Thus livestock were very seriously affected by eruptions of Hekla in 1693, 1766, 1845, and 1970, during the 1783 Laki fissure eruption and the Grimsvotn eruption of 1934. (Thorarinsson, 1970, pp.15-17; SICSLP, 1970, p.55; Nielsen, 1937, p.9). However, it seems that tephra falls with toxic concentrations of fluorine are very rare outside Iceland.

The effects of tephra fall on fish have not been well documented but only 3 cm of tephra killed many pond fish at Macassar, 400 km N of Tambora (Anon, 1816, p.253). At Tarawera (1886) many lake fish died while the survivors had a discoloured and bruised appearance (Grayland and Grayland, 1971, p.102). Turbid streamwaters resulting from the Katmai tephra fall were lethal to spawning salmon and it took a number of years for the spawning grounds to become fertile again (Erskine, 1962, pp.153, 221). The Hekla 1693 and 1766 tephras also killed many salmon and trout even where only 2-4 cm of tephra fell (Thorarinsson, 1970, p.15).

The only information available concerning the effects of tephra falls on insects stems from the eruption of Paricutin, 1943-45. Sergerstrom's (1950, p.22) analysis suggests that the selective destruction of insect populations around Paricutin was a mixed blessing. Twenty km west of the volcano, mangoes and guavas were able to grow more successfully for several years because of the temporary elimination of a destructive fruit fly. On the other hand, in the same area, the tephra fall evidently wiped out a beneficial insect which preyed on a sugar cane borer. A plague of cane borers caused a widespread loss of cane harvests in 1944 in an area that received considerably less than 10 cm of tephra (Bolt et al., 1975, p.78). Wilcox (1959) also points out that tephra fall may have killed certain insects that otherwise would have fertilised blooms, thus interrupting the reproductive cycles of some plants.

It can be seen that relatively small thicknesses of tephra can have a wide variety of effects on animals of various kinds. The data available in the literature are of insufficient quality in many cases to detail causes of death or injury, to specify the proportions of animals that were adversely affected, or to indicate thresholds of tephra thickness above which effects become serious. In these respects the literature data are similar to the legend information and we can do no more than make general comparisons.

A comparison of Table 20 and Fig. 47 with the above examples indicates strong similarities between the literature and the legends. Table 20 contains references to animals coming out into the open and into houses, to animals and birds dying, to birds having feathers filled with mud and dust, and to animals being blinded by the tephra. Such details are similar to references in the literature. Some accounts also draw distinctions between the effects of tephra fall on wild and domestic animals, the latter surviving relatively unscathed because they were in the houses (although some accounts mention that domestic animals were killed and eaten during the darkness because the people were starving. Others were sacrificed to bring about an end to the darkness).

Although the numerous references to the effects on animals can generally be regarded as accurate, some details deserve specific comments (Table 20):

> 021 and 023; it seems possible but unlikely that one species of bird became extinct.
>
> 023, 075, 093, and 098; it is very unlikely that all animals except those in houses died.
>
> 028; it seems unlikely that all pigs became vicious but they probably competed more aggressively for food.

With the exception of these minor points, the comments culled from the legends could certainly be true.

Effects on streams and drinking water

Very little information is available on the effects of tephra falls on streams and drinking water. Although references to the clogging of streams by mudflows after tephra fall are not uncommon (e.g. Anderson and Flett, 1903; Waldron, 1964), such accounts refer to the fall of considerable thicknesses of tephra. On the other hand, quite thin falls of tephra could have pronounced short term effect on water turbidity and pH. For example, the 1953 eruption of Mt Spurr in Alaska deposited 3-6 mm of tephra on Anchorage. The pH of the public water supply fell to 4.5 and then returned to 7.0 after a few hours. The turbidity of the water rose from 5 ppm to 290 ppm and took six days to return to its original level (Wilcox, 1959, p.454).

It is difficult to draw any conclusions from this one documented example. It appears that pH values would return to normal fairly quickly while turbidity levels may remain high for days or even weeks. Thus legendary accounts which mention muddied streams or refer to the poor quality of drinking water are in good agreement with what we might expect. On the other hand it seems quite unlikely that streams were blocked or landslides occurred in areas where only 6-8 cm of uncompacted tephra fell. However, some streams may have been blocked in areas in the eastern part of the distribution. Thus account 013 from near Usino may be accurate but it seems impossible that such effects occurred in the areas of 043 and 050 (Tari and Wabag).

If this analysis is correct it raises the interesting question as to how the details included in the 043 and 050 accounts arose as it is not a simple matter of exaggeration as in extending the duration of the darkness or overestimation of the thickness of the tephra fall; it is the reporting of effects which seem very unlikely without the occurrence of a much heavier tephra fall. For example, damming of the headwaters of the Laigapu River (050) could probably only occur with tephra falls of 30 cm or more instead of the 4-5 cm that actually fell. We can only speculate that perhaps one or two very minor streams (1st order streams) or even large garden drains were partially blocked by reworked tephra and that exaggeration has occurred as a result of repeated references to such phenomena.

Effects of tephra fall on people

Most people survive tephra falls. At Pompeii (AD 79) about 90 per cent of the population survived (Mauiri, 1961) a tephra fall of about 2.8 m of pumice (Lirer et al., 1973, p.759). On Sumbawa 65 per cent and on Lombok 77 per cent survived the eruption of Tambora (1815) in an area where at least 50 cm of tephra fell. In the case of Pompeii many of the dead survived nearly 2 m of pumice fall before succumbing to a nuée ardente (G.P.L. Walker, pers. comm., 1978). Around Tambora most of the people were killed, not by the tephra fall or its immediate consequences such as house collapses and tsunamis, but by subsequent starvation and disease (Neumann van Padang, 1971, p.60). In fact, of the estimated 92,000 deaths during this eruption, probably the most destructive in terms of human life ever, only about 10,000 deaths are attributed directly to the eruption (including tsunamis).

An examination of the data presented by Blong (in press) clearly indicates that tephra fall per se is a very minor cause of death during volcanic eruptions. Tsunamis, hot pyroclastic flows and subsequent mudflows are the main agents of death.

Tsunamis are limited, in our present study, to a narrow coastal strip for which we have little information. In fact information from Bilbil Island (066) specifically states that there were no deaths although tsunamis are described in this account.

Hot pyroclastic flows and mudflows were certainly limited to Long Island (and possibly Crown Island). Nuées ardentes would seem to be described in the legend from Long Island (Appendix 3) and examinations of the stratigraphy there also indicates massive reworking of the Matapun beds by mudflows.

Thus for most of the area over which the legend is known to occur the only likely causes of death are house collapse* and starvation.

*It is possible but unlikely that some houses collapsed during earthquakes prior to the tephra fall.

Comparison with other eruptions suggests that human casualties would be few in number.

In general, this view is confirmed by the data in Table 21 and Fig. 49 although there are examples of stylisation and exaggeration. Each case can be considered separately:

03; many died in many ways — my earlier comments suggest that these were coastal people and that tsunamis occurred.

012; that only 'bad men' died suggests stylisation.

013; stones could not have fallen.

049, 059, 093, 097; the number of deaths seem to be grossly exaggerated for a tephra fall of only 4 cm or less.

075; it seems unlikely that *many* people were killed when houses fell down as the tephra fall in this area cannot have been more than about 8 cm thick.

One can construct justifications for almost all of the comments taken from the legends. Many Urii (075) houses may have been in disrepair because the tephra fall occurred at a time of the year when other activities absorbed a great deal of the men's time. The Melpa around Mt Hagen (049) and the Upper Wage Enga (059) may have been fully occupied with tribal fighting before the tephra fall so that their gardens were in total disrepair. Perhaps around Koroba (012) house collapses happened to kill one or two 'bad men' and no one else. It is not our purpose to become involved in special pleading here but it is evident that particular circumstances could have markedly affected the death rate in a number of cases. We can only state that more than half of the fifteen versions of the legend which specifically mention human deaths are in accord with experiences derived from other eruptions.

Was the tephra fall harmful or beneficial?

The question, 'was the tephra fall harmful or beneficial?' is a much more esoteric question than the others considered so far, and it is perhaps much more difficult to answer because direct evidence from other eruptions is more difficult to obtain.

Most accounts of tephra falls presented in the literature emphasise the destruction of property, the deaths of humans and animals and the feelings of despair, panic and suffering common amongst the survivors. One can imagine that these feelings are exacerbated where the tephra fall is unprecedented, where there is no warning, and where no understanding of the physical reasons for its occurrence exists.

The following scenario is suggested: as the pall of darkness lifts, the landscape is revealed as a monotonous grey blanket with most of the food crops buried and with even the tall forest partially broken down and mantled with ash. This world is dominated by silence.

Under these conditions it is difficult to see how the time of darkness can be regarded as anything but harmful.

But the rain comes and clears the remaining dust from the air.

Some plants are relieved of their coating of mud as the ash is washed onto the ground. Many leaves have been burnt or perforated but others emerge relatively unscathed. Many of the taro and sweet potato tubers, protected in the ground, have not been harmed so that food is immediately available even though tubers still in the ground may deteriorate quickly in the days to come. Cuscus and kapul are easier to catch because their fur is matted with muddy ash. And the pigs have survived well because they were in the houses with the people.

As the days go by and the rain compacts the tephra and rain and wind rework it from one place to another, the grey mantle is gradually reduced, some plants appear green again, but others have died, apparently 'cooked' by the ground. Food is now harder to find because the new crops planted after the tephra fall are not ready and kapuls and cuscus are now in short supply. A *taim hungri* (famine) might ensue if the forest is remote, though for most people the diversity of forest products and greens is such that there will nearly always be something to eat. If the tephra was removed from some gardens these might have survived quite well so that not even a famine occurs. In fact in the following months it is quite remarkable just how well the crops are growing. The sweet potato and the taro seem to have received some magic fertiliser. A time of plenty ensues.

This scenario is probably fairly accurate. Odd comments can often be found in the literature which support the notion that plant growth is often encouraged by tephra fall. Varenius, writing in 1683 (p.51), commented on an eruption of Vesuvius, in the time of Vespasian: 'But then the Conflagration ceasing, and the showers watering the Sulphureous *Embers* and *Ashes,* in the Superficies of the Mountain here and there was great fertility of *Wine'*. Icelandic farmers reported improved grass growth on low lying lands following the Katla, 1918 and Hekla, 1947 eruptions (Thorarinsson, n.d., p.62) In areas around Paricutin where 3 cm of tephra fell crops of wheat and barley were reported to be excellent (Rees, 1970, p.13). Griggs' (1922) volume on the recovery of vegetation after the 1912 eruption of Katmai-Novarupta includes a revealing picture of increased increments of tree growth after the tephra fall. Griggs wrote (1918, p.6) that three years after the eruption everyone agreed that the tephra fall was 'the best thing that ever happened to Kodiak'. 'Never was such grass before, so high or as early. No one ever believed that the country could grow so many berries, nor so large, before the ash'. Similar comments were made in 1938 about Rabaul ten months after the eruption and tephra fall: 'The restoration of the Garden Town of Rabaul is truly remarkable, and it is the common belief that the volcanic dust and ash, which covered the town and tore down each vestige of greenery on the Black Saturday and Sunday in May, contained certain fertilising elements. At any rate hibiscus and other bushes have grown to greater heights and blossomed more profusely than in the pre-eruption days' (*Pacific Islands Monthly,*

March 1938, p.46).

It is not difficult to see that the Papua New Guinea agriculturalist's attitude to tephra fall might be ambivalent. The available details have been set out in Table 23. It is clear from this table that all the versions for which information is available contain comments paralleling those found in the literature. Some comments consider only a short time context while others place the event in a context of more than a year. Some versions consider only the narrow effects of the tephra fall itself; others place it in a wider cultural context. Some of the latter claims are perhaps extravagant but they at least illustrate the ways in which the occurrence of the time of darkness has been integrated into the social fabric of the society.

Summary

Each of the physical characteristics of the tephra fall can be compared with varying degrees of accuracy with data obtained from legendary accounts of the time of darkness.

More than half of the legends for which data are available provide quite accurate estimates of the uncompacted tephra thicknesses, although there is a strong tendency for slight overestimation rather than slight underestimation. Estimates of tephra thickness provided in a few versions of the legend are quite improbable, being 1 to 2 orders of magnitude higher than the field values.

The duration of the time of darkness has been quite severely overestimated by more than 60 per cent of the cases for which information is available. However, descriptions of the quality of the darkness are in good accord with those accounts of other tephra falls presented in volcanological and historical literature.

As most of the descriptions in the legends refer to the particle size of the tephra as being either sand-sized or dust or ash-like they are in reasonable agreement with the actual particle size of Tibito Tephra. However, those accounts which refer to the fall of particles greater than sand in size are clearly incorrect.

Although Tibito Tephra can be found exhibiting a narrow range of differing colours at different sites, the legends express a wide range of colours. It appears that colour of the tephra is poorly described in the legends compared with its other attributes.

The earthquakes, reported by only a few informants, are probably unrelated to the Long Island eruption, particularly in the case of earthquakes recorded in the Southern Highlands, except for two versions of the legend reporting earthquakes along the Huon-Madang coast. The two versions which mention tsunamis could be accurate reports but tsunamis have probably occurred several times along this coast in the last few hundred years. Comparison of historical records of volcanic eruptions with details mentioned in some versions of the legend demonstrate that explosions or noises like thunder emanating from Long Island could easily have been heard at distances of

500-600 km. Similarly the mention of terrible smells in several versions of the legend extending as far west as Tari is quite consistent with details presented in historical accounts of volcanic eruptions. Although other associated effects such as the occurrence of rains, winds and temperature fluctuations are mentioned in a few versions, it is difficult to find evidence to confirm or deny such occurrences except that it seems unlikely that strong winds resulting from the eruption would be experienced at any great distance from Long Island. Other reported effects such as temperature fluctuations can be easily explained.

The effects of the fall of Tibito Tephra on people, their possessions and their activities is more difficult to judge because the physical evidence on which assessment must be made is one step further removed. Interpretation can only be based on comparison of the thickness of Tibito Tephra with the effects reported in the literature relative to similar tephra falls. As much of the literature is not very specific and cultural differences almost invariably occur, generalisations are difficult.

Nonetheless it is clear that the effects on houses reported in several versions of the legend are quite consistent with published accounts stemming from similar tephra falls. We cannot, however, with the available data, assess the varying influence of different house styles and construction materials; it may be that such differences are unimportant, though some evidence (eg. Jagger, 1956; HMSO, 1903) would suggest otherwise.

Comparison of publications reporting effects on vegetation affected by tephra fall in a variety of localities but particularly in the humid tropics with data from the legends also indicates that almost all the effects mentioned are in accord with historical evidence. Similarly, comments concerning effects on animals compare favourably with those in the literature.

Although only a few accounts make any reference to effects on streams and drinking water some of these make claims that seem more in accord with much heavier tephra falls. However, the European literature is fairly reticent about such effects and it is possible that the 'clogging' of streams could occur with smaller tephra volumes than currently believed. On the other hand this aspect of some legends may represent generalisations from an isolated occurrence in a headwater stream or a garden drain.

In general, comments in versions of the legends pertaining to the number and modes of deaths are consistent with those culled from publications. Some accounts seem to overestimate the number of people killed but there may have been attendant physical or cultural circumstances which caused a high death rate. It is not possible then to state that such accounts are exaggerated.

Finally, from a consideration of the literature it is clear that a group of related people questioned about the effects of an isolated event could have quite ambivalent attitudes. That some of the legends evidently regard the event as harmful while others believe the time of darkness to have been beneficial would seem to be in harmony with the attitudes expressed by European observers.

Discussion

The very wealth of data available in the 56 versions of the legend under discussion prevents anything but en masse considerations of the time of darkness story, with only occasional references to specific accounts. More detailed analysis given adequate cultural background, although obviously practicable, is left to other observers. The broad pattern is important here, not the isolated instances. No attempt is made, therefore, to rank the veracity of the versions collected from different cultural groups.

Although it is tempting to consider such a ranking in order to establish a 'veracity index', this would seem to involve overestimating the quality of the data available. Some of the field requirements necessary for the study of oral traditions were outlined in Chapter 7. Reflection on these requirements allows the conclusion that, while most of the oral traditions which are published by the professionals do not meet the exacting specifications, neither does the present analysis. In a statistical sense, although the sample versions of the legend reported here are probably one of the largest samples pertaining to one legend ever recorded, we do not know the relationship of the sample to the population. From the information available we do know that there is a considerable variation in knowledge of the legend and its details even within the one village (see Chapter 7). A further sampling could, therefore, alter some of the details recorded from particular villages or particular groups of people. On the other hand, it would be surprising if such a sampling were to alter the general content of the legend. While it could be admitted that a further sampling might allow spatial differences in legend characteristics to be pinpointed, this seems rather unlikely in that there was very little difference in the character and amount of tephra fall across an enormous part of the area under consideration. This can be verified by examining Fig. 51; by far the greater part of the area involved received between 2.0 and 7.0 cm of uncompacted tephra. Even if the quality of the legend information could be improved by further sampling of the legend population it would be difficult to verify any spatial differences in effects that appeared for the simple reason that the comparative European literature does not adequately differentiate between the effects of 2 cm and 7 cm tephra falls.

The quality of the comparative European data requires some further investigation and illustration. For example, the 1906 eruption of Vesuvius was a much studied eruption. A manned volcanological observatory was already in existence on the mountain and a number of internationally prominent volcanologists arrived in the vicinity during or shortly after the eruption. In addition the British sent a high-ranking military officer to report back to His Britannic Majesty's Government concerning conditions in the vicinity. The town of Ottaviano on the eastern side of Vesuvius was in the area most severely affected by tephra fall. Given the analysis presented here concerning the fall of Tibito Tephra, thickness of the tephra is obviously of prime importance. Delmé-Radcliffe, the British military attaché, reported that the pumice lapilli in Ottaviano was in some places on a level with the first floors of the houses (1906, pp.3-4); 2 m might be a reasonable estimate, perhaps conservative. Lacroix (1906, p.233) noted that the lapilli was about 7 m thick, Hobbs (1906, p.640) indicated about 76 cm, de Lorenzo (1906, p.477) only 60 cm, while Jagger (1956, p.68), writing fifty years later about his observations at the time, believed the tephra fall to have been c. 1 m thick. Similarly, the tephra fall in Naples itself was 15 cm thick according to Delmé-Radcliffe (1906, p.1) but only 3 cm thick if Lacroix (1906, pp.234-5) is to be believed.

Similarly, several accounts describe the thickness of the Katmai-Novarupta tephra deposited on 6-8 June 1912 at Kodiak. Nellie Erskine, wife of one of Kodiak's prominent businessmen, in writing to her mother a few days after the event, described the tephra as about 2 feet thick. On 20 June she wrote to her mother again commenting that the tephra was 'on the level 14 inches and in places as high as your head where it is piled up' (Erskine, 1962, p.140, p.192). Captain K.W. Perry's account, published in the *Washington Sunday Sun* on 2 March 1913 but taken from his earlier official report as the senior government officer in Kodiak at the time of the eruption, gives the tephra thickness as 22 inches. Martin (1913, p.172) gives the thickness of the tephra as 10 inches in September 1912. Griggs (1918, p.3) reports that Kodiak was 'covered about a foot deep' and H. Erskine (1940) gives the thickness as 18 inches. My own observations, made 66 years after the event, indicate that the tephra has compacted to a thickness of 6-10 inches on slopes of less than 20 degrees. It is also interesting to note that the recent work on *Geological Hazards* by Bolt et al., (1975) records the thickness at Kodiak as 3 metres (p.74), between 6 inches and 1 foot (on a map, p.75) and as 25 cm (on p.76).

These examples indicate that European accounts should not be accepted uncritically as accurately recording the physical characteristics of a tephra fall.

Examples can also be selected from the literature to illustrate the point that the effects of tephra falls are also subject to selectivity of reporting, bias, or inaccuracy. Another example from the fall of Katmai-Novarupta tephra at Kodiak indicates that inconsistencies extend even to the reporting of human fatalities. H. Erskine (1940) describes the death of a tubercular Indian woman during the tephra fall and the rather humorous moment just before burial when the coffin was found to be empty, the body having been left on the *Manning* during the excitement. Hildred Erskine also describes that the woman had been left in her home by her family but later somehow found her way to the ship where she died shortly after. W.F. Erskine (1962), in a 220 page book, describes how his father stumbled over the woman in the street during the darkness and carried her to the ship. There is no mention of her tubercular condition, her death, or the excitement surrounding her burial.

Hildred Erskine also refers in some detail to the subsequent death of a man who fell into a river turned to quicksand by the tephra. W.F. Erskine (1962) does not mention this incident/death. Griggs (1918, p.41) describes the quicksand and mentions only that several men have been seriously mired in such places. Martin (1913, p.133) notes very carefully 'as far as is known it [the eruption] was not the direct and sole cause of the loss of a single human life'. However, on page 180 Martin notes: 'Two or three people died during the eruption, but their deaths are considered as being merely hastened by exposure and by breathing the dust and as not due primarily to the eruption'.

Each of these accounts could be regarded as accurately recording the effects on humans at Kodiak but the impression given by each is quite different.

Two of the trained observers around Vesuvius in 1906 have also commented on the behaviour of the people, again providing rather contrary views, Perret (1924, pp.47-8) wrote:

> the behaviour of these stricken folk was admirable, and a greater patience, resignation, and 'savoir faire' could hardly have been expected of any race. An interesting feature noted by the writer was that the children had, so to speak, taken charge; it was they rather than their elders, who were directing the flight, suggesting destinations, urging on the beasts.

Delmé-Radcliffe (1906, pp.1-2) noted that there was a disturbance in Naples with the mob endeavouring to break into the Prefecture. The whole town was immediately occupied by troops and there was no further disturbance. He also commented on the area between Terzigno and San Guiseppe:

> The troops had cleared the road partially, and then civil labour had been requisitioned, but the country folk did not display a good or self-reliant spirit. They remained looking on as long as they could at the soldiers working to save their houses, and asking how much they were to be paid for helping them. The officers several times told me that they showed no disposition to help themselves and no appreciation of all that was being done for them. Still the troops everywhere continued to work for them, and to feed them, with great consideration and patience.

It is also worthwhile recording one last example of the variously reported effects of a volcanic eruption, this time from the 1963-64 eruption of Irazú in Costa Rica. Horton and McCaldin (1964, p.928) reported that about 6000 head of cattle pastured on the slopes of the volcano had to be taken down to the plains because some 6700 ha of good pasture land had been ruined by tephra. Newsweek (7/10/63, p.65) reported that 2000 cattle had been killed while Time (1964, 83, p.31) reported that 970,000 acres of pasture for prize dairy herds was covered by fallout, that thousands of sick cattle were killed and that milk production dropped to 35 per cent of normal. U.S. News and World Report (29/6/64, pp.71-3) noted that milk production was down 35 per cent and Horton and McCaldin (1964, p.928) wrote: 'Milk production has decreased to slightly below current requirements of the community for fresh milk, but no shortage of milk is anticipated.' Given the continuation of the eruption and the different times at which these reports were written it is possible that each of these accounts is entirely accurate although the impressions produced are at variance with one another.

These examples indicate that the literature with which the time of darkness legends can be compared needs to be evaluated carefully. The quality of both the legend data and the comparative data prevents a more detailed examination of the veracity of the various legendary accounts. Given these limitations and the problems of the relationship of the sample legends to the population from which they have been drawn it seems spurious to probe further individual versions. We can only make a general assessment that the legend would seem to be an accurate report on the effects of the fall of volcanic ash. In fact, taken generally, it would seem to be as accurate as the reports with which it is being compared.

Nonetheless, one aspect of the legend seems less accurate than others. The available evidence, and on the whole it is trustworthy evidence, indicates that the duration of the time of darkness has suffered significant exaggeration, probably as a result of the disappearance of many of the external time-markers during the darkness. For example, Meggitt (1958) notes that Enga observation of the passage of short periods of time is dependent upon transit of the sun and/or the time taken to cook the contents of a ground oven. The latter period seems to be based solely on the experienced judgment of old men, who evidently need no external cues. It is not difficult to believe that, in the absence of the sun and during a period of emotional stress induced by the unique and frightening occurrence, estimates of the passage of time went seriously astray. Because the European observers who have reported darkness durations could rely on a watch or a timepiece such serious overestimates are not found in the literature. Hence, in this aspect, we find the greatest discrepancy between the legends and the European accounts.

In other areas of consideration, if falsification of information occurs, both Europeans and Papua New Guineans make similar mistakes. Thus, we generally find the details of the legend in good agreement with published observations. In the sense that European accounts of tephra falls are historically accurate, so are the various versions of the time of darkness legend. In this sense, the time of darkness story is a legend and not a myth, it is fact and not fabulous. It is, in most respects, as accurate an account as are European accounts of tephra falls. Some aspects are emphasised, some are ignored, some are distorted, some are embellished. The time of darkness legend would seem to be an accurate historical report; and it has survived as history, unwritten for several hundred years.

14 Dating the legend and the eruption

The analysis presented in earlier chapters has demonstrated not only the essential veracity of the time of darkness legends but also that most of the legends refer to the same tephra fall, namely that stemming from the cataclysmic eruption of Long Island. As the analysis also demonstrates that the eruption, the fall of Tibito Tephra and the creation of the legend are coeval, several lines of evidence assist in determining the timing of these events.

Genealogical evidence

The genealogical data available for making estimates of the time when three linked events occurred are of variable quality. Some informants have provided a genealogy indicating the ancestor during whose lifetime the time of darkness or the eruption of Long Island is purported to have occurred, and the age of their informant. In these cases a generation span of thirty years has been used to convert the data to a calendar date. The potential errors inherent in this system are obvious but it is believed that the 30-year span will generally provide an overestimate of the real age difference between parent and offspring. The effects of this overestimate will be discussed later.

Other informants have provided a calendar year estimate based on knowledge of their informants' ages and their genealogies, a technique fraught with difficulties (see for example, Nelson and Chisum, 1974), but none the less based, at least in the latter part of the genealogy, on an understanding of the individuals concerned and their culture. In this case my informant has selected an arbitrary generation gap.

Three groups of genealogical dates can be considered here: (1) dates based on Paul Mai's (1974, in press) detailed genealogies among the Enga; (2) other genealogical dates on the time of darkness legend; and (3) genealogical dates on the eruption of Long Island.

Enga genealogical dates

The data presented by Mai (in press) on the age of his informants and their genealogies back as far as the time of darkness allow twenty-two estimates to be made of the date of occurrence. Table 29 has been constructed using Mai's Table 1 and Appendix 3 (Mai, in press). Where

Table 29
Enga genealogical estimates of the date of the time of darkness

Enga Research No.	Informant's approximate date of birth	Darkness x generations earlier	Estimate of years before informants birth	Best estimate years AD
1	1914	1	30-15	1899
2	1918	2-3	70	1848
3	1919	2-3	70	1849
4	1932	3	90-15	1857
5	1915	3	90-15	1840
6	1924	2	60-15	1879
7	1917	3-4	110	1807
8	1939	3-4	110	1829
9	1917	2	60-15	1872
11	1914	1	30-15	1899
12	1930	3	90-15	1855
13	1925	3-4	110	1815
14	1934	2	60-15	1889
15	1920	1	30-15	1905
16	1919	1-2	45	1874
17	1918	3	90-15	1843
18	1922	3-4	110	1812
19	1922	3	90-15	1847
20	1916	2-3	80	1836
21	1914	2-3	70	1844
23	1908	4	120-15	1803
24	1924	3	90-15	1849

Source: Data from Mai, 1974; in press

the informant was uncertain as to which generation experienced the time of darkness, Mai indicated which generation was the more probable (in italics in Column 3 of Table 29). Column 4 has then been weighted using the more probable generation. Where Mai's informants identified only one generation, fifteen years have been subtracted from the estimate of years before the informant's birth to bring the estimated date to the mid point of the generation span believed to have experienced the event. Thus, there are many assumptions in the method and the best estimate given in Column 5 of Table 29 should be associated with an error term of at least ± 20 years. However, the field data on which these age estimates have been made are reasonably precise as the data were collected by Enga-speaking oral history students, frequently interviewing their own relatives.

Figure 57A illustrates that Enga estimates of the time of the event range right through the nineteenth century with a concentration of estimates in the period 1840-1880. Mai's (in press) analysis of his own

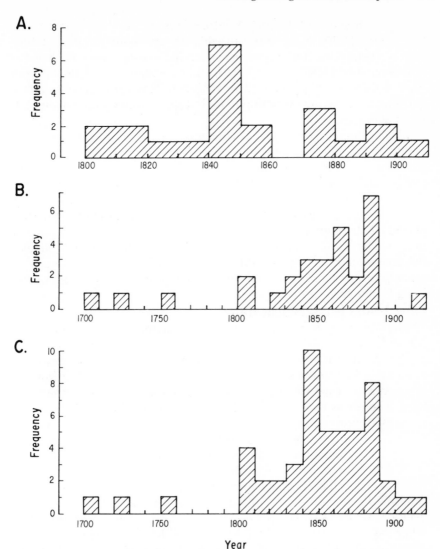

Fig. 57   *Estimates of date of time of darkness based on genealogical data: (a) estimates from Enga Province (after Mai, 1981); (b) other estimates; (c) (a) and (b) combined*

data, also using a 30-year generation span, but a different method of allowing for the uncertainties within any one generation, concluded that the time of darkness occurred in the period 1820-1860.

Other genealogical dates

Other genealogical data allowing the estimation of the date of the time of darkness have been collected in Table 30. Some estimates have been made using the same generation basis as that used for the Enga data but others are based on estimates provided by my informants or mentioned in the literature. Some informants provided more than one estimate; for example, Ben Probert's (012) informants at Tari provided three estimates: (1) a 70-75 year old man said he heard about it from his father etc. — (1880s or earlier); (2) others suggested the story went back about four generations (1977-120 = 1857); and (3) another suggested that the time of darkness happened 13 to 15 generations ago (probably just a guess as no genealogy was provided, but this implies a date about 400 years ago).

Using the basis outlined earlier most of the estimates fall in the period 1840-1890 (Fig. 57B); thus, there is substantial agreement with the estimates made from the Enga data (Figs. 57A,C). Although three groups (009, 016, 023) provide early eighteenth century estimates for the time of darkness, thirty-three out of the fifty-one estimates fall within the period 1840-1890 and all but seven estimates fall within the period 1800-1890. It may be important to note that the estimates provided by the Wanuma (094) and the Washkuk (098) may not relate to the time of darkness produced by the fall of Tibito Tephra whereas all other accounts have previously been judged to be the product of the Long Island eruption (Chapter 8).

Long Island genealogical dates

The legend of the eruption collected from Matapun on Long Island (see Appendix 3) was told in 1976 by an old man judged to be about 60 years of age. As noted in Appendix 3, Koromi came to Long Island from Tolokiwa when steam was still coming from the ground. 'After Koromi there were at least two generations before the old man's father was born. There was Koromi, then the old man's grandmother'.

Thus: informant's date of birth ~1916
informant's father's birth ~1886
informant's grandmother's birth ~1856
Koromi's date of birth ~1826

There may have been one more generation between Koromi and the informant's grandmother, pushing Koromi's date of birth back to ~1796, but Koromi was presumably a leader, at least 20 years old, when he went to Long Island. This dates Koromi's arrival on Long Island at between ~1816 and ~1846. As the ground was still steaming, he almost certainly arrived within ten years of the eruption, thus placing the eruption between ~1810 and ~1840.

A similar procedure with the Poin Kiau legend (Appendix 3) suggests a date for the eruption between 1835 and 1860.

Ball and Johnson (1976, p.144) indicate that data collected by several investigators imply that some of the people now living on Long Island are fifth and sixth generation islanders, thus placing the eruption earlier than 1815 to 1835.

Ball's (1981) annotated bibliography on Long Island lists among numerous other items Naval Intelligence Division (1945) Pacific Islands Vol. IV Western Pacific, a publication which includes two references to the last major eruption which killed all the inhabitants:

Table 30
Other genealogical estimates of the date of the time of darkness

Account No.	Informant's approx. date of birth	Darkness occurred x generations earlier	Estimate of years before informant's birth	Best estimate years AD
001	1912	≥2	60	1852
002	1907	≥2	60	1847
003				Before 1900
006				~1870
007	1922	≥2	60	1862
	1932	2	50	1882
008	1912	≥2	60	1852
009		>8	~250	1727
010				1880s
012		4	120	1857
	1905	≥1		1880s
013	1934	2	45	1889
				Before 1900
015	1922	3	75	1847
016		>7	220	1757
017	1917	≥2	60	1857
018	1932	>2	60	1872
021				~1880s
022	1898	1	30	1868
023	~1910	7	210	1700
026				1860
028				Before 1900
043				1880s
050				1820-1850 or earlier
056		5 (from 1953)	150	1803
057				1880s
059				1775-1825 or earlier
066				~1860
094	1922	≥3	100	1822
095		>2	60	1917
097	1927	~3	90	1837
098	1922	~2	60	1862

one refers to the eruption as occurring about 150 years ago (i.e. ~ 1795) while in another place the eruption is said to have occurred three centuries ago, i.e. ~ 1645 (cf. Carey, 1938). However, Ball and Hughes

(1980) have provided a detailed analysis of the available legendary information concerning both the eruption and the resettlement of the island. They suggest that 'even on the most generous age estimates' the eruption could have occurred no earlier than 1780. They also believe that resettlement of the island took place between 1830 and 1880 (probably between 1850 and 1875), 'a conclusion which is strongly supported by the degree of consistency and integration within the oral tradition of the circumstantial evidence dealing with the spread of settlement, division of resources, sequencing of villages, widely remembered genealogies and accounts of major social events'.

The genealogical data from Long Island suggest estimates for the age of the eruption ranging from ~1630 to ~1860. Most of the genealogical data place the eruption in the late eighteenth-early nineteenth century, rather earlier than the most common estimates based on the time of darkness legends. It should also be noted that if the 30-year generation span is longer than the actual generation all of the age estimates based on this span woud be overestimates. Alternatively, if the generation span was increased to forty years the mean ages calculated from the three sets of data would still fall in the early nineteenth century or in the case of the Long Island data, the late eighteenth century.

Historical evidence

A search of the readily available historical records suggests that no European navigators observed or recorded the eruption of Long Island. However, a number of navigators did pass by and comment on the island's appearance.

The earliest European navigator who may have sighted Long Island was the Spaniard Yñigo de Retes, who sailed east along the New Guinea coast as far as the Astrolabe Bay-Karkar area in 1545. Certainly de Retes observed an active volcano somewhere in this vicinity as the Herrara map of 1601 is marked 'Volcanes' in this area (Sharp, 1968, pp.12ff). However, Palfreyman and Cooke (1976, p.120) suggest that the active volcano was Manam or possibly on an island south of Manus.

A century later Abel Tasman sailed 2½ miles due north of Crown Island on 19 April, 1643, 'located three miles off the main coast of Noua Guinea . . . then made our course west South west . . .'. (Sharp, 1968, p.228). If Sharp's identification of Tasman's 'hoogh eylant' as Crown Island is correct, then Tasman must have sighted the north and north-west coasts of Long Island, mistaking the island as part of the Papua New Guinea mainland. Tasman's log evidently records no other comments on the area, though the following day he sailed past Karkar Island, reporting it to be in eruption (Sharp, 1968, p.229).

Long Island was named by William Dampier on the last day of 1700 when he sailed between the island and Crown Island:

Both these Islands appeared very pleasant having spots of green Savannahs mixt among the Woodland: The Trees appeared very green and flourishing, and some of them looked white and full of Blossoms. We past close by Crown Isle, saw many Coco-nut — Trees on the Bays and the Sides of the Hills; and one Boat was coming off from the Shore, but return'd again. We saw no Smoaks on either of the Islands, neither did we see any Plantations, and it is probable that they are not very well peopled.

Dampier also published in his log profiles of Long Island, Crown Island and Tolokiwa. Although the diagrams are not integrated with the text, commentators such as Reche (1914), Ball (1981) and R.J.S. Cooke (pers. comm.) are in agreement as to which profile shows Long Island. Cooke's reconstructed version of Dampier's drawing as reproduced in Ball (1981) is again reproduced here as Fig. 58. Long Island as it appears in profile today is also reproduced, comparison of the two figures shows little change between 1700 and the 1970s.

According to Ball (1981) the next navigator to provide any details about Long Island was J.S.C. Dumont D'Urville in August 1827. D'Urville named the two peaks Cerisy and Reaumur (Fig. 22) and wrote in his log (Ball,1981):

An hour after noon, we were already beneath the steep and rugged flanks of Mt. Reaumur which also appeared to have been a volcano, and further off, at a distance of less than two miles, we could see the deserted beaches of Long Island.

This island was quite incorrectly named by Dampier, probably because of the first view of the island which the navigator saw, because it has a rather round shape and its circumference is not less than forty miles. The ground in the vicinity of the shore appeared more arid than all the other islands and we saw neither coconut trees nor any trace of inhabitants.

Three years later A. Morell (1833), frequently regarded as quite unreliable in his comments on the north coast of Papua New Guinea (Palfreyman and Cooke, 1976, p.120; Ball, 1981), commented on the north coast of Long Island: 'We saw only a few wigwams along the shore, and some natives; but we could not conveniently land, and kept on our course until we had passed the western end of Long Island . . .'.

F.J. King sailed past Long Island in 1842 and commented on reefs extending south-east from Crown Island but he failed to mention the appearance of Long Island (King, 1844 in Ball, 1981).

For much of the period between 1871 and 1883 Nicolai Mikloucho-Maclay was resident on the Rai coast of the mainland adjacent to Long Island. He could not have failed to witness the eruption and experience the tephra fall had it occurred during his residence as Mikloucho-Maclay was a keen observer of natural phenomena, wrote a paper (1878) on the volcanoes of the Bismarck Sea,

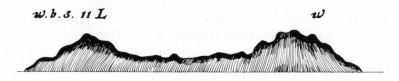

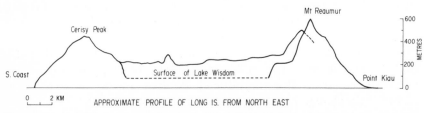

APPROXIMATE PROFILE OF LONG IS. FROM NORTH EAST

Fig. 58   *Profile views of Long Island: (a) from Dampier's log; (b)*
reconstructed from 1:63360 topographic map

and commented at length on an earthquake/tsumani which devastated
much of the Rai Coast (he believed in the 1850s) (Mickloucho-Maclay,
1975, pp.236-7), it seems unlikely that the eruption could have
occurred during the period of living memory prior to the 1870s.

During 1884 and 1885 Dr Otto Finsch visited Long Island. In 1884
he wrote: 'Long Island is mostly thickly wooded or covered with scrub
and has no coconut palms or people; or least it is very thinly peopled,
for we saw only 2 or 3 small settlements in inaccessible bays whose
inhabitants came off shore in a canoe and were difficult to persuade to
come closer' (cited from Ball, 1981). In 1885 Finsch wrote: 'The whole
island is mostly mountainous, with very little flat land and only
moderate ravines or valleys passing through it. The coast appears as
unpromising as the land itself, which should, however, be easier to
cultivate than Dampier Isl. [Karkar] since it doesn't have such thick
virgin growth but shows more under-growth-covered areas' (in Ball,
1981). In 1885 Captain Bridge of HMS *Dart* reached Long Island: 'After
examining the eastern and south-western shores without being able to
discover any natives. I directed Lieutenant Commander Moore to
return to the Southern point at which I landed, and having on a bluff
some 40 feet high above the sea set up a flag-staff, hoisted the British
flag and read the proclamation' (in Ball, 1981).

By the 1880s and 1890s there were sufficient European residents,
particularly German missionaries, on the north coast of the Papua New
Guinea mainland and on New Britain that a major eruption on Long
Island could not have gone unrecorded. Certainly the comparatively
minor eruption of Ritter Island in 1888 did not pass without
considerable comment (see Chapter 4)

Interpretation of the historical evidence

Certainly the comments of mariners and others eliminate the possibility that the eruption occurred during their sojourns in the vicinity of Long Island. Where comments have been made about the appearance of the island we can also eliminate the possibility that the eruption occurred in the years immediately before the observation as the vegetation on Long Island would have been largely destroyed by the eruption which produced Tibito Tephra. The important question then becomes, how long would it have taken for the vegetation to have recovered?

Earlier chapters have demonstrated that the eruption which produced Tibito Tephra, and gave rise to the time of darkness legend, was of the Plinian-Peléan type and that the thermal energy produced during the tephra eruption ranks the eruption as one of the great eruptions of the last millenium. Various energy calculations (Chapter 6) suggest that the eruption was at least equal in magnitude to the famous 1883 eruption of Krakatau.

Examination of the deposits produced on Long Island indicate that the eruption produced a Plinian airfall pumice deposit and finally a Peléan ignimbrite deposit many metres thick (Blong et al., 1981). Almost the whole island appears to have been mantled with these deposits. The ignimbrites, produced by incandescent gas clouds, contain numerous completely carbonised trees and there is little doubt, given the thickness of the tephra mantle and the temperature of the ignimbrites, that all the above-ground parts of the vegetation were destroyed.

However, the destruction of vegetation during major volcanic eruptions, including those of Plinian-Peléan type, is often not as great as it seems. Some slopes, such as the outer slopes of Mt Reaumur and Cerisy Peak, may have been protected from direct effects of the incandescent gas clouds and experienced only the tephra fall per se. In these relatively sheltered areas and elsewhere, particularly on the steeper flanks of the older volcanoes (Fig. 22), cloud burst rainfalls which often accompany major eruptions may have removed much of the deposit in a relatively short time (weeks or months). It is in these areas that plants are likely to have survived and from such areas that recolonisation of the rest of the island could have begun.

Such a scenario is not unparalleled by developments at other sites devasted by Plinian or Peléan eruptions. Within a year of the tephra eruption of Irazú in Costa Rica (1964) one-half to one-third of the newly fallen tephra had been removed from the upper slopes of the volcano (Waldron, 1967, p.11). Similarly, Anderson and Flett (1903, p.453) believed that more than half the new deposits around the Soufrière, St Vincent (1902), had been removed to the sea within six months of the eruption. The Soufrière eruption was identical in style, but rather smaller in magnitude to the eruption which produced Tibito Tephra.

Many plants survived the devastating nuées ardentes produced during the 1951 eruption of Mt Lamington, Papua New Guinea. At Higaturu, the temperature of the nuée ardente was estimated at about 200°C for 1.5 minutes (Taylor, 1958, p.46) and the velocities of the clouds as ~ 120 km/hr (p.44) yet:

> Five days after the eruption, taro shoots appeared through the ash near the Coffee Mill and a fortnight later similar plants had penetrated the 9 inches of ash over the gardens north of Hupo village above Higaturu . . . Within two months the monotonous grey of the devastated areas was broken by many patches of bright green where garden plants such as taro, yams, sweet potato and bananas were bursting into luxuriant growth . . .
>
> The indigenous plants returned to the area slowly. The grasses came first, spreading gradually from the margins of the devastated area [my emphasis] towards the crater. For the first year they remained the dominant vegetation and the slopes remained accessible until early 1952. During 1952, however when parts of the blanketing ejecta had been removed by erosion from the old soil horizon, the secondary growth quickly became dominant. By the end of 1952 some of the young trees were more than 15 feet high, and access to the craters up the spurs of the mountain could only be gained by laborious cutting of a track through dense vine-entangled thickets and stands of tall cane grasses. (Taylor, 1958, p.51)

Another example that provides a valuable comparison with the Long Island eruption stems from the devastation of the volcanic island at Taal in the Philippines in 1911 by a Peléan eruption. A few tree stumps were exhumed by erosion during the first rainy season and by early 1914, in the absence of human habitation, bananas, papaya, sweet potato, tomatoes, peanuts, casava and a single rice plant had become established, some shrubs such as Trema had reached 7 m, stemming from old roots (Gates, 1914). Brown et al. (1917) notes that the one area of the island that was still sparsely vegetated in 1917 had also been practically devoid of the vegetation before the eruption. While many plants, particularly crops, propagated from surviving root stocks, birds were the most important agent of dispersal, some 54 per cent of the plants present on the island in 1917 (representing about two-thirds of the species present before the eruption) could have been carried by birds, 21 per cent were apparently distributed by wind and 9 per cent by water (Brown et al., 1917, p.219). These authors also believe (p.220) that because Krakatau was much further from surviving vegetation, and because the time between ingestion and ejection of food by most birds is 1½ to 3 hours, some 72 per cent of recolonising plant species found on Krakatau probably reached the island by ocean currents. Thus at Krakatau, strand vegetation developed early on, whereas at Taal, terrestrial vegetation appeared first.

Revegetation on Krakatau certainly seems to have been slower than around the Soufrière, Mt Lamington, Taal and Mt Tarawera (New Zealand). Some evidence cited by Docters van Leeuwen (1936) indicates that Krakatau was sterilised by the 1883 eruption and that by 1921 only twenty tree species had reached the island whereas the island of Sabesy 15 km to the north which had been covered by 1-1.5 m of tephra in 1883, had forty-nine wood species on its slopes by 1921.

It is difficult to draw comparisons between these rather contrary but relevant examples and the Long Island eruption. It seems likely that much of the tephra could have been removed fairly rapidly from steep sheltered slopes and that recolonisation of the island could have begun from these source areas. In any case total destruction of the vegetation on Crown Island seems very unlikely, so that recolonisation, aided by birds and the north-west trades, may have been quite rapid.

However, much of Long Island, particularly the long gentle slopes away from the caldera, are marked with thick porous ignimbrite deposits that even today make the island more 'arid' than its neighbours Crown Island and Tolokiwa. Re-establishment of vegetation in these areas must have taken a long time.

Application of the various examples in the literature to the Long Island eruption suggests that revegetation to the state where the island's appearance would not have provoked comment from a careful observer would have taken a minimum of about 20-30 years and a maximum of perhaps 40-50 years. There would be some variation depending upon the part of the island viewed, as the outer slopes of Reaumur and Cerisy were almost certainly revegetated first.

With these comments in mind then we can interpret the remarks of passing mariners and others to determine that the eruption of Long Island could not have occurred in the periods 1680-1700 (Dampier, 1700) or 1807-1827 (D'Urville). In fact it seems impossible on the basis of historic evidence that the eruption could have occurred later than about 1807 for the island was visited by several mariners and observed for many years by Mikloucho-Maclay. These comments suggest that the eruption occurred either during the eighteenth century or prior to 1680.

Volcanic evidence

William Dampier's profile of Long Island, drawn in 1700, shows essentially the same outline as a profile taken from a modern topographic map of the island (Fig. 58). This evidence indicates that either the profile of the island was not changed by the eruption or that the eruption occurred before 1700.

As Ball and Johnson (1976, p.137) have noted it is difficult to assess the form of the central volcanic complex prior to the formation of the caldera. These authors have indicated (p.141) that the abundance of pyroclastic materials in the caldera walls suggests a series of subsidence events, each associated with a major pyroclastic eruption.

Blong *et al.* (1981) presented the evidence (see Chapter 5) for three major ignimbrite deposits dated 16,000, 4000 and ~ 300 years BP and raised the possibility that landforms and drainage networks around the present caldera suggest the existence of a caldera prior to the last ignimbrite eruption.

If a caldera did exist prior to the last ignimbrite eruption it may have been much smaller than the present Lake Wisdom and it may have been filled or partly filled by the growth of one or more pyroclastic cones (cf. Crater Lake and Wizard Island, Krakatau and Anak Krakatau, Bagiai and Karkar). Certainly any caldera filling cone must have been composed almost entirely of pyroclastics, as basalts are largely absent from the present walls. Thus, as Ball and Johnson (1976, p.137) rightly argue, the slopes of the cone or cones are likely to have been low; they suggest no more than about 10°. They argue further: 'In profile, therefore, the complex may have been low-lying and, depending on the form and distribution of its eruptive centres and on the rate at which reworked clastic deposits were redeposited at its periphery, the profile could have been more-or-less flat-topped' (p.137).

These statements raise several issues. Ten degrees is a very low slope angle even for a pyroclastic cone; there is every chance that the slope of such a cone would have been steeper and, at any rate, concave upward. Secondly that the complex, if in fact it existed at all, was not low-lying is equally possible. Thirdly, the outward redistribution of volcaniclastic materials is almost always by linear incision. At Long Island today, the profile form of the cone has been hardly touched (cf. Ollier and Brown, 1971). A final important point concerns the height of any earlier cone. A cone with 10° slopes astride the present 11 km diameter caldera rim (with its base at about 450 m asl) would reach a height of over 1300 m — not notably different in height to Mt Reaumur and certainly higher than Cerisy Peak.

If a central volcanic complex did exist, and the stratigraphy of the caldera area has not yet been examined in sufficient detail to confirm or deny the proposition, there is a chance that such a complex stood well above the present caldera rim. If such a complex did exist it had certainly vanished by AD 1700.

Although almost all authors agree that cauldron or caldera subsidence is the result of rapid evisceration of the magma chamber, particularly during an ignimbrite eruption, it is by no means certain that collapse will occur immediately. Furthermore, Johnson (1969) has argued forcefully that it may be cauldron subsidence that causes the ignimbrite eruption rather than vice versa. However, the tephrostratigraphy of Long Island indicates that at all exposures examined on the western and northern sides of the island the Plinian pumice members of the Matapun beds sit directly on a palaeosol, indicating a period perhaps of several hundred years of relative quiescence prior to the ignimbrite eruption.

No firm conclusion can be reached from these lines of evidence and on this basis it cannot be determined whether the eruption occurred before or after Dampier's passage in AD 1700.

However, it is worth recording that many versions of the legend (see Ball and Johnson, 1976, p.143; Appendix 3) record that Long Island did possess a central cone or cones ('much higher than Tolokiwa') before the eruption. As the legends seem consistent on this point, as the descriptions of the effects of the eruption on people, houses, and animals are in accord with those observed at similar eruptions, and as aspects of the story such as the island being larger now than it was before the eruption are demonstrably correct there may be much merit in accepting the notion that a large central volcanic complex existed prior to the eruption.

If the evidence from the legends is accepted then the eruption must have occurred before 1700, and on the basis of a 20-year revegetation period, before about 1680.

Lead-210 dating of lake sediments

The ^{210}Pb method of dating is based on the measurement of residual radioactivity of ^{210}Pb in sediments, the ^{210}Pb being derived from 'rain-out' onto lake surfaces. The half-life of lead-210 is 22.26 years. Laboratory methods for the measurement of lead-210 are briefly reviewed in Appleby and Oldfield (1978).

Two basic models have been developed in applying ^{210}Pb to the dating of lake sediments. The *constant initial concentration* (c.i.c.) model assumes a constant rate of input, a constant residence time, and no migration of ^{210}Pb down the sediment column, as well as assuming that there is a constant initial concentration of unsupported ^{210}Pb per unit dry weight at each stage of accumulation; i.e. each stage of initial concentration of unsupported ^{210}Pb in the sediment was constant despite any variations which may have occurred in the sediment input rate. This latter assumption is of little consequence where the accumulation rate is constant, but where the sediment input rate has fluctuated through time, the age of the sediment will be underestimated by an amount proportional to the degree of acceleration of the accumulation rate. In such cases an alternative assumption involving a *constant rate of supply* (c.r.s.) of unsupported ^{210}Pb to the sediment per unit time is to be preferred (Oldfield et al., 1978; Appleby and Oldfield, 1978).

Age/depth curves for both c.i.c. and c.r.s. models have been constructed for two cores from lakes in the Papua New Guinea Highlands (Oldfield et al., 1978). Chemical fingerprinting of a tephra layer found in each core has demonstrated that Ash Layer A/Ash 4 of Oldfield et al., (1977) is in fact Tibito Tephra (Chapter 3; Appendix 1.) In Lake Egari (Fig. 33) on the assumption that the c.i.c. model applies, Tibito Tephra has been bracketed by ^{210}Pb dates of 1805-1832 and 1848-1865. In Lake Ipea a c.i.c. age of 1815-1862 has been determined for a sediment sample from immediately below Tibito Tephra. However, ^{210}Pb concentration v. depth curves suggest that the c.r.s. model is more applicable in both lakes; this model provides age estimates of just before 1820 in Lake Egari and just after 1800 in Lake Ipea for deposition of Tibito Tephra.

More recent work by Oldfield et al., (1980) indicates that these age estimates are too young, as calculations were made assuming uniform ^{226}Ra content and hence uniform supported ^{210}Pb concentrations in each sample. New measurements indicate that Tibito Tephra has a higher ^{226}Ra content than the lake sediments above and below. Magnetic susceptibility measurements (cf. Fig. 34) indicate that samples assayed for ^{210}Pb above and below the tephra included some tephra particles and thus have abnormally high ^{226}Ra concentrations. When corrections are made for the proportions of tephra in these samples it becomes clear that there is negligible unsupported ^{210}Pb at or beneath the tephra and that Tibito Tephra is significantly older than previously calculated.

By extrapolating the age/depth curves from 85 per cent of tephra depth through ages for older tephras (including Olgaboli Tephra) determined by ^{14}C dating, (Oldfield et al., 1980) a revised age for Tibito Tephra of AD 1680-1690 is fixed. It is important to note that this age estimate is beyond the range of ^{210}Pb dating technique and is based on curve fitting through points fixed by ^{210}Pb dates at $\sim$ 130-160 years and ^{14}C dates >1000 years.

This age estimate for Tibito Tephra must be regarded as fairly crude. Minor corrections to the age of Olgaboli Tephra used by Oldfield et al. would probably make Tibito Tephra younger but other possible corrections (e.g. to the age of Ash C) might have the opposite effect.

If we believe the historical evidence and the notion that revegetation of Long Island took an absolute minimum of two decades then the ^{210}Pb age must be incorrect.

Palaeomagnetic secular variation in lake sediments

Thompson and Oldfield (1978) have shown that a close parellelism exists between measurements of magnetic inclination in the Lake Ipea (Fig. 33) sediments and the post-1650 AD secular variation in inclination for the Lake Ipea site based on all available observatory records. Matching of the two records indicates a pre-1700 AD age for Tibito Tephra (Oldfield et al., 1977; Oldfield et al., 1980).

Radiocarbon dating

In many ways the obvious method of determining the age of Tibito Tephra and the eruption of Long Island is radiocarbon dating, However, as the following discussion indicates, the answers are not as simple as they at first seem.

In numerous sections on Long Island the pyroclastic flow members of the Matapun beds include massive, completely carbonised tree trunks frequently oriented in the direction of flow with a dip on the trunk slightly greater than the slope of the depositional surface on the deposit.

Four radiocarbon dates on tree trunks believed to lie within the Matapun beds (Chapter 3) are available from Long Island. Three samples were collected by Dr I. Hughes from along the north coast west of Poin Kiau (Fig. 22). The fourth sample was collected by the late G.A.M. Taylor in 1957 from the east coast of Long Island. Although the exact collection sites are not known there is little doubt that they are from either the Matapun beds or mudflows derived from the Matapun beds. Unfortunately, the method of sample collection is not clear, and it is not known whether the assayed samples represent the outermost rings of the sampled logs. This point is not without significance as it is the outer growth rings which are the youngest and hence those closest in age to the actual eruption date. There is a possibility then that, while the trees from which samples were collected were carbonised during the eruption, the material dated could predate the event by some years.

The four dates are:

ANU — 1125   380±70 yrs BP
ANU — 1126   230±75 yrs BP
ANU — 1127   200±65 yrs BP
NZ — R332   115±40 yrs BP

Further details are presented by Polach (in press).

Six radiocarbon dates relating to the age of Tibito Tephra are available from the Kuk prehistoric site near Mt Hagen (Fig. 3):

ANU — 754A   190±65 yrs BP
ANU — 754B   >MODERN
ANU — 1052   290±60 yrs BP
ANU — 1053   240±60 yrs BP
ANU — 1054   290±60 yrs BP
ANU — 1055   480±60 yrs BP

Site details and laboratory treatment are given by Polach (in press).

There is no dateable material included within Tibito Tephra at Kuk so all samples either overlie or underlie the tephra. Some samples are separated from the tephra layer by several cm and some samples may have been of some antiquity before burial. ANU — 1052 is probably the best sample in that the age determination was made on a wooden spade and on the cellulose fraction alone. The wooden spade is almost certainly a piece of *Casuarina* containing only a few growth rings and probably close in age to its date of abandonment and burial. The assay on a cellulose fraction virtually eliminates the possibility of contamination by older or younger organic materials.

As it is quite certain that samples dating Tibito Tephra at the Kuk site and the samples dating the Matapun beds on Long Island refer to the same event we can consider all samples as one set.

There is obviously room for personal preference about the 'real' age. My own choice is based on the following reasoning:

(1)   ANU — 1126 and —1127 provide the best age estimates from Long

Island as the mean dates are close together. Combining these two results (Polach, 1969) provides a pooled mean age of 210±50 yrs BP. If ANU — 1125 and NZ — R332 were also included the pooled mean age would increase a little.

(2) ANU — 1055 is derived from disseminated fragments of charcoal 2-15 cm beneath a lens of Tibito Tephra at Kuk. ANU — 754, A and B, are from a sample of fibrous peat probably containing modern root material. None of these samples provide satisfactory age estimates.

(3) The remaining three samples, ANU — 1052, 1053, and 1054, were corrected for sedimentation rates. For example, ANU — 1052 occurred 126 cm beneath the ground surface in a drainage ditch and 24 cm below Tibito Tephra. At a constant sedimentation rate of 3.07-7.41 mm yr^{-1} (126 cm in 170-410 yrs), Tibito Tephra would be some 32 to 78 years younger than the spade. Thus a more realistic date on Tibito Tephra would be 240±60 yrs BP. Similar adjustments for ANU — 1053 and 1054 provide ages for the tephra of 250±60 yrs and 235±60 yrs BP. This 'correction' causes the three age estimates to converge.

The pooled mean of these three samples becomes 240±45 yrs BP. If the adjustments for sedimentation rate at the Kuk site had not been made the result would not be sensibly different. However, if the three samples excluded from the pooled mean were to be included the pooled mean age would increase.

(4) The pooled mean of the five samples (ANU — 1052, — 1053, — 1054, — 1126, — 1127) is now calculated as 230±40 yrs BP.

(5) However, the assays are based on radiocarbon years and there is no certain evidence that there is a one-for-one correspondence between radiocarbon years and calendar years. In fact there is considerable evidence to the contrary. A number of calibration curves have been published but these are not always in agreement and it can be difficult to choose betwen a correction curve which smoothes too much and one which shows every irregularity (Olsson, 1974). For the present case it is worthwhile comparing the results from a number of calibration corrections.*

Damon, Long & Wallick (1972): 230±40 becomes 284±58 BP = 1608-1724 AD

Ralph, Michael & Han (1973): 230±40 becomes 300-420 BP = 1530-1650 AD

Clark (1975): 230±40 becomes 270-370 BP = 1580-1680 AD

Stuiver (1978): 230±40 becomes 280-325 BP = 1625-1670 AD

Each of these calculated ranges is based on 1 σ each side of the mean. The Stuiver (1978) curve also indicates that there is a possibility that

*I am indebted to Dr R. Gillespie and Dr M. Barbetti of the University of Sydney Radiocarbon Laboratory and to John Head and Henry Polach of the ANU Laboratory for various calculations and discussions.

the calibrated date could be younger due to an ambiguity in the curve. The mean ages for the four curves are respectively 1666, 1590, 1630, 1647. These mean ages for the calibrated dates range 70 to 130 years older than the mean age of AD 1720 for the uncorrected radiocarbon dates. These calibrated radiocarbon dates place the time of darkness, the fall of Tibito Tephra and the eruption of Long Island fairly firmly in the early-mid seventeenth century. However, consideration of 2 σ each side of the mean ages indicates a possibility that the eruption occurred in the early eighteenth century or, for that matter, in the late sixteenth century.

Polach (in press) uses a rather different approach. He notes that none of the numerous calibration schemes available 'can claim to be comprehensive and none offers a unique solution' but chooses Stuiver's (1978) curve 'because it is the most precise available for the range of ages under consideration'. Polach notes some other problems in using this Pacific North West USA curve for Papua New Guinea data, rejects only ANU—754B, and concludes 'with considerable confidence that the latest catastrophic eruption of Long Island and the emplacement of Matapun beds and Tibito Tephra took place in the mid-seventeenth century'.

The ambiguities of the Stuiver curve, however, would suggest that there is also a real (but low?) probability that the eruption occurred in the eighteenth century.

Conclusions

Consideration of the dating of the time of darkness legends, the fall of Tibito Tephra and the cataclysmic eruption of Long Island has generated long (and occasionally acrimonious) debate among those with a professional interest. As not all the lines of evidence converge the weighting given to various lines of evidence is a matter of personal preference.

The strongest lines of evidence would seem to be the historical evidence and the radiocarbon dates. The historical evidence indicates that the eruption could not have taken place after about 1800 or in the period 1660-1680 to 1700, depending on the time allowed for revegetation. Combining the historical evidence with the radiocarbon dates we conclude that the eruption and associated events occurred almost certainly in the mid-seventeenth century (say 1630-1670) but we cannot totally deny the possibility that the eruption occurred post-1700.

The paleomagnetic evidence, such as it is, also supports a mid-seventeenth century age. On the other hand, the ^{210}Pb date of 1680-1690 is in direct conflict with Dampier's description of Long Island. Presumably, the lead-210 dates do not support, as yet, either a seventeenth or an eighteenth century date for the eruption. Similarly, the volcanic evidence can be used to support either argument.

Finally, almost all the genealogical dates indicate a mid-nineteenth century date for the linked events (Fig. 57). Such a date, in fact any nineteenth century date, would seem to be totally precluded by observations of passing mariners, the Rai coast sojourn of Nicolai Mikloucho-Maclay and the 20-30 years necessary for the revegetation of Long Island.

Thus the notion that Long Island erupted, Tibito Tephra fell and the time of darkness legends were generated in the mid-seventeenth century would seem to be in at least reasonable accord with all of the evidence except the bulk of the estimates based on genealogical dating. On the other hand, the notion that the linked events occurred in the early mid-eighteenth century is also in some agreement with most of the evidence except the paleomagnetic and, again, the bulk of the genealogical dates.

As it seems necessary to regard the radiocarbon dates as the soundest of the 'scientific' techniques employed here, the author's view is that a seventeenth century age is more probable than an eighteenth century date. However, it is perhaps more important to note, whichever date is 'preferred', that the genealogical dates based on the time of darkness legends are seriously in error, many of them by 200 years or more.

15 Some conclusions and some questions

The various analyses set out in this volume have demonstrated that a number of conclusions can be reached. First, field examinations and chemical analyses indicate that Tibito Tephra covered an area of more than 80,000 km² to a depth of more than 1.5 cm (compacted thickness). In all, the eruption of Long Island produced more than 10 km³ of Tibito Tephra with a thermal energy production of $\sim 10^{25}$ ergs. These conservatively estimated figures demonstrate that the Tibito Tephra eruption was one of the greatest eruptions of the last thousand years.

Second, stratigraphic considerations indicate that Tibito Tephra is the uppermost tephra layer across almost all of its currently known distribution and that the legends of a time of darkness within this area which clearly stem from a tephra fall must stem from the deposition of Tibito Tephra. Fifty-four of the versions of the legend known to the author definitely fall into this category. It is probable that many more known versions also refer to this event but current evidence is insufficient to confirm this view.

Third, despite the various emphases displayed by the numerous versions of the legend and despite evident stylisations and embellishments, comparisons with published records of the physical characteristics and effects of other tephra falls of known thickness and duration indicate that the legends can be regarded as essentially accurate historical accounts of an actual event. However, the duration of the darkness has been exaggerated in almost all versions of the legend.

Finally, the best estimates of the timing of the eruption and the tephra fall indicate a mid-seventeenth century date for the events. This evidence indicates that the genealogical dates are very seriously in error.

These conclusions are of no small significance; they relate to an area spanning almost all of the Papua New Guinea Highlands and a considerable portion of the north coast. They indicate that a seemingly unconnected set of stories have, in fact, a common origin and, more importantly, that they can be tested against the reality of the physical character of the fall of Tibito Tephra. The evidence indicates that the legends are in good accord with reality on all issues except those that involve the passage of time. The legends also demonstrate, especially when considered collectively, that unwritten history can preserve with fair accuracy events that occurred in Papua New Guinea perhaps 300 years ago. From these conclusions a number of implications and numerous questions arise.

The first set of questions are of a volcanological and physical nature. To the present, investigations of the Long Island eruption have concentrated only on the island itself and the quadrant to the south-west. No offshore investigations have been made although Krause (1965) certainly reports the presence of a grey-green sand in sediment samples from a wide area of the Bismarck Sea. Determination of the magnitude of the Tibito Tephra eruption has been based only on investigations in this area but it is possible that a large volume of tephra fell upwind from the volcano or even that surface winds were from the south-west. Examination of good sections on Tolokiwa and coring in the Bismarck Sea would allow a much more accurate determination of eruption magnitude.

Similarly, the area enclosed by the 1.5 cm isopach of Tibito Tephra (Fig. 29) has been estimated conservatively. Examination of good exposures beyond the periphery of the known distribution will again allow more accurate estimation of the true extent of the fallout. Current theoretical considerations suggest that Tibito Tephra should be recognisable as a very thin layer in little disturbed high altitude swamps as far west as Telefomin and perhaps even at the Irian Jaya border. Such an extension of the known tephrostratigraphy would be invaluable not only for various stratigraphic studies but also in elucidating the nature of time of darkness stories extant around Oksapmin and further west.

Although these volcanological questions are of some importance the conclusions reached in this volume seem also to have far reaching implications and questions for students of anthropology and oral history. The first group of questions arise from the dating of the time of darkness legend and the events which gave rise to it.

Because the time of darkness legends can now be regarded as essentially accurate historical accounts of an actual event we should ask the question: What other events recorded in Papua New Guinea legends, but generally regarded as fabulous, could have a strong basis in fact?

Oral accounts of an unusual event have survived for perhaps 300 years in the Papua New Guinea Highlands. Earlier published versions of the legend estimated that the volcanic event occurred in the 1880s because such estimates were based on genealogical evidence (Watson, 1963; Glasse, 1963; Nelson, 1971). Now that the time span that the legend has survived has been extended from 70 to 80 years to about 300 years new implications arise. Evidently all or nearly all of the communities included in the present survey 'suffer' genealogical amnesia. To what extent are other events recorded in legends much more ancient than presently supposed?

Details were set out in Chapter 11 of a number of occurrences which are reputedly temporally related to the time of darkness. For example Nelson (1971) had placed the arrival of the sweet potato amongst the Kaimbi of the Nebilyer Valley at about the same time as the time of darkness. Can these events now be more firmly fixed as having occurred about 300 years ago? Similarly Watson's pronouncement that *Casuarina oligodon* arrived in the Eastern Highlands about the same time as the time of darkness requires re-examination now that the event is known to have occurred not 90 but 300 years ago.

Although it is perhaps over optimistic to hope that the determination of the various time of darkness legends as coeval and the dating of the event at c.300 years will allow the establishment of a time plane across the highlands, it may be possible to relate events in time for relatively small areas. For example, the Waka-Enga, the west Mianmin and the Komo Huli have all migrated since the time of darkness (Chapters 8 and 11). Is it possible that these migrations all occurred at the same time and/or in response to the same pressures? Obviously very detailed investigations are required before such questions can be answered but there is now a possibility that such events can be related in time independently of genealogical criteria.

The degree to which the time of darkness can be related to other events within the society is perhaps a measure of the degree to which the legend has been integrated into the culture of the society. Thus forewarning of the eclipse of 1962 in the Eastern Highlands provoked a number of responses which stemmed directly from accounts of the time of darkness. On the other hand there is little evidence available to suggest that forewarnings of the eclipse had any effect in the Western and Southern Highlands and Enga Provinces, yet it is in the latter two provinces that memory of the legend seems to be strongest. Amongst the Tari Huli the *Dindi gamu* ceremony seems to focus on encouraging a recurrence of the fall of tephra (*Dapindu*) yet no other groups regard the tephra fall as sufficiently beneficial to wish to encourage a recurrence of the event. This is surprising because it is abundantly clear from the evidence relating to the thickness and distribution of the tephra fall that the Tari Huli's experience of the event can have been very little different from that from other groups in the Southern and Western Highlands. The evidence currently available suggests that the difference in attitude results not from some physical difference in the time of darkness but in some societal/cultural variation. Similarly, the evidence presented by Mai (in press) indicates that the time of darkness marks a turning point in Enga culture; in the aftermath dramatic improvements occurred in various aspects of cultural and economic life, evidently attributable to the time of darkness (Chapter 11). The question that arises concerns the lack of similar expressions amongst other groups and indeed the rather negative reaction of the Tairora (Eastern Highlands, J. B. Watson, pers. comm., 1978), who see themselves as physically and socially 'cold' as a result of the event. It is tempting to surmise that the sweet potato was introduced to the Enga at about the same time (c.f. Nelson, 1971 and the Kaimbi) but surely the effect of the introduction of the tuber was coincident and widespread across much of the highlands?

Certainly the memory of the time of darkness legend seems much closer to the surface amongst the Enga and the Huli than it is amongst the Melpa and the Chimbu. The Stratherns (pers. comm., 1977) found few people with much knowledge of the legend amongst the Melpa people of Mt Hagen even though Vicedom and Tischner (1948) recorded a detailed version in the 1930s. Similarly the Reverend J. Bergmann (pers. comm., 1978) and Dr Paula Brown Glick (pers comm. 1976) had not heard the story despite years of contact with Chimbu, although the legend is remembered amongst both the Dom and Salt-yui people near Gumine. These differences in memory of the time of darkness would seem to stem from cultural factors again because the tephra fall, if anything, was more severe in the Simbu and Western Highlands Provinces than in Enga and Southern Highlands Provinces. It is also possible that some groups within the area of known tephra fall (Figs. 29, 30, 31) have no memory of the event. Have these groups migrated into the area on which Tibito Tephra fell since the event, has the story really faded from memory or has the investigation so far conducted in these areas been too shallow to expose the legend? Determination of the answers to such questions is in the province of the anthropologist and the oral historian.

Several versions of the legend suggest that the people were forewarned of the event to the extent that houses were built and other elaborate preparations taking weeks or months were made, yet the volcanological evidence implies that only a few days or hours warning were possible and even then only if the portent of the warning signs was realised. Do the details of furious house construction and other preparation imply that the time of darkness fortuitously occurred at the time when the cultural cycle demanded the building of communal and other houses or do these details imply syncretism of other events with the time of darkness story? Although almost all versions of the legend indicate that the time of darkness has occurred only once, there is some evidence from amongst the Tari Huli that bingi has also occurred in earlier epochs. Amongst the Paiela the time of darkness marks both the end and the beginning of a 'ground' epoch (Dr Aletta Biersack, pers. comm., 1978). The integration of the time of darkness in the other Paiela beliefs is so strong that it is difficult to believe that a tephra fall has occurred only once. The same may be true amongst the Huli. Similarly, Mary Mennis's (1978) detailed work around Madang seems to indicate clearly that there were two times of darkness, the earlier one related to the disappearance of Yomba Island, presumed to be a Bismarck Sea volcano which vanished (total caldera collapse?) during the eruption. Certainly at the Kuk prehistoric site near Mt Hagen perhaps eight thin tephra falls have occurred in the last 6000 years, during the period of prehistoric agricultural activity at the site. At other sites throughout the highlands thin tephra layers earlier than Tibito Tephra are known to occur. One of these, Olgaboli Tephra, erupted some 1200 years ago from an undetermined Bismarck Sea volcano, and is known to have been deposited across much of at least the Eastern and Western Highlands. Could Olgaboli Tephra have been erupted from Yomba? Could two tephra falls, and the associated times of darkness, have been preserved today as a memory of only one occasion?

The answers to all these questions lie in the past. The answers, if they are obtainable at all, are only going to be determined by the detailed and persistent inquiries of geomorphologists, archaeologists, anthropologists and oral historians. Certainly the evidence already presented tells us a lot about the recent past in Papua New Guinea, a past some 300 years ago in which legend and reality are intertwined.

But these events also tell something of the future. In the longer time span recorded at the Kuk prehistoric site, the fall of Tibito Tephra was not a unique event, but an occurrence that has been repeated on average at least once every thousand years. And what of the future? There is no reason to suppose that Bismarck Sea volcanoes will not again deposit tephra across the highlands with results not dissimilar to those reported in the legend but this time complicated by the superposition of a western technology. Contingency planning for the next time of darkness, based on both the reality and the legend, should already have begun.

Appendix 1

Contents

Sample descriptions
Analytical results

```
 1    Q    KUK A9G 1F16
 2    Q    A9E W32
 3    Q    A9B/C 36E (DUPLICATE SAMPLE 184)
 4    Q    KUK A9G 1F6
 5    Q    A9E W14
 6    Z    T48/1 DILLINGHAM QUARRY KAUPENA-IALIBU 6700FT ELEV. WATER
           REWORKED AV-THICKNESS C6CM BELOW 30CM
 7    Q    A9E W30 BOTTOM
11    Z    PINDAUNDE G N-SIDE ABOVE LOWER LAKE 11600FT AV.THICKNESS 6.5
           CM VARIABLE 4-16CM FINELY LAMINATED POSSIBLE 2 GRADED BEDS
           AT 15-21 CM DEPTH (MT.WILHELM)
15    Q    PINDAUNDE F N-SIDE ABOVE LOWER LAKE 11600FT 2-3-5CM THICK
           NO CLEAR GRADED BEDDING- SURFACE AT 32.5CM (MT.WILHELM)
17    Q    A9B/C 55E+W Q (DUPLICATE SAMPLE 92)

18    Q    A9E W32 (DUPLICATE SAMPLE 107)
19    Z    KUK A9G 1F12 Z
20    Q    NM ROUNDWARA C100CM BASE BLACK SANDY ASH (MT.AMBRA)
21    Q    A9E W15 Q
25    Z    NO 3 E-W 317-3M FROM E-B,BARET FILL   Z
26    Q    A9E W48 (DUPLICATE SAMPLE 106)
28    Q    A9E W17
29    Q    A9E W39
32    Q    A9E W Q
33    Q    A9B/C 102W Q

34    Q    A9B/C 97W Q (DUPLICATE SAMPLE 90)
38    Z    41.5M FROM N END D9E WEST FACE   Z
39    Q    A9E W21
41    Q    A9E WV
43    Q    A9E WS Q
45    Z    A9B/C 104W Z
50    Q    A9B/C 34W
53    Q    A8=A9F/G 56W 2-8CM THICK TOP OF SLOT BARET
55    Q    A7=A9F/G 53XW 7CM THICK 1/2 WAY DOWN SLOT BARET
56    Q    A4=A9F/G 128E 3CM THICK STREAM CHANNEL FILL

57    Q    A3=A9E/F 11W  12CM THICK BOTTOM OF BARET FILL
58    Q    A6=A9E/F 52W HARD LAMINATED 9CM THICK BARET FILL
61    Q    S FACE DRAIN E OF JUNCTION A9E/F-STREAM CHANNEL=A10
```

```
75   Z   K52 Z (LOSS ESTIMATED)
76   Q   K116/2 (LOSS ESTIMATED) BARET FILL C9E
79   Z   LOWER MUGA-UP TO 25CM FINE SAMD-UP TO 4.5M OVERLYING SEDIMENT-LENS1.3M
81   Q   UPPER MUGA 1A LENS 2-2.5CM THICK AT DEPTH 2.74M PALE BLUE-GREY
85   Z   MAMA ASH 1 105CM DEPTH (GUMANTS)
87   Z   TIBITO A4/1 SAMPLE BASE AT 31CM
90   Q     A9B/C 97W Q (DUPLICATE SAMPLE 34)
92   Q   A9B/C 55E+W Q (DUPLICATE SAMPLE 17)

106  Q   A9E W48 (DUPLICATE SAMPLE 26)
107  Q   A9E W32 (DUPLICATE SAMPLE 18)
110  W   M2 27-31CM (MENDI)
121  W   CFP 130/2 MENDI RD 27-31CM(LOSS ESTIMATED)
123  Z   CFP 130/1 MENDI RD 1 7-13CM
124      IPAGUA 132/1 ASH1
127  W   SUGARLOAF 58/2 ASH 2
128  Z   SUGARLOAF 58/1 ASH 1
129      SUGARLOAF 58/3 ASH3
130  Z   MENDI RD 1 7-13CM

131  W   MENDI 2 27-31CM
142  Z   MT AMBRA 1 8-17CM
143  W   KUK A9G 1F10 ASH
146  W   MT AMBRA 1 40-50CM
162  Z   PINDAUNDE VALLEY NEAR TERMINAL MORAINE DEPTH C40CM (MT.WILHELM)
164  Z   SIGAL MUGAL 4 N.SIDE CIRQUE BELOW CAMP 20-30CM DEPTH.C10CM
         THICK VARIABLE. ELEV.11450FT.
172  Z   T106/1 KUMBENE-IALIBU 4-5KM FROM KUMBENE LENS  3-5CM THICK.35
         -40CM BELOW SURFACE-IN SITU THICKNESS 5CM 1 GRADED BED 7200
         FT ELEVATION
177  Q   K144/1 BARET FILL S.BDY.20M E OF A10W
178  Q   MINJIGINA SAMPLE OF BARET ASH
184  W   A9B/C 36E (DUPLICATE SAMPLE 3)

242  Z   PIPIAK B  6-8CM
243  Z   IPEA CORE 1 TOP ASH  25-27CM ASH 4
244  Z   EGARI  5 16-17CM (SEE 248)
245      QUEN 1 KM NORTH OF MENDI
246  Z   INF.IKI OLEA,KANAKIMANDA NEAR WAPENAMANDA (DUPLICATE SAMPLE 402)
247  Z   SANGULAPU NEAR WABAG (NITA PUPU)(DUPLICATE SAMPLE 403)
248  Z   EGARI  5 17-18CM (SEE 244)
249  Q   EGARI  5 64-65CM
250  Z   MARGARIMA 26-28CM BEDDED.NEW ANDEBARE RD 0.5KM N OF TENGO RD
         7200 FT ELEV.
251  W   INF. WIA TABAI,RAIAKAMA(TCHAK)(DUPLICATE SAMPLE 404)

400  Z   YUMBIS-WAGE OCCASIONAL BALLS 1-2CM THICK UP TO 50 CM BELOW
         SURFACE-REWORKED ELEV.7500-8500FT
401  Z   MARGARIMA 26-28CM BEDDED NEW ANDEBARE RD 0.5KM N OF TENGO RD
         720OFT ELEV.
402  Z   INF.IKI OLEA,KANAKIMANDA NEAR WAPENAMANDA (DUPLICATE SAMPLE 246)
403  Z   SANGULAPU  NEAR WABAG (NITA PUPU)(DUPLICATE SAMPLE 247)
404  Q   INF. WIA TABAI,RAIAKAMA(TCHAK)(DUPLICATE SAMPLE 251)
405  Z   KEGAM-DISCONTINUOUS BALLS 30CM DEPTH ELEV.10600FT
406  Z   IALIBU SUMMIT 1-2CM REWORKED-AT SURFACE OR DOWN TO 15CM
         11000FT ELEV.
410  Z   LAIAGAM,TIM PYAKALYA
419  Q   K162 W E5F/G BARET FILL 62-90CM-CEMENTED
411      EGARI 2 60-61CM ASH 2
412  W   EGARI 2 40-41CM ASH 3
413      S4 51-52CM IPEA-SIRUNKI ASH 2
414      S4 43-45CM IPEA-SIRUNKI ASH 3
415  Z   S4 24-25CM IPEA-SIRUNKI ASH 4
418  Q   K191 Q AMBRA CRATER-BASAL 4CM
420  Z   T83 1MILE FROM TOMBA ON WAP ROAD.BARET FILL UP TO 10CM THICK
         ELEV. 8400FT (DUPLICATE 417)
423  Q   K90 Q FINER THAN 3.25PHI B9E 98-113CM CHANNEL FILL
424  Q   K132/6  FINER THAN 3.25PHI
425  Q   K133/1 FINER THAN 3.25PHI S.BDY. TOP OF BARET FILL
426  Z   SIGAL MUGAL ASH 1 3-16CM FINER THAN 3.25PHI ELEV.12000FT.

427  W   SIGAL MUGAL ASH 3 8-11CM FINER THAN 3.25PHI ELEV.C12000FT.
428  Z   SIGAL MUGAL ASH 2  2-3CM. FINER THAN 3.25PHI ELEV.C12000FT.
429  Z   TAMBUL AMBUGA FLAT ASH 2
430  Z   ETPITI 1 ASH ELEV.7250FT.
431  Z   T48/2 DILLINGHAM QUARRY KAUPENA-IALIBU 6700FT ELEV. WATER
         REWORKED.AV.THICKNESS C7CM BELOW 25CM
432  Z   K90 ASH 1 FINER THAN 3.25PHI (MUST BE K90/2 OR K90/4)
454      KAINANTU W END OF AIRSTRIP C40-41CM
455      KAINANTU W END OF AIRSTRIP SAMPLE 2  35-38CM.
456      MT OTTO C11300FT Z 15-20CM DISC.LENSES
457      MT OTTO EP-LIKE TEPHRA 43-48CM
```

```
459        MT MICHAEL 3380M 5-7CM DEPTH NODULES OF Z  CFP COLLECTOR
460        MT MICHAEL 3480M SNOWPATCH HOLLOW 17CM NODULES OF Z  CFP COLLECTOR
462        MT OTTO 2  BY HUT 5-6CM Z ASH
464        USA 2 Z DISTURBED
469        SAIDOR 2 SAME AS SAIDOR 1 BUT NOT WASHED
470        SAIDOR 3 COPRA DRYER FLOOR-ACC LAPILLI 9-16CM THICK AT DEPTH 9-16CM
471        MUGIL-KARKAR COAST 16-20 CM
476        WILHELM 2750M KOMANIMAMBURO BOG,PENGAGL VALLEY (SAMPLE 11 OF JMBS)
477        WILHELM 4100M PINDAUNDE VALLEY W OF LAKES (SAMPLE 15 OF JMBS)
478        KUK 75 EW4 STH DRAIN NEAR GUGA Z ASH 1A UPPER

479        KUK 75 E44 STH DRAIN NEAR GUGA Z ASH 1B LOWER
485        KUK 75 EW ROAD 4 STH DRAIN Q ASH 1 -UPPER
489        CFP TAMBUL   ASH KAU 2 (Q)
506        KUK7 75 EW ROAD 4 STH DRAIN Q ASH 1 (LOWER)(SEE 485)
529        WAGE/PAOWII ASH 25CM 4/26/75
531        WABI 1
533        TAMBUL AMBUGA FLAT ASH 2
536        YUMBIS-WAGE Z-1
538        AIYURA-EAST SIDE OF AIRSTRIP 48-57CM
540        GOGOL FLOODPLAIN ASH G1/1 COLLECTOR  CFP 16-21CM IN BACKSWAMP
541        LONG IS. MALASIOLA BARET  MATAPUN  BEDS
542        LONG IS. NORTH JCB BASE MATAPUN   FLOW
543        LONG IS. MATAPUN    ACC. LAPILLI FROM COAST N. OF MATAPUN
544        LONG IS. MALASIOLA BARET  BILIAU BEDS
545        LONG IS. MAROI MAI BILIAU BEADS
546        CROWN IS. C1/2 LOWER UNIT
547        CROWN IS. C1/1 UPPER UNIT WITH ACCRETIONARY LAPILLI
548        LONG IS. MATAPUN 2 FROM MATAPUN NTH.ACC.LAP.IN BEDDED DEPS.4M.A.S.L.
549        LONG IS. SAUKOU VALLEY KIAU BEDS PYROCLASTIC FLOW
550        LONG IS. MALALA JABI GREY FINE ASH BETWEEN 1ST   2ND PALEOSOLS IN
                 BILIAU SEQUENCES
551        CROWN IS. C2/1 MIDDLE LAPILLI UNIT-FOR MAX.PARTICLE SIZE ANALYSIS
552        CROWN IS. C2/2 MUDDY UNIT ABOUT 80CM. BETWEEN THE 2 LAPILLI UNITS.
559        Q OR Z SIRUNKI
572        MADANG KRANKET ISLAND E COAST TOPSOIL
575        BAIYER R 1  19-21CM
576        BAIYER R 2  24-28CM
577        T83A   Z
578        T83A   Q
579        MOGOROFUGA NW KOROBA 4-5CM DOWN 1-4CM THICK
580        TARI GAP  13KM PEG W SIDE  24-26.5CM
581        SNOS CORNER C6KM E OF TARI GAP Z  1-2CM THICK 5-6CM DEPTH IN CLAYEY PE
582        LAIGAM - SIRUNKI
583        NIPA 30-33/34CM  W.SIDE OF AIRSTRIP
584        SIRUNKI X CORE 5  ASH 9-13CM ABOVE MIXED SILT   D.WALKER
587        YANAMUGI YAN MCI 49-51CM (SUSPECTED Z ASH ) S.GARRETT-JONES
588        KONDO Z ASH NR KANDEP INFORMANT PITA TAMBULI
589        KONDO ROAD BARET 60CM DEPTH 3-6CM THICKNESS
```

A=SAMPLE WITH MAGNETIC FRACTION REMOVED

B=VALUES DETERMINED USING COMPTON SCATTER AND LOSS ON IGNITION
    CORRECTION

C=VALUES DETERMINED USING MEASURED MASS ABSORPTION COEFFICIENT AND
    NO LOSS ON IGNITION CORRECTION

D=SINGLE DETERMINATION ONLY-NO DUPLICATE

E=50 PERCENT QUARTZ ADDED TO SINGLE DETERMINATION

G=SAMPLE IGNITED AT 800 DEGREES C, MEASURED MA

H=SAMPLE IGNITED AT 800 DEGREES C, COMPTON SCATTER.

SAMPLE	SR	ZR	RB	Y
SAMPLE	SR	ZR	RB	Y
SAMPLE	SR	ZR	RB	Y
SAMPLE	SR	ZR	RB	Y
SAMPLE	SR	ZR	RB	Y
SAMPLE	SR	ZR	RB	Y

1B	270	85	16	24
2B	257	81	14	29
2C	252	77	15	23
3B	255	74	16	26
4B	286	86	17	30
5B	192	119	10	30
6B	622	62	28	27
6C	608	64	27	23
7B	341	63	21	26
11B	610	59	28	26
11C	653	67	31	25
15B	358	55	22	24
15G	365	49	21	27
17B	202	92	12	25
17C	188	86	13	20
17G	227	97	14	27
18B	302	75	17	27
19B	550	96	30	29
19C	509	69	28	24
20B	382	53	22	24
21B	333	69	19	27
25B	614	69	30	28
25C	562	69	28	23
26B	204	101	11	30
28B	218	124	14	25
29B	302	70	16	28
32B	322	66	18	27
32C	312	65	17	24
33C	314	71	20	24
33C	313	67	19	23
34B	233	62	15	22
38B	592	75	34	32
39C	326	71	19	24
41B	278	75	15	25
43B	325	71	18	26
43C	302	67	18	23
43G	326	60	21	27
45B	580	74	27	27
50B	251	83	14	26
53B	321	78	19	31
55B	226	120	12	29
56B	169	141	10	30
57B	227	105	11	29
58B	182	125	10	29
61B	237	106	13	32
76B	348	70	20	28
79B	649	65	31	27
81B	660	72	30	32
81G	618	59	30	30
85B	567	77	26	32
87B	662	70	39	28
87GD	655	60	37	28
90B	320	82	18	29
92B	137	69	8	21
106B	232	87	13	27
107B	268	74	16	27
110B	268	66	17	21
121B	314	68	20	26
123B	610	62	29	26
124B	392	101	34	25
124C	350	98	30	20
124C	346	99	30	21
127B	310	58	20	27
127GD	333	59	19	30
128B	642	66	31	26
130B	630	62	32	26
131B	334	53	21	26
142B	652	61	27	29
143B	171	126	10	33
146B	334	56	19	26
162B	676	60	34	26
162C	622	65	31	24
164C	672	58	33	27
164GD	655	53	33	26
172B	663	65	32	28

172G	656	59	31	28
177B	152	86	9	14
178B	363	52	24	29
17BC	330	57	22	23
184B	217	68	12	24
242C	564	74	28	22
242C	560	70	27	23
243C	554	75	32	22
243C	548	60	31	21
244C	626	68	31	25
244C	633	71	31	25
245C	511	75	26	23
245C	511	73	25	23
246C	624	66	32	24
247C	514	80	31	25
248C	642	68	31	25
249C	344	53	20	23
250C	565	66	29	22
251C	260	65	17	24
400ADE	645	61	32	11
401AC	563	64	25	24
401G	634	60	31	28
402AC	631	62	29	24
402C	625	66	31	19
403AC	510	99	28	23
403C	519	81	30	20
404AC	239	58	15	26
404C	256	67	18	22
405AC	639	71	33	23
406AC	617	57	29	20
410C	606	68	39	24
410C	591	67	40	22
411DC	247	113	18	39
411DC	249	107	19	35
412CD	347	57	21	24
412DC	349	56	22	21
413CD	131	75	16	33
413DC	136	67	15	30
414DC	60	38	14	23
415CD	487	65	27	25
415DC	484	60	29	23
418C	325	56	19	21
419C	328	67	22	26
420C	644	66	30	23
423C	344	67	20	23
424C	610	73	29	22
425C	321	59	19	22
426C	660	73	31	24
427C	376	51	23	21
428C	665	75	32	26
429C	551	71	27	23
430C	648	63	34	24
431C	602	69	29	22
432C	536	83	26	24
454C	214	133	23	41
455C	241	95	19	27
455G	248	74	19	26
456C	628	56	34	25
456C	618	46	33	23
456C	616	57	33	25
456C	562	70	34	27
457C	314	94	18	26
457C	269	87	16	22
459C	581	77	29	25
459C	604	69	29	24
460C	610	69	31	24
462C	496	83	26	26
462C	487	81	25	27
462G	572	94	29	31
464C	551	68	27	25
464G	599	68	30	27
469G	631	58	28	26
470C	556	54	28	25
471C	695	48	28	26

471C	685	37	29	20
471G	713	57	30	27
476C	578	51	31	23
476G	635	64	35	27
477C	592	52	30	25
478C	609	68	31	28
479C	610	57	32	26
485C	256	64	15	28
489G	201	260	15	35
506C	247	72	15	29
529C	8	178	9	59
529G	12	268	6	93
531C	22	133	5	17
533C	443	78	29	32
533G	353	54	22	27
536G	505	274	30	40
538C	255	199	9	48
540C	624	68	25	27
540G	663	55	29	29
541C	650	76	34	29
541G	651	57	33	31
542C	653	66	25	25
542C	629	73	37	28
543C	641	73	30	28
543G	655	46	32	30
544C	587	74	41	28
545G	612	48	36	29
546C	626	55	20	20
546G	624	31	20	21
546G	633	32	22	20
547C	616	70	29	26
547G	644	46	30	28
548C	616	80	32	28
549C	582	68	31	27
549G	596	57	31	29
550C	577	63	24	24
551C	616	52	22	19
551GD	616	31	21	21
552C	623	71	32	26
552G	652	52	31	30
559GD	389	172	20	40
572G	618	59	24	33
575H	80	314	24	29
576H	104	299	29	29
576H	104	303	29	30
577H	675	57	36	28
578H	373	59	26	27
579H	613	64	35	28
580H	622	105	36	26
581H	616	63	36	26
582H	158	184	18	35
583H	596	73	33	31
584H	643	122	64	23
587H	661	51	34	25
588H	621	62	40	26
589H	335	58	29	28

Appendix 2
**Analysis of factors influencing the spread of values in samples field
identified as Olgaboli Tephra**

Contents

Figures

Tables

2.0 Introduction

Three factors are considered:

1. Particle size variations
2. Loss on ignition content variations
3. Presence of more than one tephra.

Values of Rb and Sr for field identified samples of Olgaboli Tephra from the Upper Wahgi Valley vary from 8 to 22 (Rb) and from 137 to 382 (Sr). The range of values for Zr is 53 to 125 while Y ranges from 14 to 32 ppm.

2.1   Particle size variations
A first approximation would suggest that:

    Sr occurs principally in plagioclase and glass;

    Rb in K-feldspar, glass and biotite;

    Y in clinopyroxene; and

    Zr in zircons and in biotite (as small inclusions).

With density sorting of the ash during airfall various distributions can be expected — basically lightest particles go furthest. This is essentially irrelevant in the present situation as most samples considered come from the small area of the Upper Wahgi Valley. However, winnowing of fines by water action influences concentration of each particle size in a sample. It is this variation which is considered here.

Table 2.1 lists mean settling velocity for twelve samples of Olgaboli

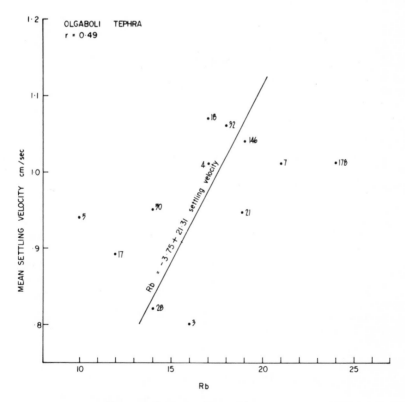

Fig. 2.1   Mean settling velocity versus Rb

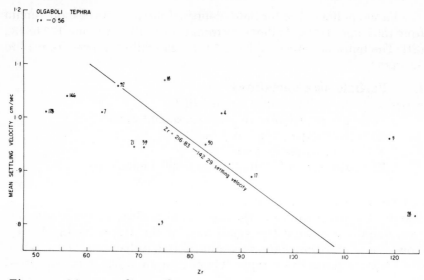

Fig. 2.2   Mean settling velocity versus Zr

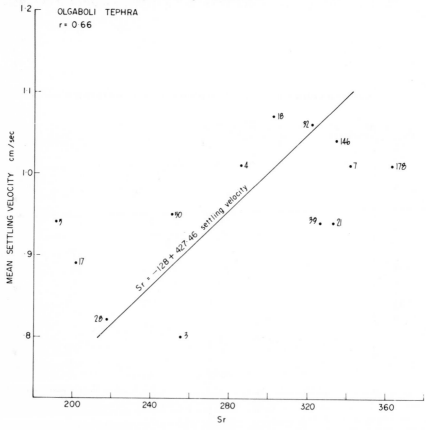

Fig. 2.3   Mean settling velocity versus Sr

Tephra from the Upper Wahgi Valley, together with trace element concentrations determined using the one analytical method. Values of mean settling velocity are plotted against Rb (Fig. 2.1), Zr (Fig. 2.2) and Sr (Fig. 2.3). Sample numbers refer to Appendix 1.

Figure 2.1 indicates a tendency for Rb to increase with increasing mean settling velocity. The correlation coefficient $r = 0.49$. For Zr, $r = -0.56$ and for Sr, $r = 0.66$.

These trends are perhaps in accord with the data plotted in Fig. 9, where known, coarse, dark-coloured samples such as 20, 146 and 7 certainly plot at the high end of the Olgaboli Tephra ellipse. Furthermore, the data listed in Table 2.3 (see below) are listed in approximate decreasing order of Sr and Rb values, and show that Zr is concentrated in those samples with rather lower Sr and Rb values. If all the variations in the data were explainable in terms of particle size variations, then lower mean settling velocities should be associated with increasing Zr contents. This is clearly the case as $r = -0.56$, but as $r^2 = 0.31$ some 70 per cent of the variance is unaccounted for and other factors must also pertain.

Table 2.2 provides a little more information using two paired samples* (one of Tibito Tephra). Values for Sr, Rb and Y show no or little variation from coarse to fine while the trend in Zr values is contrary for the two samples.

Table 2.1
Settling velocities and trace element concentrations —
Olgaboli Tephra, Upper Wahgi samples

Sample No.	Mean settling velocity cm/sec	Sr	Zr	Rb	Y
5B	.940	192	119	10	30
17B	.893	202	92	12	25
50B	.954	251	83	14	26
18B	1.073	302	75	17	27
178B	1.011	363	52	24	23
4B	1.008	286	86	17	30
28B	.818	218	124	14	25
3B	.797	255	74	16	26
21B	.944	333	69	19	27
7B	1.012	341	63	21	25
32B	1.059	322	66	18	27
146B	1.037	334	56	19	26

2.2   Loss on ignition variations

From Table 2.3 it appears that samples with low Sr and Rb values tend to have higher loss on ignition values than those which plot at the

*In each case the sample has been divided in the field into a coarse basal layer and an upper finer layer.

Table 2.2
Trace element concentrations in coarse and fine fractions of tephra

		Sample No.	Sr	Zr	Rb	Y
Olgaboli	— fine fraction	485C	256	64	15	28
	coarse fraction	506C	247	72	15	29
Tibito	— fine fraction	478C	609	68	31	28
	coarse fraction	479C	610	57	32	26

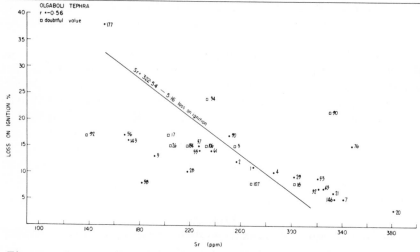

Fig. 2.4   *Loss on ignition values versus Sr*

higher end of the ellipse (Fig. 9). This is shown also on Fig. 2.4, while Fig. 2.5 illustrates the relationship between Zr and loss on ignition values. Though there is a scatter of points, note that there is a definite trend of values with increasing Zr with increasing loss on ignition (r = 0.17).

This trend is the opposite to that which could be expected if the variation in Zr values was due to a straight mass absorption factor, or in fact from errors (overestimates) of loss on ignition.

The loss on ignition would seem to have two components: (a) absorbed water which can be driven off at high (105°C) temperatures and (b) organic matter content which can be ashed at high (>500°C) temperatures, driving off the volatile component but leaving any mineral material concentrated in the ash residue.

It is fair to conclude that samples with high ignition loss were those with either (a) high clay contents and hence much absorbed water or (b) those with much included organic material. As geomorphic processes at the Kuk prehistoric site would be more likely to winnow than to concentrate clays within the tephra samples the second explanation would seem more likely, though it should be noted that the crushing of samples prior to the manufacture of pressed pellets creates

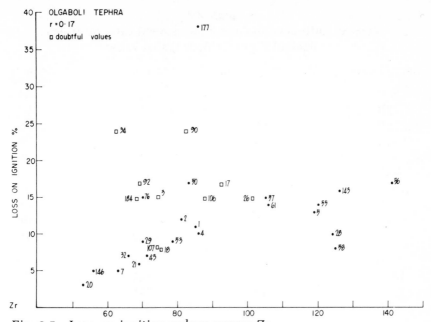

Fig. 2.5   *Loss on ignition values versus* Zr
large surface areas available for water absorption.*

If in fact high Zr values result from the presence of large amounts of
organic material in the sample, the question arises, how?

Analyses of some environmental materials from the Kuk swamp as
presented in Table 2.4 provide some clues.

That the losses on ignition for samples 168 and 169 might be
seriously in error does not matter unduly; these two highly organic
samples are clearly low in Zr. Even if Zr values for sample 169 were
multiplied by 2.5 and for sample 168 by 4 (to give ignition losses of 100
per cent), Zr values would still only be equal to mean values for
Olgaboli Tephra.

It is clear that if high Zr values for some Olgaboli Tephra samples
have derived via contamination, then it is not contamination, by organic
residues but by other sediments derived from older tephra (samples
170, 512, 521, represent the Highlands Tephra >50,000 years in age —
see Pain and Blong, 1976), their redeposited derivatives (K139/6 — grey
clay sample 175), or reworked garden material (K117/1, sample 237),
the mineral component of which must ultimately have been derived
from the older Highlands Tephra. However, contamination by
Highlands Tephra such as samples 512 and 521 would also increase the
Sr content of Olgaboli Tephra. On the other hand admixture with either
baret fill material (237) and/or grey clay (175) and some organic
material could increase the Zr values and dilute Sr and Rb values at the
same time.

*This effect can be avoided by keeping samples in airtight containers and
desiccating jars.

Table 2.3
Loss on ignition values and trace element concentrations
Olgaboli Tephra, Upper Wahgi Valley

Sample No.	Loss on ignition %	Sr(ppm)	Zr(ppm)
20B	3	382	54
7B	5	341	63
76B*	15	348	70
53B	9	321	78
21B	6	333	69
43B	7	302	71
90B*	24	320	82
32B	7	322	66
4B	10	286	86
18B*	8	302	75
29B	9	302	70
107B*	8	268	74
1B	11	270	85
3B*	15	255	74
34B*	24	233	62
2B	12	257	81
50B	17	251	83
28B	10	218	124
61B	14	237	106
106B*	15	232	87
17B*	17	202	92
184B*	15	217	68
55B	14	228	120
57B	15	227	106
26B*	15	204	100
5B	13	192	119
58B	8	182	125
56B	17	169	141
143B	16	171	126
177B	38	152	86
92B*	17	137	69

For example, if we take sample 418, the basal 4 cm of a thick Olgaboli Tephra from the little disturbed Mt Ambra environment, as type Olgaboli Tephra and dilute this sample so that its composition is
    50% Olgaboli Tephra
    20% baret fill (sample 237)
    30% grey clay (sample 175)
a new composite sample would have values as set out in Table 2.5.

*Samples on which loss values could be for duplicate analyses.

Table 2.4
Trace element concentrations for various materials
at Kuk prehistoric site

Sample No.		Sr ppm	Zr ppm	Rb ppm	Y ppm	Loss on ignition %
237	K117/1 (single analysis baret fill only)	230	111	8	24	loss estimated 25
175	K139/6 centre of grey clay	172	134	6	47	21
168	wood (K139/2)	111	14	0	6	loss estimated 25
169	K139/1 brown peat with grey-brown tephra (black organic clay)	77	21	1	6	loss estimated 40
170	K138/4 (top of tephra column)	280	253	11	12	14
512	T75 WST 6 (tephra)	611	176	17	18	<5%
521	T71 Tomba 1 (tephra)	916	225	18	22	<5%

Table 2.5
Trace element concentrations for a composite sample

418	Sr	Zr	Rb	Y
	325	56	19	21
50% of 418	162	23	8.5	10.5
30% of 175	57	45	2	16
20% of 237	46	22	1.6	5
100%	265	90	13	31

Such a composite sample differs but little from many of the lower value Olgaboli Tephra samples plotted in Fig. 10.

Unfortunately there is little that can be done to avoid this sort of sample contamination. Careful collection of samples in the field is necessary; diligent removal of obvious organic contaminants is also required.

2.3   **Presence of more than one tephra**

Figure 10 lends no support to the possibility that more than one tephra is present within the ellipse of Olgaboli Tephra. However, Fig. 2.6, a frequency diagram for Zr values of putative Olgaboli samples, indicates a polymodal distribution.

Similarly, as shown on Fig. 2.7 (Sr-Zr plot for Tibito and Olgaboli Tephras), Olgaboli appears to be composed of two subsets; there is a

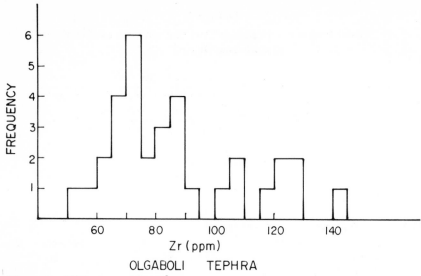

OLGABOLI   TEPHRA

Fig. 2.6   Histogram–Zr values

particularly clear dividing line if sample 106 (which may have an incorrect loss on ignition value) is ignored. Furthermore the Sr/Zr plot against altitude and sample environment (Fig. 2.8), particularly at the 1500m (5000 ft) level shows a similar gap (again with sample 106 in the middle). The samples that plot to the left of the gap in Fig. 2.8 also plot high (as expected) on Fig. 2.6 and are listed low in Table 2.2. Fig. 2.9 illustrates a similar division. While there is some virtue in regarding these samples (Nos. 56, 143, 58, 28, 177, 92, 55, 26, 17, 57, 61 and 5) as representative of a separate tephra, there is no conclusive evidence to support such a view.

If in fact Olgaboli Tephra is really two separate tephras, the two tephras must have been closely spaced in time as no stratigraphic distinction has been recognised in the intensive investigations at the Kuk prehistoric site. Samples from Block A9E at Kuk, a small area only 220 x 250 m, occur in both groups, and in fact samples from each group alternate along barets A9E and A9b/c. Even if two tephras were closely tied in time there should still be stratigraphic differences observable at the Kuk prehistoric site. A gap of tens of years (or even years?) would allow continued baret infilling, renewed gardening activity, further sedimentation and so on. No such differences have been recognised, or where they have been, they are not consistent with or related to the possible groupings noted here.

2.4   **Summary**

Particle size variations do influence trace element concentrations and it seems certain that varying admixtures of organic material and stratigraphically adjacent layers also influence element concentrations. On the other hand more than one tephra layer could be included in the sample although this seems very unlikely given the intensity of field

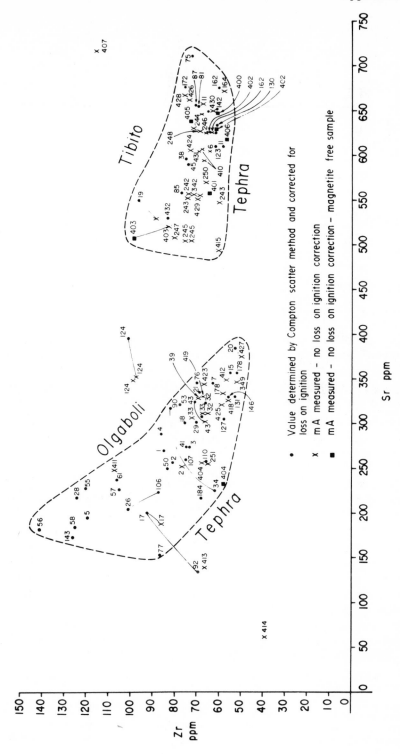

Fig. 2.7   Sr versus Zr–Olgaboli and Tibito Tephra

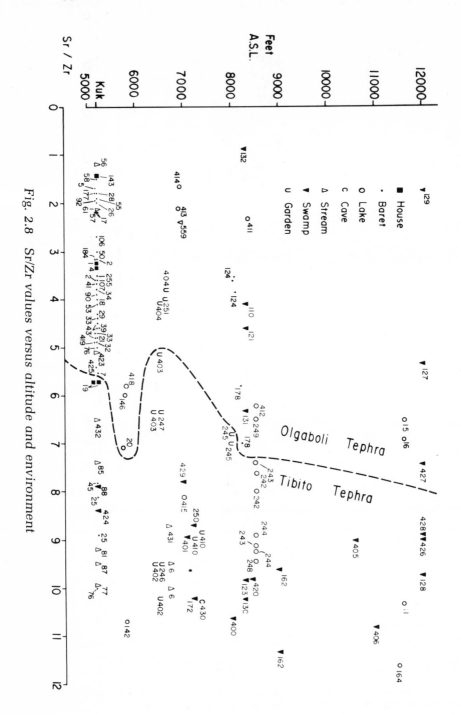

Fig. 2.8   Sr/Zr values versus altitude and environment

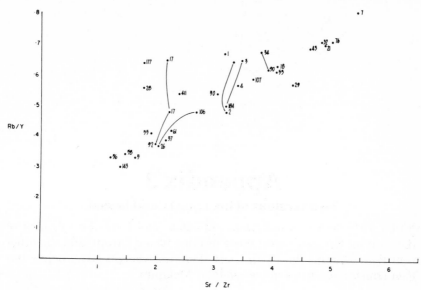

Fig. 2.9   *Rb/y versus Sr/Zr*
investigation at the Kuk site.

The samples included within the Olgaboli Tephra ellipse on Fig.
2.9 are regarded as belonging to the one tephra.

Appendix 3
Two versions of the Long Island legend

During 1976 two versions were collected; one from the villagers of Matapun on the south-west coast of Long Island (Arop), and the other from Poin Kiau on the north coast. The first version given below has been constructed from notes made at Matapun.

The people came to Arop from West New Britain. They sailed to Bara Point (near Bok). Some people also came here to trade pigs for the obsidian they brought. More people lived at Matapun then than today.

Iramo, the leader, came to steal women. He was going to kill them but they speared him through the head and put a tanket through the hole from one side to the other. The wound did not kill Iramo and he took his friends and left the island saying that he would be back and that the people of Arop had better kill their pigs and take their food and enjoy themselves before he returned.

Straight away big tidal waves came and the slopes collapsed. There were continuous earthquakes and a big rain — many mosquitoes came afterwards and then a bush fire burnt the houses. All of the houses and all the bush were burnt. No one knows how the fire started, but it wasn't fire from the mountain. The people didn't go away. Malala and Bok, as well as Matapun, were wiped out by the fire. There the people stayed away for three days.

Two men came in a canoe, we don't know where from. They found everybody dead at Malala and everywhere else. The people were dead but their hearts were still beating. [One old woman thinks the fire was accompanied by ash but others say the ash came later.] The two men called on the mountain to cover all the bodies up, then the two men went back to wherever they came from.

Before the eruption there was a big mountain where the lake is now. The mountain was much bigger than Cerisy and Reaumur. We don't know whether it was dark or not on Arop or Tolokiwa when the eruption occurred. And we don't know how long the eruption lasted [in answer to question].

Bodies were buried, houses were buried, coconuts were buried by the ash. The island was smaller before the eruption — like Tolokiwa. The erupted material went in all directions. All the animals and birds were killed by the fire; by the fire not by the eruption.

Koromi came to Arop from Tolokiwa. When he came steam was still coming from the ground. His fire went out. The first village was Malala. Vegetation started to come up but all the trees were stunted; the trees, not the grass.

After Koromi there were at least two generations before the *lapun's* [old man's] father was born. There was Koromi then the *lapun's* grandmother.

After the eruption there was no water in the lake. Water comes up in the wet season and covers the place where the boat is now. When the *lapun* was a boy, the lake level was the same as now. A tidal wave only occurred once (?).

Motmot Island wasn't there when the *lapun* was a boy, or when his sons were boys. When the war was on there was no island — just a reef. There was lots of smoke; black, white and red.

The gardens are just the same now as they were before the big eruption.

Ash fell on Tolokiwa during the big eruption but it didn't break down houses or destroy gardens. The skin of the people turned black because of the dust. Stones fell too. It was a white dust, and it happened only once.

The second version, collected at Poin Kiau, is similar in many respects. It was told by Koio, an old man, and translated into Neo-Melanesian Pidgin by the captain of the MV *Berana*, an Arop Islander from Poin Kiau. The reconstruction made here is based on notes.

Iramo (or Dramo) came in his canoe. Talmai from Arop was sleeping in his house. The canoe came close and the people got ready to kill Iramo with bows and arrows. He goes along the beach and they spear him through the brow. They put a tanket in the hole but he doesn't die. Iramo tells Talmai to kill his pigs and to sleep. Iramo is going and he will come back. Rain, wind and earthquakes are coming to kill the people on Arop. It didn't worry the people on Arop but then a high water came. It was a very big high water; only one.

Iramo went to get his father. The two come back together to work magic. There is a fire on the mountain Cerisy. The fire comes down below to the beach. The two sailed around the island. The father was sleeping and the son forgot to wake him up when fire got to a certain point so that the father could stop the fire. Only Malala, Bok and Matapun were supposed to be burnt but the fire burnt everybody. Iramo and his father sailed away — we don't know where to. They came back in three days to wake the people up but all the people are dead. They are rotten on the side down on the ground. They call on the ground to cover up the bodies. The ground fell from the sky, not from the mountain. There was very much ground, the same as we see today in the cliffs [i.e. Matapun beds]. Before the earth fell from the sky, the ground was red brown. There are trees and bones down below. The ground that fell from the sky was dark. The island has no men now.

Then people came from Tolokiwa. Koromi came. There was still smoke coming from the fire at this time on the beach and on the mountain — from everywhere. No grass had come up yet. Made a fire by getting bits of wood from the canoe and putting them in the ground to cook food. They jumped in canoe and went around the island. There was nobody on Crown Island either. They came back and then went to Tolokiwa. They brought everything to Arop to build houses. They went to Malala to live with their wives and children . . .

In answer to questions Koio said that people had lived on Crown Island before the eruption. When the fire came people went to the mainland and to Karkar Island. No ground fell at Crown Island but heat from the fire killed gardens and burnt the houses. This was true of the whole Crown Island not just the side near Arop. Nobody went back to Crown Island — they don't know why.

On Long Island a strong wind came with the fire.

Our informants did not know whether there was a lake or not before the eruption. When the people went hunting after the eruption, when the whole place was covered with thick bush, they found the lake. It was the same amount of water now as when Koio was a boy. Before the lake there were two mountains between Cerisy and Reaumur. Koio said there were two mountains before the fire and that the two mountains disappeared in the fire.

'When ground fell from the sky it didn't fall on Tolokiwa or the mainland or on Crown Island.'

Appendix 4

Questionnaire distributed in 1976-77

QUESTIONNAIRE

1. Name:

2. Address:

3. Organisation/Affiliation:

4. Distance and direction from nearest town or patrol post:

5. Number of years you have lived in this area:

6. Name of local language:

7. Did you question informants in local language or in pidgin?:

(Where applicable encircle responses or cross out incorrect answers.)

8. Do the local people have a story about a 'time of darkness'?
   Yes / Not to my knowledge / No

9. Is the story widespread / known to only a few people?

10. Is the story an important one from local people's point of view?
    Yes / No

11. Had you heard the story before the arrival of this Questionnaire?
    Yes / No
    If yes, how long ago?

12. How many hours or days did darkness last?

13. Describe the quality of the darkness, preferably in local people's words (e.g., like a night with no moon, or couldn't see hand at

arm's length).

14.   Did the people see the darkness approaching? Yes / No
If yes, from which direction (e.g. north, south-east, etc.):

15.   Was it daytime or night-time when 'darkness' first fell?

16.   Were any preparations made before 'darkness' arrived?

17.   Was the darkness preceded by a noise? Yes / No
                                by a wind? Yes / No
If yes to either questions, please describe.

18.   Was it raining at time 'darkness' fell? Yes / No

19.   Did ash (or sand, or broken-up-sky) fall during the time of
'darkness'? Yes / No
If yes, describe (e.g. sand, clay, mud?)
                colour: green, white, brown, other?
How thick did this material lie on the ground?
                        (in inches or cm)

20.   Did people stay inside houses during time of
darkness? Yes / No

21.   Did anyone go outside? Yes / No
If yes, describe relationship to head of house and indicate
reasons for leaving house.

22.   Did people perform any ceremony to bring about end of
darkness? Yes / No
If so, describe.

23.   What effects did the darkness have on the houses? Did any
houses collapse? If yes, why?

24.   What effects did darkness have on trees? (If necessary, use
local language names for specific trees or plants.)

25.   What effects did darkness have on crops? (Specify which
crops and what effects.)

26.   What effects did darkness have on animals? (Ask about
specific animals if necessary — e.g. pigs, cuscus, etc.)

27.   What effects did darkness have on birds? (Specify which

birds, using local language names if necessary. Ask about
muruk (cassowary).)

28.   What effects did darkness have on gardens? (Differentiate, if
      possible, between short-term and long-term effects. Also
      differentiate, if possible, between gardens on steep slopes and
      gardens on gentle slopes.)

29.   In general, do people believe that time of darkness was
      beneficial or harmful?

30.   Did darkness affect drinking water or streams in general?
      Yes / No   If yes, state how.

31.   Did people die during darkness? Yes / No
      If yes, how?

32.   Did people die after the darkness? Yes / No
      If yes, how?

33.   Were people forced to migrate because of darkness?
      Yes / No
      If yes, why exactly? (e.g., famine?)

34.   Was it hot or cold or just the same as usual when darkness fell?

35.   Was there a terrible smell during darkness? Yes / No
      If yes, describe it.

36.   Were optical effects such as brilliant sunsets or blue moons
      observed after darkness? Yes / No
      If yes, state effects.

37.   When did time of darkness occur? (i.e. How many generations
      ago?)

38.   Do local people associate other events with arrival of time of
      darkness (in the sense that they occurred at about the same
      time)? (e.g., arrival of sweet potato, arrival of other plants (or
      animals?), arrival of malaria, etc.)

39.   Do people live in same place now as they did when time of
      darkness fell? Yes / No

40.   Can anyone still identify the stuff that fell from the sky?
      Yes / No

If yes, please collect a sample in a plastic bag (about ½ lb/ 200 gm weight) and mail or airfreight it to me at this address:

C/- Dr C. F. Pain,
Department of Geography,
University of Papua New Guinea,
Box 4820, University PO,
Papua New Guinea.

Please make sure that sender's name is clearly labelled on sample.

I will reimburse any costs.

41.   Has darkness occurred more than once?   Yes / No
If yes, how many times?
Was it the same each time?

42.   Do local people expect time of darkness to occur again?
Yes / No
What will they do if it does?

Any comments you have to make on the following would be of major assistance to me:

.......Do you think the story has been embellished by religious teachings or other additions?

.......Do the local people have numerous stories about the sun, the sky, the stars, the moon, etc., or do they generally appear fairly uninterested in the heavens?

.......If local people live on or near the coast, are there associated/related stories about explosions, tidal waves, land rising or sinking, etc.?

Glossary of Volcanic Terms

Some of the definitions included here have been taken from the *Dictionary of Geological Terms*, American Geological Institute, Dolphin Books, and Bullard, F. M., *Volcanoes of the Earth*, University of Texas, Austin.

acidic: a descriptive term applied to those igneous rocks which contain more than 66 per cent SiO_2, as contrasted with intermediate and basic rocks.

accretionary lapilli: spherical bodies greater than about 4 mm in diameter formed by the accretion of concentric layers of tephra when rain falls through a tephra cloud.

allophane: an amorphous hydrated gel of variable composition; a frequent early breakdown product of the weathering of volcanic glass.

andesite: a lava of intermediate composition, usually light grey in colour; SiO_2 content 52-53 per cent to 66 per cent.

ash flow: See nuée ardente, pyroclastic flow.

basalt: a dark-coloured, usually fine-grained lava, of basic composition; SiO_2 content <52-53 per cent.

basic: descriptive term for those igneous rocks that generally have less than 52-53 per cent SiO_2.

caldera: a large, more or less circular, depression formed by volcanic explosion or collapse.

co-ignimbrite airfall tephra: the upper dilute part of a pyroclastic flow formed from column collapse which becomes disassociated during the emplacement of the ignimbrite forming a fine tephra layer depleted in crystals; the layer is usually thin and well-bedded. See ignimbrite.

colluvial: refers to deposits produced by the downslope movement of rock and soil debris.

crater: a steep-sided conical depression formed by an eruption.

dacite: the extrusive equivalent of a rock intermediate in composition between a rhyolite and an andesite.

fumarole: a vent from which fumes or vapours issue.

ignimbrite: flow deposits laid down by hot to incandescent clouds of gas and pyroclastic material; deposits resulting from flows formed from the collapse of an eruption column.

intermediate lava: a lava containing between 52-53 and 66 per cent SiO_2.

isopach: a line on a map, drawn through points of equal tephra thickness.

K-Ar ages: radioactive age based on the determination of the potassium 40 -argon 40 ratio.

lahar: a flow of water-saturated volcanic debris down the slope of a volcano; a mudflow; a type of landslide.

lapilli: volcanic ejecta or tephra ranging in size from about 4 to 32 mm.

lithic: refers to sediments composed predominantly of rock fragments rather than crystals or pumice.

maar: a relatively shallow, flat-floored crater formed by violent explosion; commonly occupied by a circular lake.

nuée ardente: a highly heated, incandescent mass of gas and pyroclastic material which flows down the slopes of a volcano following eruption column collapse. Temperatures may reach 600°C or more while velocities may exceed 200 km/hr. The deposit resulting from a nuée is called an ignimbrite.

paleosol: a buried soil; in this case, buried by further tephra falls or pyroclastic flows.

palynology: study of pollen and other spores and their dispersal.

parasitic cone: a volcanic vent developed on the flank of a larger volcano.

Peléan: an eruption style of extreme violence typified by the 1902 eruption of Mt Pelée on Martinique; results from eruption column collapse. Characterised by hot pyroclastic flows (nuées ardentes) and the deposition of ignimbrites.

phreatic explosion: an explosion caused by the conversion of ground water to steam, resulting from the mixing of volcanic gases or magma with ground water.

Plinian: an eruption style characterised by the production of a strong eruption column as in the AD 79 eruption of Vesuvius described by Pliny the Younger. Upward momentum of the eruption cloud results initially from the gas thrust phase and subsequently from the convective thrust phase. Column height may reach 50 km in exceptionally strong eruptions.

pumice: a highly vesicular, frothy natural glass, frequently with a high silica content; normally light in colour, pumice will float on water.

pyroclastic: a general term applied to detrital volcanic materials that have been explosively ejected from a volcanic vent.

scoria: slaggy volcanic debris usually of basic composition.

solfatara: a volcanic vent from which only sulphurous gases and aqueous vapours are emitted; frequently indicative of the last phases of volcanic activity.

stratovolcano: a volcanic cone, usually of large size, built of alternating layers of lava and pyroclastic materials.

subduction zone: the zone, according to plate tectonic theory, where the crustal layer descends into the mantle.

tephra: a collective term for all airborne pyroclastic material. Includes both airfall and flow pyroclastic material but frequently used to indicate only airfall pyroclastics.

tephrochronology: a chronology based on the measurement, connection and dating of tephra layers. In particular, tephrochronology is concerned with the establishment of a chronosequence of geological events based on the unique characteristics of tephra layers.

tephrostratigraphy: interpretation of the sucession of deposits based on the recognition of tephra layers.

tsunami: a sea wave produced by a submarine earthquake or volcanic eruption; often improperly called a tidal wave.

tuff: a rock composed of compacted volcanic fragments, generally smaller than about 4 mm in diameter; compacted tephra.

volcanic ash; See tephra.

volcanic mudflow: See lahar.

References

Anderson, T. and Flett, J.S., 1903, Report on the eruptions of the Soufriere in St. Vincent, and on a visit to Montagne Pelee in Martinique. Pt I. Roy. Soc. Lond. Phil. Trans., A 200, 353-553.

Anderson, T. and Bonney, T.G., 1917, Volcanic studies in many lands, vol. 2, John Murray, London.

Anon, 1816, Miscellaneous observations on the volcanic eruptions at the island of Java and Sumbawa, with a particular account of the mud volcano at Grobogar, Quart. Jnl Sci. Arts, 1, 245-58.

Appleby, P.G. and Oldfield, F., 1978, The calcuation of lead-210 dates assuming a constant rate of supply of unsupported ^{210}Pb to the sediment, Catena, 5, 1-8.

Aramaki, S., 1956, The 1783 activity of Asama volcano, Pt I, Jap. Jnl Geol. & Geogr., 27, 189-229.

Ball, E.E., 1981, Annotated bibliography of references relating to Long Island, PNG, Record of the Australian Museum, 34.

Ball, E.E. and Glucksman, J., 1975, Biological colonization of Motmot, a recently-created tropical island, Proc. Roy. Soc. London, B, 190, pp.421-42.

Ball, E.E. and Hughes, I.M., 1981, Long Island PNG — People, resources and culture, Record of the Australian Museum. 34.

Ball, E.E. and Johnson, R.W., 1976, Volcanic history of Long Island, Papua New Guinea, in Johnson, R.W. (ed.), Volcanism in Australia, Elsevier, Amsterdam, 133-47.

Ball, R.S., 1906, In starry realms, Pitman, London, 371p.

Barth, F., 1975, Ritual knowledge amongst the Baktaman of New Guinea, Yale U.P., New Haven, Conn. 291p.

Blake, D.H. and Löffler, E., 1971, Volcanic and glacial landforms on Mt. Giluwe, Territory of Papua and New Guinea, Bull. Geol. Soc. Am., 82, 1605-14.

Blong, R.J., 1975, The Krakatoa myth and the New Guinea Highlands, J. Poly. Soc., 84(2), 213-17.

Blong, R.J. 1979a, Huli legends and volcanic eruptions, Papua New Guinea, Search, 10(3), 93-4.

Blong, R.J. (ed), 1979b, Time of darkness legends from Papua New Guinea, Oral History, 7(10). 1-135.

Blong, R.J. (in press), Tephra fall-out from Karkar volcano, Papua New Guinea; a first approximation of volcanological papers (ed. R.W. Johnson), 85-93. Cooke-Ravian Memorial Volume, PNG Geological Surv. Memoirs 10.

Blong, R.J. (in press), Tephra eruptions and human activity, in J. Green (ed.) Encyclopedia of Volcanology, Hutchinson Ross, Stroudsburg, Penn. 34.

Blong, R.J., Pain, C.F. and McKee, C.O., 1981, Long Island, Papua New Guinea — aspects of the landforms and tephrostratigraphy, Record of the Australian Museum, 34.

Bolt, B.A., 1976, Nuclear explosions and earthquakes, the parted veil,

Freeman, San Francisco, 309p.

Bolt, B.A., Horn, W.L., Macdonald, G.A. and Scott, R.F., 1975, *Geological hazards*, Springer-Verlag, New York, 328p.

Bond, A. and Sparks, R.S.J., 1976, The Minoan eruption of Santorini, Greece, *Jnl Geol. Soc. London*, **132**, 1-16.

Borchardt, G.A. and Harward, M.E., 1971, Trace element correlation of volcanic ash soils, *Proc. Soil Sci. Soc. Am.*, **35**, 626-31.

Branch, C.D., 1967, Volcanic activity at Mount Yelia, New Guinea, in Short papers from the Volcanological Observatory, Rabaul, New Britain, *Bur. Min. Res. Aust. Rep.*, **107**, 35-9.

Brookfield, H.C., 1961, The Highlands people of New Guinea, *Geog. Jnl*, **127**, 436-8.

Brookfield, H.C. and Hart, D., 1971, *Melanesia, a geographical interpretation of an island world*, London, Methuen.

Brooks, R.R., 1972, *Geobotany and biogeochemistry in mineral exploration*, Harper & Row, New York, 290p.

Brown, W.H., Merrill, E.D. and Yates, H.S., 1917, The revegetation of Volcano Island, Luzon, Philippine Islands, since the eruption of Taal Volcano in 1911, *Philip. Jnl Sci.*, 12C(4), 177-248.

Bullard, F.M., 1976, *Volcanoes of the earth*, University of Texas Press, Austin, 579p.

Caldcleugh, A., 1836, Some account of the volcanic eruption of Coseguina, in the Bay of Fonseca, on the western coast of Central America, *Phil. Trans.*, **1**, 27-30.

Cann, J.R., 1970, Rb, Sr, Y, Zr and Nb in some ocean floor basalt rocks, *Earth Planet. Sci. Letters*, **10**, 7-11.

Carey, S.W., 1938, The morphology of New Guinea, *Aust. Geogr.* **3**, 3-31.

Cilento, R., 1937, The volcanic eruption in Blanche Bay, Territory of New Guinea, May, 1937, *Hist. Soc. Qld Jnl*, **3**, 37-49.

Clark, R.M., 1975, A calibration curve for radiocarbon dates, *Antiquity*, **49**, 251-65.

Coleman, S.N., 1949, *Volcanoes, new and old*, Museum Press, London, 212p.

Cooke, R.J.S. and Johnson, R.W., 1978, Volcanoes and volcanology in Papua New Guinea, *PNG Geol. Survey Rept*, 78/2, 49p.

Curtis, G.H., 1968, The stratigraphy of the ejecta from the 1912 eruption of Mount Katmai and Novarupta, Alaska, *Geol. Soc. Am. Memoir*, **116**, 153-210.

Damon, P.E., Long, A. and Wallick, I.E., 1972, Dendrochronologic calibration of the carbon-14 time scale, *Proc. 8th Int. Conf. Radio Carbon dating*, Wellington, NZ, October 1972, A28-A43.

Day, A.L., and Allen, E.T., 1925, The volcanic activity and hot springs of Lassen Peak, *Carnegie Inst. Wash. Publ.*, No. 360, 190p.

de Lorenzo, G., 1906, The eruption of Vesuvius in April 1906, *Quat. Jnl Geol. Soc. London*, **67**, 476-83.

Delmé-Radcliffe, C., 1906, Report by Lt.-Col. Delmé-Radcliffe on conditions following the eruption of Vesuvius in 1906, HMSO, London, 9p.

Denham, D., 1969, Distribution of earthquakes in the New Guinea-Solomon Islands region, *J. Geophys. Res.*, **74**, 4290.

Docters von Leeuwen, W.M., 1936, Krakatau 1883-1933, *Annales du Jardin Botanique de Buitenzorg*, 46-7, E.J. Brill, Leiden, 506p.

Dorson, R.M., 1973, Sources for the traditional history of Scottish Highlands and western islands, in R.M. Dorson (ed.), *Folklore and traditional history*, Mouton, The Hague, 75-112.

Duncan, A.R. and Vucetich, C.G., 1970, Volcanic activity on White Island, Bay of Plenty, 1966-69, Part 2 — Tephra eruptions — stratigraphy and petrography, *N.Z. Jnl Geol. & Geophys.*, **13**, 969-79.

du Toit, B.M., 1969, Misconstruction and problems in communication, *Am. Anthropologist*, **71**, 46-53.

Eggler, W.A., 1948, Plant communities in the vicinity of the volcano el Paricutin, Mexico, after two and a half years of eruption, *Ecology*, **29**, 415-36.

Eggler, W.A., 1963, Plant life of Paricutin volcano, Mexico, eight years after activity ceased, *Am. Midl. Nat.*, **69**(1), 38-68.

Erskine, H.D., 1940, Katmai's black out, *Alaska Sportsman*, 16-17, 22.

Erskine, W.F., 1962, *Katmai*, Abelard-Schuman, London, 223p.

Faustino, L.A., 1929, Mayon volcano and its eruption, *Phil. Jnl Sci.*, **40**(1), 1-43.

Fieldes, M. and Perrott, K.W., 1966, The nature of allophane in soils, Part 3. Rapid field and laboratory test for allophane, *NZ Jnl Sci.*, **9**, 623-9.

Fisher, N.H., 1957, Catalogue of the active volcanoes of the world, including solfatara fields — Pt V, Melanesia, *Int. Volc. Assoc. Naples.*

Francis, P., 1976, *Volcanoes*, Penguin, London, 368p.

Furneaux, R., 1965, *Krakatoa*, Secker and Warburg, London.

Galanopoulos, A.G. and Bacon, E., 1969, *Atlantis; the truth behind the legend*, Bobbs-Merrill, New York, 216p.

Gates, F.C., 1914, The pioneer vegetation of Taal volcano, *Philip. Jnl Sci.*, **9C**(5), 391-434.

Gehberger, J., 1938 and 1940, *The myths of the Samap* translated from German by J.T. Tschauder and P. Swadling, Inst. PNG Studies, 1977.

Giddings, R.J., 1966, When snow fell in the Goroka Valley, *Pacific Islands Monthly*, **37**, 85-7.

Glasse, R.M., 1963, Bingi at Tari, *J. Poly. Soc.*, **72**, 270-1.

Glasse, R.M., 1965, The Huli of the Southern Highlands, in P. Lawrence and M.J. Meggitt (eds.), *Gods, ghosts and men in Melanesia*, OUP, Melbourne, 27-49.

Glasse, R.M., 1973, Volcanoes and virtue, an ecological interpretation of sex ambivalence in New Guinea, 72nd Ann. Meeting Am. Anthropological Assn, New Orleans, 11p.

Goldstein, K.S., 1964, A guide for field workers in folklore, *Memoirs of Am. Folklore Soc.*, **52**, 199p.

Golson, J., 1977, No room at the top: agricultural intensification in the New Guinea Highlands, in J. Allen, J. Golson, and R. Jones (eds.), *Sunda & Sahul*, Academic Press, London, 601-38.

Golson, J., 1978, Archaeology and agricultural history in the New Guinea Highlands, in G. de G. Sieveking, I.H. Longworth, and K.E. Wilson (eds.), *Problems in economic and social archaeology*, Duckworth, London, 201-20.

Gorshkov, G.S., 1959, Gigantic eruption of volcano Bezymianny, *Bull. Volc.*, **20**, 77-109.

Gorshkov, G.S. and Dubik, Y.M., 1970, Gigantic directed blast at Shiveluch Volcano (Kamchatka), *Bull. Volc.*, **24**, 261-88.

Grayland, E. and Grayland, V., 1971, *Tarawera*, Hodder and Stoughton, Auckland, 158p.

Greenway, J. (ed.), 1966, *The anthropologist looks at myth*, U of Texas, Austin 323p.

Griggs, R.F., 1918, The recovery of vegetation at Kodiak, *Ohio Jnl Sci.*, **19**(1), 1-57.

Griggs, R.F., 1919, IV, The character of the eruption as indicated by its effects on nearby vegetation, *Ohio Jnl Sci.*, **19**(3), 173-209.

Griggs, R.F., 1922, *The Valley of Ten Thousand Smokes*, Natl Geog. Soc., Washington DC. 340p.

Healy, J., Vucetich, C.G. and Pullar, W.A., 1964, Stratigraphy and chronology of Late Quaternary volcanic ash in Taupo, Rotorua, and Gisborne districts, *NZ Geol. Surv. Bull.*, n.s. **73**, 88p.

Hedervari, P., 1971, Energetical calculations concerning the Minoan eruption of Santorini, *Acta Thera 1st Congr.*, 257-76.

Heilprin, A., 1903, *Mount Pelee and the tragedy of Martinique*, Lippincott, Philadelphia, 335p.

Henning, R.A., Rosenthal, C.H., Oldo, B. and Reading, E. (eds.), 1976, Alaska's Volcanoes, *Alaska Geographic*, **4**(1), 1-88.

Herbet, D. and Bardossi, F., 1968, *Kilauea: case history of a volcano*, Harper & Row, New York, 191p.

HMSO (His Majesty's Stationary Office), 1903, *Further correspondence relating to the volcanic eruptions in St. Vincent and Martinique, in 1902 and 1903*, 193p.

Hobbs. W.H., 1906, The grand eruption of Vesuvius in 1906, *J. Geol.*, **14**, 636-55.

Horton, R.J.M. and McCaldin, R.O., 1964, Observations on air pollution aspects of Irazu volcano, Costa Rica, *Publ. Health Repts Wash.*, **79**(10), 925-9.

Huggins, P.F., 1902, *Report on the Soufrière*, Saint Vincent, British West Indies, 30p.

Jack, R.N. and Carmichael, I.S.E., 1969, The chemical 'fingerprinting' of acid volcanic rocks, *Short Contrib. Calif. Geol. Spec. Rept*, **100**, 17-32.

Jagger, T.A., 1924, Sakurajima, Japan's greatest volcanic eruption, *Natl Geog. Mag.*, **45**, 441-70.

Jagger, T.A. 1945, *Volcanoes declare war, logistics and strategy of Pacific Volcano Science*, Paradise of the Pacific Ltd, Honolulu, 166p.

Jagger, T.A. 1956, *My experiments with volcanoes*, Hawaiian Volcano Research Assn, Honolulu, 198p.

Johnson, R.W., 1969, Volcanic geology of Mt. Suswa, Kenya, *Phil. Trans. Roy. Soc. London*, **265A**, 383-412.

Johnson, R.W., 1970, Ulawun Volcano, New Britain: geology, petrology and erupture history between 1915 and 1967, *Bureau Min. Resources Record*, 1970/21, 43p.

Johnson, R.W. (ed.), 1976a, *Volcanism in Australasia*, Elsevier, Amsterdam, 405p.

Johnson, R. W., 1976b, Late Cainozoic volcanism and plate tectonics at the southern margin of the Bismarck Sea, Papua New Guinea, in Johnson, R.W. (ed.),) *Volcanism in Australasia*, Elsevier, Amsterdam, 101-16.

Johnson, R.W., 1977, Late Cainozioc volcanoes at the southern margin of the Bismarck Sea, Papua New Guinea. Part 1, Distribution and major element chemistry of late Cainozoic volcanoes at the southern margin of the Bismarck Sea, Papua New Guinea, *B.M.R. Aust. Rept.*, **188**, 170p.

Johnson, R.W., Mackenzie, D.E., and Smith, I.E., 1971, Seismicity and late Cenozoic volcanism in parts of Papua New Guinea, *Tectonophysics*, **12**, 15-22.

Johnson, R.W., Taylor, G.A.M. and Davies, R.A., 1972, Geology and petrology of Quaternary volcanic islands off the north coast of New Guinea, *B.M.R. Record*, 1972/21, 127p.

Judd, J.W., 1888, On the volcanic phenomena of the eruption and on the nature and distribution of the ejected materials, in Royal Society Committee, *The eruption of Krakatoa and subsequent phenomena*, pp.1-46.

Juhle, W. and Coulter, H.W., 1955, The Mount Spurr eruption, July 9, 1953, *Am. Geophys. Un., Trans.*, **36**, 199-202.

Kircher, A., 1665, *Mundus subterraneus*, J. Waesberge, Amsterdam.

Kjartansson, G., 1951, The eruption of Hekla 1947-48; II, 4; Water flood and mud-flows, *Societas scientiarum Islandica*, 51p.

Knox, J.B. and Short, N.M., 1964, A diagnostic model using ashfall data to determine eruption characteristics and atmospheric conditions during a major volcanic event, *Bull. Volc.*, **27**, 5-24.

Kohn, B.P., 1970, Identification of New Zealand tephra-layers by emission spectrographic analysis of their titanomagnetites, *Lithos*, **3**, 361-8.

Krause, D.C., 1965, Submarine geology north of New Guinea, *Bull. Geol. Soc. Am.*, **76**, 27-42.

Kuschel, R. and Monberg, T., 1977, History and oral traditions; a case study, *J. Poly. Soc.*, **86**(1), 85-95.

Lacroix, A., 1906, The eruption of Vesuvius in April, 1906, *Smithsonian Inst. Ann. Rept*, 223-48.

Lamb, H.H., 1970, Volcanic dust in the atmosphere; with a chronology and assessment of its meteorological significance, *Phil. Trans. Roy. Soc.*, **266**, 425-533.

Lawrence, P., 1964, *Road belong cargo*, Melbourne University Press. 293p.

Leppmann, W., 1966, *Pompeii in fact and fiction*, Elek, London, 189 p.

Lerbekmo, J.F., Hanson, L.W. and Campbell, F.A., 1968, Application of particle size distribution to determination of source of a volcanic ash deposit, *23rd Int. Geol. Congr.*, **2.**, 283-95.

Lirer, L. Pescatore, T., Booth, B. and Walker, G.P.L., 1973, Two Plinian pumice-fall deposits from Somma-Vesuvius, Italy, *Bull. Geol. Soc. Am.*, **84**, 759-72.

Löffler, E., 1976, Potassium-argon dates and pre-Würm glaciations of Mount Giluwe volcano, Papua New Guinea, *Zeitschrift für Gletscherkunde und Glazialgeologie*, **12**(1), 55-62.

Luce, J.V., 1969, *The end of Atlantis*, Paladin, London 187p.

Macdonald, G.A., 1972, *Volcanoes*, Prentice Hall, New Jersey, 510p.

McElhanon, K.A. (ed.), 1976, *Legends from Papua New Guinea*, Summer Institute of Linguistics, Ukarumpa.

McKee, C.O., Cooke, R.J.S., and Wallace, D.A., 1976, 1974-75 eruptions of Karkar Volcano, Papua New Guinea, in R.W. Johnson (ed.), *Volcanism in Australasia*, Elsevier, Amsterdam, 173-90.

Mackenzie, D.E., 1973, Quaternary volcanoes of the central and southern Highlands of Papua New Guinea, *B.M.R. Record*, 1973/89, 65p.

Mackenzie, D.E., 1976, Nature and origin of late Cainozoic volcanoes in western Papua New Guinea, in R.W. Johnson (ed.), *Volcanism in Australasia*, Elsevier, Amsterdam 221-38.

Mackenzie, D.E. and Chappell, B.W., 1972, Shoshonitic and calc-alkaline lavas from the highlands of Papua New Guinea, *Contr. Mineral. & Petrol.*, **35**, 50-62.

Mai, P., 1974, The time of darkness, Enga Research Programme, 18p. (unpubl.).

Mai, P., in press, The time of darkness or Yuu Kuia, in D. Denoon and R.J. Lacey (eds.), *Oral traditions in Melanesia*. University of Papua New Guinea, Port Moresby.

Marinos, G. and Melidonis, N., 1971, On the strength of seaquakes (tsunamis) during the prehistoric eruptions of Santorin, *Acta 1st Int. Sci. Congr. Volcano Thera*, Greece, 15-23 Sept. 1969, Athens, 1971 — Arch. Services of Greece, 277-82.

Markhinin, Y., 1971, *Pluto's chain*, Progress Publ., Moscow, 214p.

Martin, C., 1911, Observations on the recent eruption of Taal volcano, *Philip. Jnl Sci.*, **6**(2), 87-90.

Martin, G.C., 1913, The recent eruption of Katmai volcano in Alaska, *Natl. Geog. Mag.*, **24**(2), 131-81.

Mauiri, A., 1961, Last Moments of the Pompeians, *Natl Geog. Mag.*, **120**(5), 651-69.

Meggitt, M.J., 1957, House-building among the Mae Enga, Oceania, **27**, 161-76.

Meggitt, M.J., 1958, Mae Enga time-reckoning and calendar, New Guinea, Man, 86-7, 74-7.

Meggitt, M.J., 1973, The sun and the shakers: a millenarian cult and its transformations in the New Guinea Highlands, Oceania, **44**(1), 1-37; (2) 109-26.

Mennis, M., 1978, The existence of Yomba Island near Madang: Fact or fiction, Oral History, **6**(6), 2-81.

Mikloucho-Maclay, N., 1878, Uber vulkanische Erscheinungen an der nord ostlichen Kuste New Guineas, Petermann's Mitt. **24**, 408-10.

Mikloucho-Maclay, N., 1975, New Guinea diaries, 1871-1883, trans, from Russian by C.L. Sentinella, Kristen Pres, Madang, 355p.

Mintz, Y., 1954, The observed zonal circulation of the atmosphere, Bull. Am. Met. Soc., **35**(5), 208-14.

Moore, J.A., 1967, Base surge in recent volcanic eruptions, Bull. Volc., **30**, 337-63.

Moore, J.G., Nakamura, K. and Alcaraz, A., 1966, The 1965 eruption of Taal volcano, Science, **151**, 955-60.

Morell, A., 1833, Narrative of a voyage to the Ethiopic and South Atlantic Ocean, Indian Ocean, Chinese Sea, North and South Pacific Ocean in the years 1829, 1830, 1831, J. & J. Harper, NY.

Morell, B., 1832, A narrative of four voyages to the South Sea, J. & J. Harper, NY.

Murai, I. and Hosoya, Y., 1964, The eruptive activity of Mt. Asama from 1958 to 1961 and the associated minor pyroclastic flows, Bull. Earthquake Res. Inst., **42**, 203-36.

Naval Intelligence Division, 1945, Pacific Islands, vol. 4, Western Pacific (New Guinea and islands northward), Geographical Handbook Series.

Nelson, H.E., 1971, Disease, demography and the evolution of social structure in Highlands New Guinea, J. Poly. Soc., **80**, 204-16.

Nelson, H., and Chisum, G.L., 1974, A computer-assisted method for age-determination in non-literate populations, Bijdragen tot de taal-, Land- en Volkenkunde, **130**, 132-7.

Neumann van Padang, 1971, Two catastrophic eruptions in Indonesia, comparable with the Plinian outburst of the volcano of Thera (Santorini) in Minoan time, Acta 1st Int. Sci. Congr. of Volcano Thera, Greece, 15-23 Sept., 1969, Archaeological Services of Greece, 51-63.

Nielsen, N., 1937, A volcano under an ice-cap. Vatnajokull, Iceland, 1934-36, Geog. Jnl, **90**(1), 6-23.

Ninkovich, D. and Heezen, B.C., 1965, Santorini tephra, in Whittard, W.F. and Bradshaw, R. (eds.), Submarine geology and geophysics, Colston Papers, **17**, 413-53.

Norrish, K. and Chappell, B.W., 1967, X-ray fluorescence spectrography, in Zussman, J. (ed.), Physical methods in determinative mineralogy, Academic Press, London, 161-214.

Oldfield, F., 1976, Recent ecological history of small drainage basins in the Western and Southern highlands of Papua New Guinea (unpublished research report), 58p.

Oldfield, F., Appleby, P.G., Brown, A. and Thompson, R., 1977, Recent lake sediment studies in the Highlands of Papua New Guinea (Paper read to INQUA Congress — unpublished), 23p.

Oldfield, F., Appleby, P.G. and Battarbee, R.W., 1978, Alternative ^{210}Pb dating: results from the New Guinea Highlands and Lough Erne, Nature, **271**, 339-42.

Oldfield, F., Appleby, P.G. and Thompson, R., in press, Palaeo-ecological studies of three lakes in the Highlands of Papua New Guinea, 1, The chronology of sedimentation, *J. Ecol.*,

Ollier, C.D. and Brown, M.J.F., 1971, Erosion of a young volcano in New Guinea, *Zert. Geomorph.*, **15**, 12-28.

Ollier, C.D., and MacKenzie, D.E., 1974, Subaerial erosion of volcanic cones in the tropics, *J. Trop. Geog.*, **39**, 63-71.

Olsson, I.U., Some problems in connection with the evaluation of C^{14}. dates, *Geologiska Föreningens i Stockholm Fördhandlingar*, **96**, 311-20.

Page, R.W. and Johnson, R. W., 1974, Strontium isotope ratios of Quaternary volcanic rocks from Papua New Guinea, *Lithos*, **7**, 91-100.

Pain, C.F., 1973, The late Quaternary geomorphic history of the Kaugel Valley, Papua New Guinea, unpublished PhD thesis, ANU, 226p.

Pain, C.F. and Blong, R.J., 1976, Late Quaternary tephras around Mt. Hagen and Mt. Giluwe, Papua New Guinea, in Johnson, R.W. (ed.), *Volcanism in Australasia*, Elsevier, Amsterdam, 239-51.

Pain, C.F. and Blong, R.J., 1979, The distribution of tephras in the Papua New Guinea Highlands, *Search*, **10**(6), 228-30.

Pain, C.F. and McKee, C.O., in press, Late Quaternary eruptive history of Karkar Island, *Cooke-Ravian Memorial Volume*, PNG Geological Survey.

Pain, C.F. and Wood, A.W., 1976, Tephra beds and soils in the Nondugl-Chuave area, western highlands and Chimbu Provinces, Papua New Guinea, *Science in New Guinea*, **4**(3), 153-64.

Pain, C.F., Blong, R.J. and McKee, C.O. (in press), Pyroclastic deposits and eruptive sequences on Long Island, Papua New Guinea, *Cooke-Ravian Memorial Volume*, PNG Geological Survey.

Palfreyman, W.D. and Cooke, R.J.S., 1976, Eruptive history of Manam Volcano, Papua New Guinea, in R.W. Johnson (ed.) *Volcanism in Australasia*, Elsevier, Amsterdam, 117-31.

Perret, F.A., 1924, The Vesuvius eruption of 1906, *Carnegie Inst. Wash. Publ.*, **339**, 151p.

Perret, F.A., 1937, The eruption of Mt. Pelee, *Carnegie Inst. Wash. Publ.*, **458**, 126p.

Perret, F.A., 1950, Volcanological observations, *Carnegie Inst. Wash. Publ.*, **549**, 162p.

Petroeschevsky, W.A., 1949, A contribution to the knowledge of the Gunung Tambora (Sumbawa), *Ned. Aardrijksundig Genootschap, Tijdschrift*, ser. 2, **66**, 688-701.

Pettijohn, F.J., 1957, *Sedimentary rocks*, 2nd ed., Harper, New York, 718p.

Polach, H.A., 1969, Optimisation of liquid scintillation radiocarbon age determinations and reporting of ages, *Atomic energy in Australia*, **12**(3), 21-8.

Polach, H.A., in press, Radiocarbon dating of Long Island and Tibito Tephras, *Cooke-Ravian Memorial Volume*, PNG Geological Survey.

Pond, J.A. and Smith, S.P., 1886, Observations on the eruption of Mount Tarawera, Bay of Plenty, New Zealand, 10th June, 1886, *NZ Inst. Trans. & Proc.*, **19**, 342-71.

Pratt, W.E. 1911, The eruption of Taal Volcano, January 30, 1911, *Phil. Jnl Sci.*, **6A**(2), 63-83.

Purey-Cust, H.E., 1895? Report on the eruption of Ambrym, New Hebrides, October and November, 1894, HMSO, 26p.

Raffles, T.S., 1830, *The history of Java*, 2 vols., John Murray, London.

Ralph, E.K., Michael, H.N. and Han, M.C., 1973, Radiocarbon dates and reality, *MASCA Newsletter*, **9**(1), 1-19.

Reche, O., 1914, Dampier's Route langs der Nordkuste von Kaiser-Wilhelms-Land, *Petermanns Geog. Mitt.*, **60**, 223-5

Rees, J.D., 1970, Paricutin revisited: a review of man's attempts to adapt to ecological changes resulting from volcanic catastrophe, Geoforum, 4, 7-25.

Rittman, A., 1962, Volcanoes and their activity, trans. E.A. Vincent, Interscience Publ., NY, 305p.

Rose, W.I., 1972, Notes on the 1902 eruption of Santa Maria volcano, Guatemala, Bull. Volc., 36, 29-45.

Ross, J.T., 1816, Narrative of the effects of the eruption from the Tomboro mountain in the Sumbawa on the 11th and 12th of April 1815, Lembaga Kebudajaan Indonesia Verhandelingen, 8, 343-9, 450-60.

Royal Society Committee, 1888, The eruption of Krakatoa and subsequent phenomena, ed. G.J. Symons, Trubner, London.

Sapper, K., 1927, Vulkankunde, Engelhorn Verlag, Stuttgart.

Sekiya, S. and Kikuchi, Y., 1889, The eruption of Bandai-san, Jnl College Sci. Imperial University, Japan, 91-172.

Sentinella, C.L. (ed.), 1975, New Guinea diaries of Mikloucho-Maclay, 1871-1883, Kristen Pres. Madang, 355p.

Sergerstrom, K., 1950, Erosion studies at Paricutin, State of Michoacan, Mexico, U.S.G.S. Bull., 965-A, 164p.

Sharp, A., 1968, The voyages of Abel Janszoon Tasman, OUP, London, 375p.

Shimozuru, D., 1972, A seismological approach to the prediction of volcanic eruptions in The surveillance and prediction of volcanic activity, UNESCO, 19-45.

SICSLP (Smithsonian Institution Center for short-lived phenomena), 1970-1972 Annual Repts.

Skeldon, R., 1977, Volcanic ash, hailstorms and crops: oral history from the Eastern Highlands of Papua New Guinea, J. Poly. Soc., 86(3), 403-9.

Smith, R.L. and Bailey, R.A., 1968, Resurgent cauldrons, in R.R. Coats et al. (ed.), Studies in volcanology, Geol. Surv. Am. Memoir, 116, 613-62.

Sparks, R.S.J. and Walker, G.P.L., 1977, The significance of vitric-enriched air-fall ashes associated with crystal-enriched ignimbrites, J. Volc. & Geothermal Res., 2, 329-41.

Sparks, R.S.J. and Wilson, L., 1976, A model for the formation of ignimbrite by gravitational column collapse, J. Geol. Soc. London, 132, 441-51.

Spinden, H.J., 1919, Shattered capitals of central America, Natl. Geog. Mag., 35, 185-212.

Stanley, E.R. 1923, Report on the salient geological features and natural resources of the New Guinea Territory, Rep. on the Territory of New Guinea 1921-22, Aust. Parl. Papers. Sessions 1923-24, vol. 4, General App. B.

Steinhauser, R., 1892, The tidal wave and the relief expedition from Finschhafen to the south-west coast of New Britain, Westermann's Illustriere Deutsche Menutschefte, vol. 71.

Stuiver, M., 1978, Radiocarbon timescale tested against magnetic and other dating methods, Nature, 273, 271-4.

Symons, G.J. (ed.), 1888, The eruption of Krakatoa and subsequent phenomena, Royal Society of London.

Taylor, G.A.M., 1958n The 1951 Eruption of Mount Lamington, Papua, Aust. Bur. Min. Res. Bull., 38, 117p.

Taylor, G.A.M., 1971, An investigation of volcanic activity at Doma Peaks, Bur. Min. Res. Aust. Rec., 1971/137, 15p.

Thompson, R. and Oldfield, F., 1978, Evidence for recent paleomagnetic secular variation in lake sediments from the New Guinea Highlands, Physics of the Earth & Planetary Interiors, 17, 300-6.

Thorarinsson, S., 1954, The tephra-fall from Hekla on March 29th, 1947, *Soc. Sci. Islandica*, Reykjavik 68p.

Thorarinsson, S., 1958, The Oraefajökull eruption of 1362, *Acta Naturalia Islandica*, **2**(2), 1-99.

Thorarinsson, S., 1967, The eruptions of Hekla in historical times, *Soc. Sci. Islandica*, Reykjavik, 183p.

Thorarinsson, S. 1970, *Hekla, a notorious volcano*, Almenna Bokafelagid, Reyjavik, 61p.

Thorarinsson, S. 1971, Damage caused by tephra fall in some big Icelandic eruptions and its relation to the thickness of the tephra layers, *Acta 1st Int. Sci. Congr. on Volcano Thera*, Greece 15-23 Sept. 1969, Archaeological Services of Greece, 213-36.

Thorarinsson, S. and Sigvaldason, G.E., 1972, The Hekla eruption of 1970, *Bull. Volc.*, **36**, 269-88.

UNDRO, 1976 (Office of the UN Disaster Relief Co-ordinator.) *Disaster prevention and mitigation, a compendium of current knowledge, vol. 1. Volcanological aspects*, UN, Geneva, 38p.

Vansina, J., 1965, *Oral tradition, a study in historical methodology* (Trans, H.M. Wright), Penguin, Harmondsworth, 226p.

van Bemmelen, R.W., 1971, Four volcanic outbursts that influenced human history — Toba, Sunda, Merapi, and Thera, *Acta 1st Int. Sci. Congr. of Volcano Thera*, Greece 15-23 Sept. 1969. Archaeological Services of Greece, 5-49.

Varenius, B., 1683, *Cosmography and geography*, S. Roycroft (Richard Blome edition).

Verbeek, R.D.M., 1885, *Krakatau*, Batavia, Lansdrukkerij.

Vicedom, G.F. and Tischner, H., 1943, *Die Mbowamb* Hamburg Museum für Volkenkunde Monographien zur Volkenkunde Nr. 1, 3 vols.

Vitaliano, D.B., 1973, *Legends of the earth*, Indiana UP Bloomington, 305p.

Vitaliano, D.B. and Vitaliano, C.J., 1971, Plinian eruptions, earthquakes and Santorin: a review, *Acta 1st Inst. Sci. Congr. Volcano Thera*, Greece 15-23 Sept. 1969, Archaeological Services of Greece, 88-108.

Vucetich, C.G. and Pullar, W.A., 1969, Stratigraphy and chronology of late Pleistocene volcanic ash beds in central North Island, New Zealand, *N.Z. J. Geol. Geophys.*, **12**, 784-837.

Waldron, H.H., 1967, Debris flow and erosion control problems caused by the ash eruptions of Irazu Volcano, Costa Rica, *U.S.G.S. Bull.*, 1241-I, Il-I 37.

Watkins, N.D., Sparks, R.S.J., Sigurdsson, H., Huang, T.C., Federman, A., Carey, S. and Ninkovich, D., 1978, Volume and extent of the Minoan tephra from Santorini Volcano: new evidence from deep sea sediment cores, *Nature*, **271**, 122-6.

Watson, J.B., 1963, Krakatoa's echo? *J. Poly. Soc.*, **72**, 152-5.

Watson, J.B., 1967, Horticultural traditions of the Eastern New Guinea Highlands, *Oceania*, **38**(2), 81-98.

Westgate, J.A., Smith, D.G.W. and Tomlinson, M., 1970, Late Quaternary tephra layers in southwestern Canada, *Proc. 2nd Ann. Paleo-environmental workshop of Uni. Calgary Arch. Assoc.*, Students' Press, Calgary, 13-34.

Wexler, H., 1951, Spread of the Krakatoa volcanic dust cloud as related to the high level circulation, *Bull. Am. Met. Soc.*, **32**(2) 48-51.

Wharton, W.J.L., 1888, On the seismic sea waves caused by the eruption of Krakatoa, August 26th and 27th, 1883 in Symons, G. (ed.), *The eruption of Krakatoa and subsequent phenomena*, 89-107.

Whittaker, J., Gash, N., Hookey, J. and Lacey, R.J., 1975, *Documents and readings in New Guinea history*, Jacaranda, Brisbane.

Wichmann, A., 1909-1910, *Nova Guinea*, 3 vols., Leiden.

Wilcox, R.E., 1959, Some effects of recent volcanic ash falls with especial reference to Alaska, *U.S.G.S. Bull.*, 1028-N, 409-74.

Williams, H., 1941, Calderas and their origin, *U. Calif. Geol. Sci. Publ.*, **25**, 239-346.

Williams, H., 1952, The great eruption of Coseguina, Nicaragua, in 1835, *U. Cal. Publ. Geol. Sci.*, **29**(2), 21-46.

Wilson, L., 1972, Explosive volcanic eruptions — II The atmospheric trajectories of pyroclasts, *Geophys. J. Roy. Astr. Soc.*, **30**, 381-92.

Wilson, L., 1976, Explosive volcanic eruptions — III Plinian eruption columns, *Geophys. J. Roy. Astr. Soc.*, **45**, 543-56.

Young, M.W., 1971, *Fighting with food*, CUP, London, 282p.

Subject index

Placenames and Linguistic Group index

Author and Informant index